ASTA String Curriculum

Standards, Goals, and Learning Sequences

for

Essential Skills and Knowledge

in

K-12 String Programs

Stephen J. Benham

Mary L. Wagner

Jane Linn Aten

Judith P. Evans

Denese Odegaard

Julie Lyonn Lieberman

2011 Edition

© 2011 American String Teachers Association
All Rights Reserved
Printed in the United States of America

ISBN 978-0-615-43901-3

Table of Contents

Preface

The ASTA National Executive Board shares in the excitement of seeing the first national string curriculum go from an idea to a reality. What an invaluable resource for string teachers throughout the United States! Many thanks go to the members of the Committee: Jane Aten, Judy Evans, Julie Lyonn Lieberman, Denese Odegaard, Mary Wagner, and chaired by Stephen Benham. Each is a highly respected teacher and together they represent many facets of American string teaching. When they began this project they had no idea of the size of the job they were undertaking or that it would require the investment of several years' work, but it has culminated in the creation of a masterpiece. We take pride in them as representatives of ASTA, and we congratulate each committee member on a magnificent job well done.

Providing a basis for agreement among teachers as well as a starting point for discussion, this curriculum will be useful in many ways. It can help set standards and guidelines in the development of string programs as well as educate administrators, board members, parents and students. It can also serve as a needed tool for administrators and teachers to use in evaluation.

Recognizing that successful teachers may use differing approaches, this curriculum includes many schools of thought and provides a comprehensive approach. Setting standards for instruction and outcomes will benefit us all and now that these ideas are in print, they can act as a starting point for further development. We view the curriculum as a living document that will evolve over time.

In the introductory material, the Committee presents an extensive rationale and background for the curriculum and provides many ideas for its implementation in the real-world classroom. With its logical layout, clear language and degree of detail, this curriculum can aid any teacher, from a first year initiate to an experienced veteran who wants to improve.

The ASTA national curriculum is a necessity for every string teacher!

Kirk Moss, ASTA President
Bob Phillips, ASTA President-Elect
Jeffrey Solow, ASTA Past President

Note from the Committee Chair

We are extremely excited about the publication of this first national-level curriculum under the auspices of the *American String Teachers Association*. As is true with many documents like this, the project grew in scope and depth as the committee surveyed current curricular practices, discussed the project aims with experts in the field of string education and curriculum in general education, and as we determined how to best meet the needs of the K–12 strings and orchestra teacher. From the first discussion of the project until its release, nearly three-and-a-half years have passed, a longer time period than any of us first anticipated. However, we did not want to rush the final project, as we recognized that this curriculum is an important initial step in curricular development within our profession. We also recognized that this work would be critically reviewed by other educational experts beyond the field of string teaching, and so it has been our desire to present a curriculum that is based on outstanding research and curricular design models while being extremely accessible and practical for the teachers in the classroom or studio. To the extent that we were successful in achieving our aims, our audience will have to judge! We anticipate that the curriculum will undergo revision in coming years and that supplemental documents will become available as needs are expressed by those in our string teaching community.

As the lead author and editor of this work, I want to acknowledge the substantial contributions of the excellent team of authors that we had, including Jane Aten, Judy Evans, Julie Lyonn Lieberman, Denese Odegaard, and Mary Wagner. Their experience in teaching, curriculum design, and knowledge about string pedagogy is outstanding and this document could not have been written without their specific input. It is better because of their contributions! Our discussions were frank, critical, respectful, and always held with the idea of how do we best serve our constituents with this document. I am proud to be associated with them!

I also want to express my gratitude directly to the leaders of ASTA who saw the need for a curriculum of this nature and responded by directly supporting the project in ways such as providing travel support for the writing team and administrative and conceptual support from the ASTA board and administrative staff. Throughout this process, we have been blessed by strong leadership from our association, and I want to directly thank Mary Wagner, Kirk Moss, Bob Phillips, Jeff Solow, Donna Sizemore Hale, Mary Jane Dye, and Sky Henderson, for their support and input.

Ultimately, I hope that this curriculum is useful and will serve as a tool for helping teachers in their quest for excellence.

Stephen Benham, Chair, ASTA K–12 Curriculum Committee

Special Note to Teachers

Dear Teachers,

We are extremely pleased to share this curriculum with you and hope that you will find it to be a useful and practical document. Our writing team includes teachers who have substantial experience in teaching in public schools, private institutions, and the studio, from pre-K through the university level. During each phase in the development of this curriculum, we continuously evaluated how teachers would use the curriculum on a daily basis to meet the needs of their individual classrooms and students. We recognize the many challenges faced in the life of the string teacher, including traveling between multiple buildings, teaching several instruments to students with a wide range of skill levels at the same time, in addition to concert scheduling, instrument repair, inventory management, and planning lessons and rehearsals for multiple grade levels, just to name a few! We also have seen the increasing focus on curriculum and assessment from district, state, and even federal agencies and know that there are substantial pressures on string programs even in locations where there is strong community support.

We also recognize that string teachers are a diverse group, with greatly varying levels of preparation and experience in the field of string pedagogy and teaching. Teacher preparation programs in colleges and universities vary widely in the amount of emphasis that is placed on the unique needs of string educators in the area of sequential pedagogy, lesson planning, knowledge of secondary instruments, and teaching in heterogeneous group and ensemble settings.

With that in mind, our desire was to provide a curriculum that was both easy to use (with a clear and concise scope-and-sequence) and comprehensive (with more than 200 specific learning tasks). This curriculum is not just the work of our team of authors, but is based on the outstanding teaching traditions in our field and the contributions of many earlier authors, educators, and researchers. We hope that you find this curriculum to be a useful tool to you at multiple levels, from designing the overall K–12 string program in your school system to planning daily lesson plans.

Thank you for your ongoing commitment to excellence!

Stephen Benham, Chair
ASTA K–12 Curriculum Committee

Special Note to Administrators

Dear Administrators,

First, thank you! If you are reading this letter we recognize that you have taken the time to familiarize yourself with this first full-length comprehensive curriculum for string education in K–12 school systems. We appreciate your commitment to providing support for those teachers and students involved in your string program.

Primary responsibilities for administrators generally include the evaluation of teacher performance and the oversight of curriculum. This particular document is designed to be a model for the local school district to write its own curriculum. Though the curriculum may be adopted as is for a specific school district, the local school will need to determine the specific grade levels for each of the benchmarks and also appropriate the appropriate amount of time required to achieve the performance tasks and benchmarks.

We encourage the regular and ongoing evaluation of string teachers, but believe that evaluation should be done within the context of a program that has adequate time for instruction, appropriate administrative support (policy, finances, and scheduling). The activities that take place during a string class or rehearsal may look very different from those activities that take place during another type of academic class (such as math or science). The music-making process is highly interactive, but should also have a clear structure and high expectations. Rehearsals and classes should have clearly stated and measurable performance outcomes that are regularly assessed by the teacher. In other words, teacher evaluation should also reflect the performance of the students within the individual class.

In the absence of a written curriculum, it is difficult to assess teacher performance (or to adequately understand if students are meeting any specific goals at all). We hope that this curriculum will serve as an impetus for the development of a local curriculum and also encourage districts to provide for additional professional development for teachers if it becomes apparent that teachers or students aren't meeting performance standards because the curricular outcomes are not being met. We also encourage administrators to consider that other reasons may also exist for lower than expected performance in the string classroom, including the lack of instructional time, scheduling conflicts, inferior instruments or equipment, or inadequate rehearsal space.

As you likely already know, teaching string instruments requires a unique specialized skill set, which includes knowledge of sequential pedagogy for multiple instruments, an understanding of instructional design for a wide range of classes (from small group lessons to large ensemble rehearsals), the ability to manage and coordinate a program at multiple grade levels, an understanding of how to assess the wide range of skills and knowledge students must have to perform at a high level, an understanding of strategies for effective student recruitment and retention, and the ability to deliver instruction in a way that engages student attention and provides for consistent growth and high achievement. We encourage you to see the curriculum and assessment section of our resource list for materials related to the assessment of music teachers and music performance.

This curriculum also underscores the need for trained specialists in the area of string education. It isn't possible or realistic to expect students to pay for private lessons outside of the school day to replace the training that they should be receiving in their school program. Performance of orchestral stringed instruments requires specialized knowledge about each of the instruments and substantial training in the area of pedagogy and teaching strategies.

We also want to solicit your feedback or advice regarding the use of this curriculum. If you have any questions or would like additional information, we encourage you to contact the ASTA national office.

Thank you for your ongoing support of string students in your district!

About the Curriculum Authors

In fall 2007 the ASTA Board developed an ad hoc committee, the Curriculum Committee, for the express purpose of writing this document. Mary Wagner, then ASTA president was charged with the process of appointing a committee chair. Additional committee members were selected based on recommendations by leaders in the ASTA community, with an emphasis placed on past experience with curriculum writing efforts, a record of successful public school and/or studio teaching experience, substantial prior leadership, and the willingness to commit to a lengthy writing process.

Stephen Benham was appointed chair of the committee in fall 2007. Mary Wagner continues to serve as liaison to the ASTA Executive Board. Additional remaining committee members were appointed by spring 2008, and were subsequently approved by the ASTA Executive Board.

Committee Members:

- Chair, Stephen Benham—B.S.M.E, University of Minnesota, MM, University of Michigan, Ph.D., Eastman School of Music; Associate Professor of Music Education, Duquesne University, Pittsburgh, Pennsylvania. Past-President, Pennsylvania-Delaware String Teachers Association. Taught thirteen years at public school level (Michigan, Oregon, and New York), more than twenty years of studio teaching experience, 14 years of university-level teaching experience.

- Jane Linn Aten—graduate, University of Texas String Project; B.S.M.E., Abilene Christian University; M.M., University of Texas in Austin; Texas Mid-Level Management Certificate, Texas Women's University; Studio Teacher, String Curriculum Consultant (Dallas Independent School District); Curriculum Team (Dallas Symphony Orchestra); previously strings teacher/orchestra conductor in New Mexico and Texas; past-president of the Texas Chapter of ASTA; developed urban education music project; elementary school principal; editor of *String Teaching in America: Strategies for a Diverse Society.*

- Judy Petersen Evans—B.M.E., Baldwin Wallace Conservatory; M.M., Florida Atlantic University; Adjunct Faculty (String Education), Bower School of Music (Florida Gulf Coast University); String Consultant for Title I Elementary String Programs (Orlando, Immokalee, FL); Program Director, *Enhanced Learning Through Music* (Collier County, FL); 30+ years of teaching experience, Pre-K–12 in Ohio and Florida, past-president of the Florida chapters of NSOA, FOA and ASTA, past ASTA National Secretary, past editor of NSOA *Bulletin.*

- Julie Lyonn Lieberman—B.A., Sarah Lawrence College, M.A., Gallatin at New York University; author of eight books, six DVDs, two National Public Radio series, and a national project, *The Green Anthem* (facilitated by MENC); 30+ years private teaching, residencies in schools across America, eclectic styles teacher training, and former faculty member, Juilliard, Manhattan School of Music, Mannes, The New School Jazz Program, and Jazz at William Paterson College. Specialist in creative musicianship for Carnegie/Weill Hall/Juilliard's "The Academy," Carnegie Hall Link-Up Program, National Young Audiences, and The Associated Board of the Royal Schools of Music.

- Denese Odegaard—B.M., University of Wyoming; drama and music curriculum specialist for the Fargo Public Schools; 30+ years of string teaching experience; President-Elect of MENC North Central Division; author, *Simply Strings* beginning string method book and *Music Curriculum Writing 101 (GIA)*; past-secretary of ASTA, past-president of NDMEA and past-president of NDSTA.

- Mary Wagner—30+ years of teaching experience in Fairfax County Public Schools (FCPS); mentor teacher, FCPS (retired); co-author, FCPS Program of Studies; university supervisor, James Madison University; consultant, FJH New Directions Series; past-president and advocacy chair, ASTA; chair, Fairfax Arts Coalition for Education.

Part I—Designing the Curriculum

About the ASTA Curriculum

This curriculum was developed under the direction of the ASTA Board of Directors, who recognized the need for a published curriculum to specifically meet the requirements of strings and orchestra teachers. There have been several excellent publications in the past that have dealt with curricular issues in strings and orchestra, and the teacher's manuals for many elementary- and middle-school method books also contain strong curricular components. In general, these resources either address curriculum within a specific age level (i.e., elementary, or first-year students) or give a broad overview (such as a scope-and-sequence), without addressing the topics such as teaching strategies and evaluation. Our goal, therefore, has been to develop a document that:

- is comprehensive, relevant, and practical
- is based upon excellent sequential string pedagogy
- is flexible and can be used or adapted to a wide range of curricular standards (at national, state, or local levels)
- is structured in a way that conveniently provides for differentiated instruction
- contains specific teaching sequences for curricular knowledge and skills
- facilitates the measurement and evaluation of curricular knowledge and skills
- reflects current language used in curriculum development throughout the profession
- is relevant to the skills and knowledge required for twenty-first century learners

The task of writing a national curriculum for ASTA is complex and not without hazards! First, we recognize that there is a wide range of thought based on the various technical "schools" that exist in our profession. These schools of thought have developed based on traditions established over centuries of performance and reflect the individualities of great teachers and pedagogical practice. Lack of agreement on such fundamentals is to be expected in our profession, and is part of the underlying dichotomy and tension of ideas that urges progress and continued evolution of musical and technical achievement. At the same time, our profession has historically shown itself to be open to new ideas, incorporating the work of Shinichi Suzuki, Paul Rolland, Kato Havas, among others (this list is short and by no means exclusive!).

With that in mind, this document is not meant to be exhaustive. We anticipate that it will undergo continuous revision and updating, based on current thought, new research, and best practice. Further, we believe that any curriculum is only useful to the extent that it is implemented in the classroom or studio and can be adapted by the local teacher for specific use in a given teaching context.

Ultimately, our desire is for this curriculum to reinforce the high standard for teaching strings and orchestra that exists in many places across the country. We hope that the curriculum will help reinforce the understanding that the teaching and playing of strings and orchestra requires expert knowledge and trained teachers, who understand the comprehensive and sequential nature of string pedagogy. We also anticipate that this curriculum document will help clarify and standardize some of the terminology used in our field. Last, we recognize that this curriculum will serve as a tool of advocacy, both for enhancing existing programs and to underscore the importance of specialized teachers.

Intended Audience

Our goal in developing this document was to serve a broad audience involved with string music education programs. While teachers are perhaps the most obvious to benefit from this curriculum, we also believe that this document will be useful as well to administrators, parents, and students. At all levels, our belief is that this document will help 1) provide additional support to programs that already have a record of excellence and 2) serve as a tool of increased accountability for programs that are in need of improvement.

1. For teachers: Our goal is assist all teachers, regardless of experience, in their ongoing efforts to either design for the first time, or revise existing, curriculum documents. Our profession sees an increasing number of string teachers whose primary instrument is not a string instrument. In addition, there is a growth in the number of string players entering the string education field who receive post-baccalaureate or alternate certification and may have reduced preparation in pedagogy and methodology. Finally, the majority of music teacher preparation programs do not have a specific course dedicated to sequential string pedagogy. For string and non-string players alike, this curriculum will serve as an invaluable tool as they enter the profession. We also hope that this

document will assist studio teachers and collegiate music educators (and teacher trainers) in guiding curriculum development and preparing future educators.

2. <u>For administrators</u>: administrators vary widely in their level of preparation in the area of evaluating music teachers and curriculum. When the focus is narrowed to string teachers and string curriculum, the number of administrators who have the specialized understanding needed to effectively measure student learning and teacher effectiveness in strings and orchestra is even smaller. We hope that this document will provide administrators with a framework for helping string teachers formulate or revise curriculum, develop lesson plans, create appropriate assessments, and ultimately evaluate student progress against a specific standard.

3. <u>For parents</u>: The absence of a written curriculum calls into question the academic validity of any program. Music programs as a whole, and string programs specifically, are at greater risk for elimination in an environment of constant educational reform and economic restriction. When a curriculum has been approved by the local school board, and when the curriculum contains standards and tasks that are specific, achievable, and measurable, the academic standing of the program is greatly enhanced. Further, strings and orchestra as subjects move from being simply an extra- or co-curricular activity to something worthy of rigorous study, commitment of district resources (time, money, staffing), and an educational priority.

4. <u>For students</u>: We believe that students achieve best when they know the standards and expectations for performance. Further, student learning is significantly increased when students are involved in self-assessment and establishing goals for improvement. In addition, this document demonstrates the significant endeavor and challenge in which students are engaged.

Rationale

Why do we need a written model curriculum at the national level? Though it is true that many excellent local curricula models exist, particularly at the district level, the majority of school districts in the US do not have a written curriculum for strings or orchestra instruction. In addition, we noted the following trends within the string teaching profession, which underscore the need for a curriculum at this particular time:

- Participation in strings and orchestra programs continues to grow across the United States.

- There is a shortage of available string teachers, resulting in an increased number of teachers who have entered school strings and orchestra education programs in non-traditional ways, such as those who have come from fields of performance, music technology, general education, arts education, or other non-string specialized fields.

- Increasing numbers of teachers without a background in strings are now responsible for teaching strings and orchestra either as a full- or part-time assignment. This includes teachers who did not play a string instrument as a primary instrument, are teaching in dual-assignments (band/strings or general music/strings), or those who developed a strong interest in teaching strings because of internship opportunities, teacher training programs, or other experiences.

- The majority of music education/teacher certification programs in the United States do not have full-time string specialists; in other programs, string pedagogy and education classes are simply clustered together as part of a general "instrumental music education" sequence. Little attention is given to the unique needs of string teachers and the comprehensive and sequential nature of string pedagogy. In other programs, the string methods courses are taught by performers who may have excellent pedagogical background, but do not have public school teaching experience.

- Several past and current excellent models for strings and orchestra curriculum, program, design, and related information do exist, including *Teaching Stringed Instruments: A Course of Study*, which was developed by the MENC Task Force on String Education; *The Complete String Guide: Standards, Programs, Purchase and Maintenance* (jointly published by ASTA and MENC), *TIPS: Establishing a String and Orchestra Program* (compiled by Jacquelyn Dillon-Krass and Dorothy A. Straub); and *Strategies for Teaching Strings: Building a Successful String and Orchestra Program* (by Donald L. Hamann and Robert Gillespie). The proposed curriculum will fill a specific niche by:

- updating existing models to reflect current pedagogical thought and contemporary developments (such as alternative or eclectic strings)[1]
- providing a sequential curriculum that is based not on graded repertoire, but on executive (i.e., technical), musical, and artistic development
- providing a resource equally usable by the studio and school strings teacher
- directing the teacher to outstanding additional resources and method books for the specific needs of individual classroom and studio.
- developing a curriculum that may be easily linked to national and/or state-level curriculum standards.

- General curriculum models, such as the *National Standards for Music Education* (NSME), do not adequately address the unique nature of string pedagogy and performance. The NSME content standards, for example, do not provide any specific outcomes for stringed instruments. Even the NSME achievement standards, which are benchmarked at specific grade levels, are not comprehensive and not always easily adaptable for string instruction.

- Related to the above, benchmarking string performance at specific grade levels, such as happens in the NSME and in some state and district curricula, does not reflect the wide range of starting points that occur in our profession (e.g., from early-age Suzuki programs to middle- or high-school level starting experiences). This curriculum reflects specific achievement points, rather than grade levels. In the committee's review of national- and state-level documents, we found that few curricula offer a clear-cut and comprehensive approach that is specifically tied to string performance.

Connecting to National, State, and Local Standards

Our committee spent substantial time discussing how best to link this curriculum to existing national, state, and local standards. We spent considerable time discussing the role of the NSME in terms of the ASTA curriculum and determined that while we wanted our document to be compatible with the NSME, we did not want to be limited by the structure and specific content of those standards. We recognized the all-encompassing nature of the NSME, but also understood that the content standards are very broadly designed, encompassing what comprises the overall experience in music education for every student.

We also asked several other curricular experts in addition to string teachers who saw earlier drafts of this document at national and state conventions for input on this particular issue. Though varying opinions did exist, the overall consensus was as follows:

- The most commonly understood standards are the NSME. However, these standards are voluntary and are not assessed as part of current federal legislation. In addition, the man states already have written separate standards and have not universally accepted the NSME for implementation.
- The NSME are currently under review and it is highly likely that there will be substantial changes made to those standards in the relatively near future. National, state, and local standards are all subject to frequent and ongoing revision, a process that will continue in the future as well.

- Language used for the development of standards has shifted dramatically to a greater emphasis on *21st Century Skills*. Creativity, in general, is receiving greater attention, but there is still a wide range of opinion on how standards should be written. Terminology is not universal and the format of standards and curriculum is variable between states and local communities.

- In addition, though the arts are considered part of the "core curriculum" (under the *Goals 2000: Educate America Act*), there is still not a universally accepted philosophy about the role of the arts in education as a whole. Though music educators generally believe that the arts are central to a child's development, we still see an ongoing emphasis on how the arts help achievement in other academic areas. We do not want to tie this curriculum to documents or policy statements that place music or other arts at a subservient level, as several recent publications have done.

---

[1] There is not a commonly accepted usage yet for the field that is collectively known as alternative or eclectic strings, which include non-classical styles such as various fiddling styles (American, Celtic, Bluegrass, etc.), jazz, blues, rock, or various styles of ethnic, folk, or world music.

We did not find in national or state standards any specific curricular area that dealt with the idea of artistic expression, and yet this is one of the main reasons that many of us are involved with string instruments. This document, therefore, includes specific elements related to artistic expression.

With the above in mind, we determined to not link this curriculum to any specific national, state, or local standards. We believe that this curriculum should be *linkable*, but that determining *what* and *how* to do that is best left to local teachers, as they are the ones who ultimately are accountable to their districts and schools for achieving specific standards.

Curriculum Development Process

An initial organizational meeting was held at the ASTA National Convention in March 2008 (Albuquerque, New Mexico). At that meeting the committee discussed the parameters and goals for the project, the specific needs of the ASTA community, the rationale for the development of the project, and what the limits and expectations of this project would be. We recognized the need for a broad-based curriculum that reflected the diverse nature of string education as it exists in the United States today. At that meeting, as part of our due diligence process, the committee determined to search for and review existing curriculum documents, including state arts standards, model curricula from school districts, and any other related documents that would guide us in the development of this curriculum. This work was completed by July 2008.

Following the review of state and district documents, the committee held a working session at Duquesne University (Pittsburgh, Pennsylvania) in July 2008. During our meetings, we discussed the extremely wide-range of practices between states and districts that we found in our review of curriculum documents. We also recognize that each state has its own set of standards. In some cases, states adopted the NSME in their entirety. In other cases, the national standards were used as a guiding document for the development of state or district standards. These practices fell into three general categories:

1. The majority of states had very broad arts standards, of which music performance was just one small part, if it was mentioned at all.
2. A smaller portion of states had specific music standards, with some level of measurable outcome.
3. A limited number of states (at the time of this writing, Georgia, Iowa and Rhode Island) had no specific standards for music and/or the arts.

During the July 2008 meeting, our committee determined a structure for the curriculum that seemed to be logical and based on the best practice of previously published curricula and also reflected the language found in many state and district standards documents. We divided writing assignments between committee members (at least two committee members were responsible for each area) and determined a timeline for the writing process.
From September 2008–January 2009, we continued to review curriculum models and began the writing process. This initial process proved to be more tedious than expected. First, it was clear that there is a wide range of word usage in our profession as it relates to pedagogy. Next, it was evident that we had to more distinctly limit the scope of this project. Finally, the challenges of writing curriculum with only limited face-to-face meetings added to the time-intensive nature of the project.
In March 2009, we presented a draft of general curriculum organization to ASTA membership with sample level I benchmark documents. Based on the feedback we received from those who reviewed the document, we made several changes, including the development of a scope-and-sequence, addressing eclectic string styles, and expanding the learning tasks.

In July 2009, our committee met again, developed the initial scope-and-sequence, and began the process of writing the learning tasks that are part of this document, a process that continued through summer 2010.

An updated draft of the curriculum was presented at the national ASTA conference in February 2010, and feedback from that conference (plus other state conferences where the curriculum was presented) was incorporated into the current curriculum document.

The final draft was completed in August 2010 and sent out for advance review to our curricular advisory committee. Final revisions were made in late 2010 and early 2011.

We expect that this curriculum will undergo regular review and revision, which is normal for curriculum documents as standards, expectations, and practices change.

Organization of the Curriculum

We've organized this curriculum based on the unique priorities and needs of strings and orchestra teachers. We surveyed several different curricula models, both from the field of music and also from other academic areas, such as language arts, math, and science. In addition, we also surveyed outstanding curricular models from numerous school districts. A primary goal in writing this curriculum was that it clearly identified the skills, tasks, and knowledge needed at any given point throughout the performer's development.

The curriculum itself is organized into a clear *scope-and-sequence*, showing the progression within specific skill areas and also at increasing levels of ability. We recognize that some skills and knowledge are closely related while others are more distinct. Some skills may be just in the beginning stages while other skills may be more developed. For example, a student may have excellent aural skills, but may not have similarly high aptitude or achievement in rhythmic skills. Student progress is likely to vary within each category, and teachers should pay close attention to making sure that some skills that need remedial attention are not skipped in order to move students towards a more advanced level of achievement before they are actually ready to do so. Because much more information on musicianship and artistic skills may be found within curricula in the broader music education profession, our emphasis in this document is weighted towards executive skills. There is greater detail, therefore, on learning sequences and processes related to executive skill items. The three primary categories (or strands) of skills and knowledge that serve as the foundation for this curriculum were chosen because they reflect the broad and comprehensive nature of string performance.

Some curricula end with the scope-and-sequence, but our review of existing curricula nationwide, together with our understanding that there is a great diversity in the types of preparatory experiences string teachers have, influenced us to move one step further and develop *learning tasks*. Each learning task reflects a specific element found within the scope-and-sequence and contains a suggested sequence of teaching activities plus the indicators of success for that particular element. In addition, the teacher will find space at the bottom of each learning task template to add their own notes about specific connections to national, state, or local standards and also a place to note specific resource material for that element. See Figure 1 (below) for a diagram of the overall structure of the curriculum.

Figure 1. General Organization of ASTA Curriculum

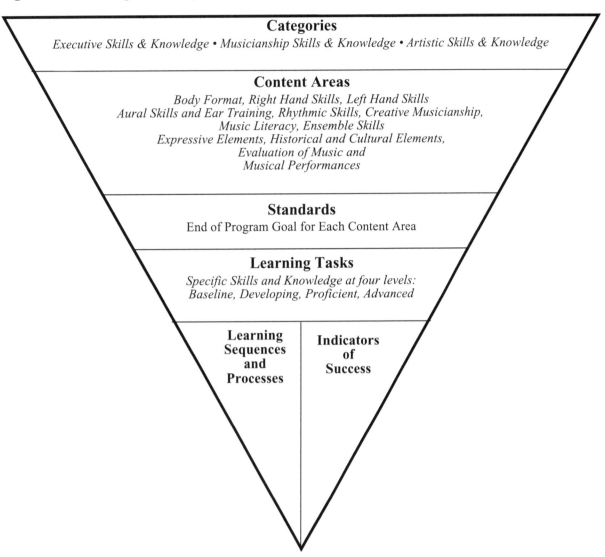

As shown above, the curriculum contains five general components:

    A. Categories of Skill and Knowledge
    B. Content Areas
    C. End-of-Program Standards
    D. Learning Tasks (divided into four additional levels)
    E. Learning Sequences and Process & Indicators of Success (Assessment)

Each of these components is described in more detail below:

A. Categories of Skills and Knowledge

    We divided this curriculum into three categories, reflecting the skills and knowledge that should be present in the strings studio or classroom:

    1. Executive Skills and Knowledge—those technical skills and understandings required to physically perform on the instrument, such as body format, bowings, etc.

    2. Musicianship Skills and Knowledge—those elements, such as understanding of rhythms, aural skills, note-reading skills, etc., that relate to musical understandings.

    3. Artistic Skills and Knowledge—those elements that relate to the creative and expressive side of music-making, beyond mere performance, such as improvisation, performance with artistic understanding, etc.

B. Content Areas

Each of the three categories above was divided into smaller content areas. While it may have been possible to create even smaller or larger categories, our committee determined that these specific areas were logical breakpoints for the curriculum.

1. Executive Skills and Knowledge—Body Format, Right Hand Skills, Left Hand Skills

2. Musicianship Skills and Training—Tonal Aural Skills and Ear Training, Rhythmic Skills and Ear Training, Creative Musicianship, Music Literacy, Ensemble Skills

3. Artistic Skills and Knowledge-- Expressive Elements, Historical and Cultural Elements, Evaluation of Music and Musical Performance

C. Standards

Rather than writing standards based on specific grade levels or years of study, this curriculum includes a single standard statement that serves as target for all levels of performance. In this approach, all levels of achievement in all content areas are measured in the context of the ultimate goal of performing at the level indicated in the standards.

1. **Standards Category 1: Executive Skills and Knowledge**

Content Area 1A—Body Format

Students perform with a lengthened and balanced posture; support instrument without tension, demonstrate ease of motion; format is adjusted for physiological changes due to growth; control of weight distribution, unilateral movement, bilateral movement, in sitting and standing position.

Content Area 1B—Left Hand Skills and Knowledge

Students perform with the correct placement and angle of the left arm-wrist-hand-fingers to the instrument; demonstrate position that is balanced and free of tension; play with independence of fingers, ease of motion and control of finger weight; produce characteristic tone, with vibrato (as appropriate); show understanding and ability to apply fingerings, finger patterns, shifting, extensions.

Content Area 1C—Right Hand Skills and Knowledge

Students perform with fluent bowing motion, control of variables (weight, angle, speed, and placement), in a variety of bowing techniques and articulations, with characteristic tone.

2. **Standards Category 2: Musicianship Skills and Knowledge**

Content Area 2A—Tonal Aural Skills & Ear Training

Students demonstrate the following abilities: matching and manipulating pitch, playing with a sense of tonality, tonal--melodic and tonal--harmonic function (horizontal and vertical relationships/functions of tonality), ear-to-hand skills, aural and kinesthetic awareness of pitch accuracy and intonation, including and related to improvisation.

Content Area 2B—Rhythmic Aural Skills and Ear Training

*Students perform simple and complex **rhythm** patterns/functions, with steady pulse/beat, correct sense of meter, metric organization and phrasing, in a variety of meters.*

Content Area 2C—Creative Musicianship

*Students demonstrate **creative musicianship** skills at all stages of development, including the ability to improvise variations of rhythmic, melodic, and harmonic patterns, within the traditions and standards of a variety of genres and practices; arrange and compose melodies and harmonies according to specific criteria and guidelines.*

Content Area 2D—Music Literacy

Students demonstrate sequential music literacy skills (decoding and comprehension), defined as an association of sound-to-symbol, in a given musical context, which includes: predictive components (understanding of reading based on audiation of written material) and knowledge of symbols and notation related to pitch, rhythm, dynamics, tonality, clef, articulation, etc.), based on the principle that sound comes before sight.

Content Area 2E—Ensemble Skills

Students perform in an ensemble, demonstrating sensitivity and the ability to adjust and maintain a uniform sense of rhythm, tempo, articulation, tone, blend, balance, and dynamics; understand conducting gestures, follow conductor and section leader, and are able to synchronize bowings.

3. **Standards Category 3: Artistic Skills and Knowledge**

Content Area 3A—Expressive Elements

Students employ expressive elements of music to communicate abstract thoughts, ideas, and meaning; to share the depth of the human experience; and for self-expression and understanding.

Content Area 3B—Historical and Cultural Elements

Students listen to, respond to, and perform music from a wide range of genres in a culturally authentic manner, reflecting the diverse nature of people groups and cultures across the world and in the US; performances demonstrate an understanding of historical and cultural contexts and reflect stylistic traditions and practice.

Content Area 3C—Evaluation of Music and Musical Performance

Students evaluate and analyze music for executive skill, musicianship, and artistic considerations; evaluate and analyze the individual and group performances based on appropriate criteria.

D. Learning Tasks

The learning task is the specific performance task or skill required at a given point. We have divided our learning tasks into four smaller levels: baseline, developing, proficient, and advanced. We anticipate that there will be discussion and perhaps energetic disagreement among our profession about the choice of these words, as there was even among our own committee! However, we hope that by defining these four levels that we can provide a useful working document for our profession.

Note: These tasks are not tied to a specific age, grade level, or number of years of performance. This is due to the fact that there is great diversity and disparity in our profession in the following areas:

- Starting age and grade
- Number of lessons or rehearsals per week
- Individual versus group instruction
- Prior learning, general musical environment, amount of home support
- Availability of instruments for practice outside of school
- Availability of qualified string teachers

These levels are not necessarily intended for those in studio-intensive or private-lesson intensive programs, where rates of progress may be much faster.

Baseline: This is typically found during the first- and/or second-year of instruction, depending on items listed above. These skills must be mastered in order for additional techniques to be learned. These are the basic, priority-level items for any beginning student.

Developing: This level is an extension of beginning-level technique; demonstrates more mastery of basic skills, moving into intermediate-level playing skills.

<u>Proficient</u>: At this level, students demonstrate mastery of beginning and intermediate-level skills, and performs with fluency and understanding. Should typically be found at middle-school level, but depending on items above, may not be found until high school level.

<u>Advanced</u>: These are upper level skills that should provide the student with the essential ability to perform on his or her instrument with musical and artistic understanding beyond the school years. This is the goal for all students at the exit-point from the public school program.

The learning task examples we have provided in this curriculum are intended to be representative of sample activities teachers might use in their classroom. There are excellent resources of other teaching strategies and activities already published and we highly encourage teachers to take advantage of them (we've included a resource list as part of this publication).

E. <u>Learning Sequences and Processes</u>

These are detailed descriptions for the teacher and/or student about how to perform or teach the given learning task. We have provided a parallel column for assessment points or indicators of success. For example, a description of how to initiate the basic beginning bow hold is included, with specific indicators of success that are understandable by the teacher and the student.

Summary

The curriculum is both sequential and developmental, moving from larger categories of skills and knowledge to specific learning tasks within each category. Figure 2 demonstrates how this works for the area of body format.

Figure 2: Specific Example for Category 1—Executive Skills and Knowledge, Content Area 1—Body Format

Category	Executive Skills and Knowledge	
Content Area	**Body Format**	
Standard	*Students perform with a lengthened and balanced posture; support instrument without tension, demonstrate ease of motion; format is adjusted for physiological changes due to growth; control of weight distribution, unilateral movement, bilateral movement, in sitting and standing position.*	
Example Learning Tasks	Rest Position	
	Attention Position	
	Playing Position	
	Weight Distribution	
	Posture	
	Unilateral movement	
	Bilateral movement	
	Sequential movement	

How to Use This Curriculum

One of the great challenges in designing a curriculum for national use is that there is great variety across the nation in the composition of string programs, starting age, state and district requirements and standards, community traditions and expectations, and cultural context for strings. While a district could adopt this curriculum as a model as written, we believe that the curriculum is best used when the teacher is able to adapt lesson plans and sequencing based on local needs. Because of this diversity, our curriculum is designed with the following characteristics:

1. Comprehensive: Covers all areas of string performance
2. Sequential: Demonstrates the appropriate sequence and hierarchy of skills and knowledge related to performing on a string instrument.
3. Flexibility: Levels can be adjusted and tasks may be adapted for local needs
4. Open-ended: Provides for extensions in technique, repertoire, skills, and understandings beyond what is written

Our goal was not to write all possible learning tasks and lesson plans for teachers, nor to provide a master list of all possible resources. Instead, we want this curriculum to outline the most essential concepts to serve as a launching pad for the expert teacher's own ideas and creativity.

Assessment of Student Performance

A curriculum that is not assessed is essentially a useless document. As we developed this curriculum, we wrote every standard, concept, learning task, and sequence asking the question *How will this item be assessed?*

Assessment occurs both formally and informally. Assessment is strategic and intentional and is the ultimate test of how well a curriculum works, and whether or not the students are actually learning anything along the way. For each of the learning tasks in this document, you will find a list of indicators of success. These are just some of the primary diagnostic indicators that the teacher should look for as students perform.

This curriculum does not address *dispositions* in assessment, by which we mean items such as *attendance, attitude, practice charts,* or *effort*. Those items are difficult to assess and do not always directly relate to actual achievement on the specific performance tasks. Instead, we focus on items related to the scope-and-sequence only, which are specifically linked to performance on the instrument itself within the categories of executive skills and understandings, musicianship skills and understandings, and artistic skills and understandings.

We strongly recommend that teachers develop a consistent system for evaluating student performance for the primary purpose of helping the teacher, parent, and student understand areas of mastery, areas of needed attention, and areas of severe deficiency. Regular, performance-based assessment is a characteristic of excellent string programs.

Sample Assessment Tools

There are several outstanding examples of performance-based rubrics available in the assessment part of the resource list at the end of the curriculum. However, the following examples provide a basic overview of how rubrics might be used in evaluating student performance. The *additive* (or *checklist*) rating scales emphasize elements equally, while a *continuous* rating scale emphasizes sequential skill motion and function and is more useful once students have mastered the basic skills outlined in the additive scales.[2]

Figure 1. *Right Hand: Bow Hold Rating Scale—Additive (5 points)*

Criteria	Points
Thumb bent at both knuckles	1
Index finger placed on side, between base knuckle and top knuckle	1
Middle fingerpad contacts frog, across from thumbnail	1
Ring fingerpad contacts frog, in concavity below stick	1
Little finger rests on top of bow stick	1
Total	

---

[2] All examples taken from Stephen Benham. "Musical Assessment as an Impetus for Strategic, Intentional, and Sustainable Growth in the Instrumental Classroom," in *The Practice of Assessment in Music Education: Frameworks, Models, and Designs*, ed. Timothy Brophy. (Chicago: GIA Publications, 2010), 145–169. Used by Permission.

Figure 2. *Right Hand: Bowing Motion Rating Scale—Continuous (5 points)*

Criteria	Points
Fingers display functionality (purposeful flexion/not tense)	1
Fingers passively flex inward at change to down-bow	2
Fingers passively flex outward at change to up-bow	3
Elbow joint opens/closes with bow change	4
Direction change is sequential (anticipated in upper-arm, leading to elbow, wrist, fingers)	5
Total	

Figure 3. *Left Hand: Instrument & Arm Placement Rating Scale—Additive (8 points)*

Criteria	Points
Body is balanced and centered over feet	1
Body is lengthened	1
Instrument falls naturally between shoulder and chin in playing position	1
Instrument is angled to provide ease of access for bowing and fingering	1
Elbow falls over left foot, under instrument	1
Left hand is balanced on arm (i.e., hand does not lean back or forward, providing access for finger extensions both directions, plus ease of motion for vibrato)	1
Hand is angled to allow all fingers to contact string while maintaining curved knuckles	1
Hand contacts neck slightly above base knuckle of index finger	1
Total	

The rating scale on the following page (Figure 4) may be used to evaluate individual student performance in an ensemble setting, i.e., how students perform on their individual parts within the ensemble. The goal here is not to assign a grade (though the teacher may decide to do so), but to determine the specific general level of performance that student has achieved on the assigned material. This should guide the student, teacher, parent, and administrator in understanding the specific needs of the student. See the following page for a definition for the criteria for each category.

Figure 4. *Individual Student Performance in an Ensemble—Check-box Style*

City High School
Student Performance Rating Sheet

Name_____ Date_____

Instrument_____Music Selections_____

Fundamentals: 1 2 3 4

Right Hand Position ☐ ☐ ☐ ☐

Left Hand Position ☐ ☐ ☐ ☐

Posture/Instrument Position ☐ ☐ ☐ ☐

Musical Criteria:

Rhythm ☐ ☐ ☐ ☐

Tone Quality ☐ ☐ ☐ ☐

Accuracy of Notes ☐ ☐ ☐ ☐

Accuracy of Bowing ☐ ☐ ☐ ☐

Intonation ☐ ☐ ☐ ☐

Expression ☐ ☐ ☐ ☐

Comments:

Definitions of Rating Scale Points for Individual Student Performance Rating Sheet

Right Hand Position
1   Student does not demonstrate correct placement of fingers or functional bow hold
2   Student demonstrates some correct finger placement, but not all aspects are correct
3   Student has correct finger placement, but does not demonstrate functional bow hold or fluidity
4   Student demonstrates consistent finger placement and functional bow hold

Left Hand Position
1   Left hand and arm is completely incorrect
2   Left arm is in correct position but wrist/hand do not address instrument correctly
3   Left arm, wrist, and hand are in correct position, but are not flexible
4   Left arm is fully functional

Posture/Instrument Position
1   Posture is not lengthened or balanced
2   Posture is lengthened and balanced, but instrument is not held correctly
3   Posture and instrument position are basically correct but student does display mobility/functionality
4   Posture and instrument position are consistently correct and functional

Rhythm
1   Student does not keep a steady beat
2   Student keeps a steady beat but does not display a sense of meter
3   Student keeps steady beat and displays sense of meter
4   Student plays both macrobeats and microbeats with precision

Tone Quality
1   Tone quality is unfocused; surface sound; or inconsistent
2   Student produces correct basic tone
3   Tone quality is consistent, student is able to control tone using bow placement, speed, or weight
4   Tone quality is full and consistent, and colors are controlled. Vibrato is used

Accuracy of Notes
1   Multiple errors are present; student unable to play notes correctly; may indicate lack of preparation or material that is too difficult
2   Student performs with control, although some errors are present
3   Student performs with fluency; errors are infrequent
4   Student performs with complete mastery of notes; no errors

Accuracy of Bowing
1   Bowing and articulation markings are not followed
2   Student plays with correct bowings
3   Student plays with correct bowings and articulations
4   Student plays with correct bowings, articulations, bow distribution

Intonation
1   Intonation is consistently incorrect
2   Student has general sense of intonation, but is inconsistent in finger placement
3   Finger placement is consistent and basic intonation is accurate
4   Student adjusts intonation for color and tonality

Expression
1   Student plays without expression or phrasing
2   Basic elements of phrasing are correct
3   Student plays with correct phrasing and style
4   Student plays with correct phrasing, style, and articulation

Part II—Curriculum Documents

Scope and Sequence, Page 1

Category 1: Executive Skills and Knowledge	Baseline	Developing	Proficient	Advanced
Content Area 1A—Body Format *Students perform with a lengthened and balanced posture; support instrument without tension, demonstrate ease of motion; format is adjusted for physiological changes due to growth; control of weight distribution, unilateral movement, bilateral movement, in sitting and standing position.*	1.1—Establish posture (sitting and standing) on all instruments. 1.2—Basic playing position for violin and viola. 1.3—Basic playing position for cello. 1.4—Basic playing position for bass.	2.1—Unilateral movement (connected to bowing motion) 2.2—Bilateral movement (connected to bowing motion) 2.3—Continue Baseline criteria, monitoring and adjusting to physical characteristics of individual students.	3.1—Continue previous criteria, monitoring and adjusting to physical characteristics of individual students.	4.1—Continue previous criteria, monitoring and adjusting to physical characteristics of individual students.
Content Area 1B—Left Hand Skills and Knowledge *Students perform with the correct placement and angle of the left arm-wrist-hand-fingers to the instrument; demonstrate position that is balanced and free of tension; play with independence of fingers, ease of motion and control of finger weight; produce characteristic tone, with vibrato (as appropriate); show understanding and ability to apply fingerings, finger patterns, shifting, extensions.*	1.1—Initial left hand finger placement 1.2—Initial finger patterns a. Violin/Viola b. Cello/Bass 1.3—Lateral finger movement 1.4—Vertical technique	2.1—Extensions a. Violin/Viola b. Cello/Bass 2.2—Introduction of positions a. Violin/Viola b. Cello/Bass c. Half Positions 2.3—Refinement of shifting a. Violin/Viola b. Cello c. Bass 2.4—Harmonics 2.5—Finger substitutions 2.6—Simple double-stops (one open string, one fingered string) 2.7—Chromatic alterations (F–F#) 2.8—Extension of vertical technique	3.1—Initial vibrato development 3.2—Advanced positions (5th and higher) 3.3—Complex double stops (two fingered strings) 3.4—Advanced finger patterns—Violin/Viola (e.g., augmented and chromatic patterns) 3.5—Extension of vertical technique	4.1—Artistic development and applications of vibrato. 4.2—Extension of vertical technique

Scope and Sequence, Page 2

Category 1: Executive Skills and Knowledge	Baseline	Developing	Proficient	Advanced

Content Area 1C—Right Hand Skills and Knowledge
Students perform with fluent bowing motion, control of variables (weight, angle, speed, and placement), in a variety of bowing techniques and articulations, with characteristic tone.
	1.1—Perform pizzicato in guitar position—Violin/Viola
	1.2—Perform pizzicato in playing position
	  a. Violin/Viola
	  b. Cello/Bass
	1.3—Establishing initial bow hold – all instruments
	  a. Violin/Viola
	  b. Cello/Bass (French bow)
	  c. Bass (German bow)
	1.4—Perform pre-bowing exercises
	  a. Violin/Viola
	  b. Cello/Bass (French bow)
	  c. Bass (German bow)
	1.5—Perform with simple connected (détaché) bow strokes.
	  a. Violin/Viola
	  b. Cello/Bass (French bow)
	  c. Bass (German bow)
	1.6—Perform with simple separated (staccato) bow strokes.
	1.7—Direction changes
	1.8—Short slurs
	1.9—String crossings
	1.10—Basic bow distribution
	1.11—Intro to weight, angle, speed, and placement (contact point and part of bow).
		2.1—Extending the détaché bow stroke.
		2.2—On-string strokes
		  a. Martelé
		  b. Slurred Staccato
		  c. Hooked Bowings
		  d. Longer slurs (three or more notes)
		  e. Accented Détaché
		2.3—Off-string strokes
		  a. Brush stroke
		2.4—Simple double stops
		2.5—Extension of technique related to control of bowing variables (weight, angle, speed, and placement)
			3.1—More advanced détaché bowings:
			  a. Louré
			  b. Détaché Lancé
			  c. Portato
			  d. Rapid Détaché
			  e. Tremolo
			3.2—Off-string strokes
			  a. Spiccato
			3.3—Special effect bowings
			  a. Flautando
			  b. Sul ponticello
			  c. Sul tasto
			  d. Col legno
			3.4—Chords
			3.5—Extension of technique related to control of bowing variables (weight, angle, speed, and placement)
				4.1—Ricochet bowing
				4.2—Sautillé
				4.3—Flying Spiccato
				4.4—Extension of technique related to control of bowing variables (weight, angle, speed, and placement)

Category 2: Musicianship Skills and Knowledge	Baseline	Developing	Proficient	Advanced
Content Area 2A—Tonal Aural Skills & Ear Training *Students demonstrate the following abilities: matching and manipulating pitch, playing with a sense of tonality, tonal–melodic and tonal–harmonic function (horizontal and vertical relationships/functions of tonality), ear-to-hand skills, aural and kinesthetic awareness of pitch accuracy and intonation, including and related to improvisation.*	1.1—Students perform, by ear, *melodic* tonal patterns (simple patterns and melodies within a tetrachord), in major and minor tonalities (vocally, pizzicato, and/or arco; neutral syllable, then solfege) 1.2—Students identify whether two performed *melodic* tonal patterns are the same or different. 1.3—Students correctly associate the words *high* and *low* with relative pitch differences (e.g., with the use of Curwen hand symbols and vocal solfege) 1.4—Students correctly identify direction of *melodic* motion (within a tetrachord). 1.5—Students alter melodies and harmonies (major-to-minor, minor-to-major) 1.6—Students perform, by ear, primary (tonic and dominant) *harmonic* tonal patterns (vocally, pizzicato, and/or arco; neutral syllable, then solfege) 1.7—Students improvise (vocally, pizzicato, and/or arco) *melodic* tonal patterns (within a tetrachord; neutral syllable, then solfege)	2.1—Students perform, by ear, *melodic* tonal patterns (patterns and melodies within a one-octave scale) in major and minor tonalities (vocally, pizzicato, and/or arco; neutral syllable, then solfege) 2.2—Students manipulate single pitches to adjust intonation and listen for "ringing tones" (resonance, sympathetic vibrations). 2.3—Students perform, by ear, primary (tonic, dominant, and subdominant) *harmonic* tonal patterns (vocally, pizzicato, and/or arco; neutral syllable, then solfege) 2.4—Students improvise (vocally, pizzicato, and/or arco) *melodic* tonal patterns (within an octave) 2.5—Students improvise (vocally, pizzicato, and/or arco) *harmonic* tonal patterns (vocally, pizzicato, and/or arco; neutral syllable, then solfege) 2.6—Students alter melodies and harmonies (major to minor and vice versa) 2.7—Students use fine tuners to adjust strings to match an external tonal reference	3.1—Students perform, by ear, *melodic* tonal patterns (patterns and melodies with chromatic alterations) in major and minor tonalities (vocally, pizzicato, and/or arco; neutral syllable, then solfege) 3.2—Students perform primary and secondary (ii, vi, vii) tonal patterns (vocally, pizzicato, and/or arco; neutral syllable, then solfege) 3.3—Students improvise (vocally, pizzicato, and/or arco; neutral syllable, then solfege) melodies and patterns, using chromatic alterations or simple modulations (e.g., major to relative/parallel minor). 3.4—Students improvise (vocally, pizzicato, and/or arco; neutral syllable, then solfege) simple accompaniments to melodies 3.5—Students use fine tuners and/or pegs to tune strings, in fifths, to an external tonal reference	4.1—Students perform, by ear, melodies and accompaniments in various modes and scales (e.g., Dorian, Mixolydian, Blues, etc.) and harmonies. 4.2—Students improvise melodies and accompaniments in various modes and scales (e.g., Dorian, Mixolydian, Blues, etc.) and harmonies.

Scope and Sequence, Page 4

Category 2: Musicianship Skills and Knowledge (cont.)	Baseline	Developing	Proficient	Advanced
Content Area 2B—Rhythmic Aural Skills & Ear Training *Students perform simple and complex rhythm patterns/functions, with steady pulse/beat, correct sense of meter, metric organization and phrasing, in a variety of meters.*	1.1—Students will maintain a steady pulse while *singing* or *chanting* rhythm patterns 1.2—Students will demonstrate a sense of meter while *singing* or *chanting* rhythm patterns 1.3—Students will maintain a steady pulse while *playing* rhythm patterns 1.4—Students will demonstrate a sense of meter while *playing* rhythm patterns 1.5—Students will perform rhythm patterns containing rests 1.6—Students will perform rhythm patterns containing ties 1.7—Students will perform rhythm patterns containing upbeats 1.8—Students will improvise rhythm patterns corresponding to Learning Tasks 1.1–1.7	2.1—Students will perform rhythm patterns containing subdivisions 2.2—Students will perform rhythm patterns containing elongations 2.3—Students will perform rhythm patterns containing rests 2.4—Students will improvise rhythm patterns corresponding to Learning Tasks 2.1–2.3	3.1—Students will perform rhythm patterns in asymmetrical and unusual meters 3.2—Students will perform rhythm patterns containing hemiolas 3.3—Students will perform rhythm patterns containing enrhythmic notation 3.4—Students will improvise rhythm patterns corresponding to Learning Tasks 3.1–3.3	4.1—Students will perform rhythmic patterns in irregular meters and polymeters 4.2—Students will perform rhythm patterns in mixed meters 4.3—Students will perform rhythm patterns containing syncopation within a single macrobeat 4.4—Students will improvise rhythm patterns corresponding to Learning Tasks 4.1–4.3

Scope and Sequence, Page 5

Category 2: Musicianship Skills and Knowledge (cont.)	Baseline	Developing	Proficient	Advanced
Content Area 2C—Creative Musicianship *Students demonstrate **creative musicianship** skills at all stages of development, including the ability to improvise variations of rhythmic, melodic, and harmonic patterns, within the traditions and standards of a variety of genres and practices; arrange and compose melodies and harmonies according to specific criteria and guidelines.*	1.1—Rhythmic: Students derive rhythm patterns from speech and environmental sounds and link them with the motion of the bow-hand 1.2—Tonal (Melodic & Harmonic): Students create one-note solos against a class-generated accompaniment 1.3—Textural: Students reproduce sound effects from their environment on their instruments (exploratory focus) 1.4—Compositional: Students invent scoring techniques based on common objectives 1.5—Creative Leadership: Students invent their own physical language for conducting	2.1—Rhythmic: Students teach each other short original rhythmic phrases through call-and-response 2.2—Tonal (Melodic & Harmonic): Students use the root, third, and fifth of a chord to solo over student-generated accompaniment 2.3—Textural: Students translate a visual or experiential narrative into original sounds on their instruments (music as storytelling) 2.4—Compositional: Students add traditional notation into their original scores 2.5—Creative Leadership: Students rehearse conducting the group with individually created hand signals	3.1—Rhythmic: Students layer individual rhythmic phrases to create an original group piece 3.2—Tonal (Melodic & Harmonic): Students create solos using the notes of the scale as stepping-stones between chord tones 3.3—Textural: Students translate a visual or experiential narrative into original sounds on their instruments and add rhythmic components (rhythmic focus) 3.4—Compositional: Students add a second instrument to their original scores 3.5—Creative Leadership: Student conductors lead extemporaneous sound stories using nonverbal signals	4.1—Rhythmic: Students analyze rhythmic phrases for tonal content and improvise over class-generated accompaniments 4.2—Tonal (Melodic & Harmonic): Students create solos using three scales over class-generated three-chord harmonic motion 4.3—Textural: Students improvise descriptive stories, including melody and harmony (harmonic focus) 4.4—Compositional: Students add third and fourth parts to their original scores 4.5—Creative Leadership: Students combine original scores with student-conducted improvised sections

Scope and Sequence, Page 6

Category 2: Musicianship Skills and Knowledge (cont.)	Baseline	Developing	Proficient	Advanced
Content Area 2D—Music Literacy *Students demonstrate sequential music literacy skills (decoding and comprehension), defined as an association of sound-to-symbol, in a given musical context, which includes: predictive components (understanding of reading based on audiation of written material and knowledge of symbols and notation related to pitch, rhythm, dynamics, tonality, clef, articulation, etc.), based on the principle that sound comes before sight.*	1.1—Students correctly identify and perform basic music notation and symbols associated with the following skills and understandings to each corresponding curricular level (see list in learning tasks) 1.2—Students sight-read basic music notation and symbols 1.3—Students understand chord symbols (root only) 1.4—Students correctly identify the following key signatures: C, G, D, and F Major (with their relative minors) 1.5—Students correctly identify accidentals (♮, ♭, ♯) 1.6—Students correctly identify musical forms: *AB* and *ABA*	2.1—Students correctly identify tonality (including key signature) and perform repertoire through three sharps and three flats 2.2—Students correctly identify interval labels (numbers only) 2.3— Students correctly identify musical forms: *Theme and Variations*, *Rondo* and *Minuet and Trio*	3.1—Students correctly identify and perform chords from chord symbols (tonic, dominant, and subdominant) 3.2—Violists correctly identify and perform the pitches found on the treble-clef staff, for the D- and A-strings, through 3rd position 3.3—Cellists correctly identify and perform the pitches found on the tenor-clef staff, for the D- and A-strings, through 4th position 3.4—Bassists correctly identify and perform the pitches found on the tenor-clef staff, for the D- and G-strings 3.5—Students correctly identify and perform double-flats and double-sharps 3.6—Students correctly identify tonality (including key signature) and perform repertoire through four sharps and four flats 3.7—Students correctly identify musical form: *Sonata-Allegro*	4.1—Students correctly identify tonality (including key signature) for all major and minor keys 4.2—Students correctly identify and perform in modes and scales: Dorian, Mixolydian, and Blues) 4.3—Students understand are able to perform notation associated with non-classical styles (e.g., twentieth century/modern, world music, other special effects

39

Scope and Sequence, Page 7

Category 2: Musicianship Skills and Knowledge (cont.)	Baseline	Developing	Proficient	Advanced
Content Area 2E—Ensemble Skills *Students perform in an ensemble, demonstrating sensitivity and the ability to adjust and maintain a uniform sense of rhythm, tempo, articulation, tone, blend, balance, and dynamics; understand conducting gestures, follow conductor and section leader, and are able to synchronize bowings.*	1.1—Students match pulse and rhythm to stay together as an ensemble. 1.2—Students adjust pitch within the ensemble. 1.3—Demonstrates self-discipline by working cooperatively with peers to produce a quality musical performance. 1.4—Display appropriate etiquette for style and venue of musical performance (classical concert *vs.* fiddle jam session). 1.5—Demonstrates well-disciplined personal demeanor during rehearsals and performance.	2.1—Students perform various tempos with a steady pulse. 2.2—Students adjust pitch within the ensemble. 2.3—Students demonstrate understanding of appropriate balance of the melody and accompanying lines. 2.4—Students imitate rhythm patterns at slow, medium, fast tempos following a conductor's beat pattern and cues. 2.5—Students match bow usage to section/ensemble.	3.1—Students follow section leader. 3.2—Students perform with style, articulation and pitch including adjusting dynamics according to musical function of their part (i.e. melody, harmony, counterpoint, etc.) 3.3—Follow conductor's more complex beat patterns, cues and expressive gestures.	4.1—Students adjust pulse, rhythm, pitch and dynamics within the ensemble. 4.2—Students demonstrate: preparation, balance, blend, style, interpretation and music sensitivity.

Scope and Sequence, Page 8

Category 3: Artistic Skills and Knowledge	Baseline	Developing	Proficient	Advanced
Content Area 3A—Expressive Elements *Students employ expressive elements of music to communicate abstract thoughts, ideas, and meaning; to share the depth of the human experience; and for self-expression and understanding.*	1.1—Students shape phrases with simple dynamic variation 1.2—Students alter tone by modifying bow technique (WASP—weight, angle, speed and point of contact) 1.3—Students perform with articulations corresponding to baseline-level right-hand technical skills	2.1—Students evaluate and demonstrate multiple ways of performing a single melody 2.2—Students apply knowledge of performance practice to selected repertoire. 2.3—Students perform with articulations corresponding to developing-level right-hand technical skills	3.1—Students perform with an expanded range of dynamics, tempos, and timbre/tone color 3.2—Students perform with a characteristic tone at all dynamic levels 3.3—Students apply knowledge of performance practice to selected repertoire 3.4—Students perform with articulation corresponding to proficient-level right-hand technical skills 3.5—Students use vibrato, when appropriate, to enhance timbre and tone	4.1—Students perform with consistent timbre and tone quality at all dynamic levels 4.2—Students independently interprets and performs selection applying appropriate dynamics, tempos, and timbre 4.3—Students apply knowledge of performance practice to selected repertoire 4.4—Students perform with articulations corresponding to advanced-level right-hand technical skills 4.5—Students employ various styles of vibrato for enhancing the artistic interpretation of the piece, according to accepted performance practice 4.6—Students use ornamentation, as appropriate to the performance practice and conventions of the period and style

Repertoire Note: As students progress throughout the four levels, the range of repertoire and styles should increase and become more eclectic. At the beginning level, the scope of music may be more limited, for example, to beginning folk songs. However, even these beginning level songs should reflect the local community and diverse cultural heritage.

Scope and Sequence, Page 9

Category 3: Artistic Skills and Knowledge	Baseline	Developing	Proficient	Advanced
Content Area 3B—Historical and Cultural Elements *Students listen to, respond to, and perform music from a wide range of genres in a culturally authentic manner, reflecting the diverse nature of people groups and cultures across the world and in the US; performances demonstrate an understanding of historical and cultural contexts and reflect stylistic traditions and practice.*	1.1— Students listen to selected music from diverse cultures and musical eras 1.2— Students identify, describe and compare distinguishing characteristics of composers and styles from selected repertoire 1.3— Students perform music from diverse styles	2.1— Students listen to selected music from diverse cultures and musical eras 2.2— Students identify, describe and compare distinguishing characteristics of composers and styles from selected repertoire 2.3— Students perform music from an expanding repertoire of diverse styles	3.1— Students listen to selected music from diverse cultures and musical eras 3.2— Students analyze and classify music according to style, composer, and genre 3.3— Students perform music from a large repertoire of diverse styles	4.1— Students listen to selected music from diverse cultures and musical eras 4.2— Students analyze and classify music according to style, composer, and genre 4.3— Students perform a comprehensive repertoire of eclectic styles in a manner that reflects understanding of cultural and stylistic traditions

Repertoire Note: As students progress throughout the four levels, the range of repertoire and styles should increase and become more eclectic. At the beginning level, the scope of music may be more limited, for example, to beginning folk songs. However, even these beginning level songs should reflect the local community and diverse cultural heritage.

Category 3: Artistic Skills and Knowledge	Baseline	Developing	Proficient	Advanced
Content Area 3C—Evaluation of Music and Musical Performance *Students evaluate and analyze music for executive skill, musicianship, and artistic considerations; evaluate and analyze the individual and group performances based on appropriate criteria.*	1.1—Students evaluate individual and group performance using established criteria. 1.2—Students describe personal preference in music listening and group performance.	2.1—Students evaluate individual and group performance using established criteria. 2.2—Students describe personal preference in music listening and group performance 2.3—Students, with teacher assistance, establish criteria for evaluating individual and group performances based on the level of music performed	3.1—Students evaluate individual and group performance using established criteria. 3.2—Students describe personal preference in music listening and group performance 3.3—Students, with teacher assistance, establish criteria for evaluating individual and group performances based on the level of music performed 3.4—Students compare and contrast performances of various interpretations of the same piece, using appropriate terminology and informed value judgments	4.1—Students evaluate individual and group performance using established criteria. 4.2—Students describe personal preference in music listening and group performance 4.3—Students, with teacher assistance, establish criteria for evaluating individual and group performances based on the level of music performed 4.4—Students compare and contrast performances of various interpretations of the same piece, using appropriate terminology and informed value judgments

Content Area 1A—Body Format

Students perform with a lengthened and balanced posture; support instrument without tension, demonstrate ease of motion; format is adjusted for physiological changes to growth; control of weight distribution, unilateral movement, bilateral movement, in sitting and standing position

Learning Tasks

1.1   Establish posture (sitting and standing) on all instruments
1.2   Basic playing position for violin and viola
1.3   Basic playing position for cello
1.4   Basic playing position for bass
2.1   Unilateral movement
2.2   Bilateral movement
2.3   Continue baseline criteria, monitoring and adjusting to physical characteristics of individual students.
3.1   Continue previous criteria, monitoring and adjusting to physical characteristics of individual students.
4.1   Continue previous criteria, monitoring and adjusting to physical characteristics of individual students.

Category 1:	Executive Skills and Knowledge
Content Area:	1A. Body Format Skills and Knowledge
Benchmark:	*Students establish a lengthened and balanced posture; support instrument without tension, demonstrate ease of motion; format is adjusted for physiological changes due to growth; control of weight distribution, unilateral movement, bilateral movement, in sitting and standing position.*
Learning Task:	1.1—Establish Basic Posture (all instruments)

Learning Sequences & Processes	Indicators of Success
Prior Knowledge and Precursors • Performing with good posture is foundational to all future success on the instrument. Emphasizing the development of good posture and body format will assist students in developing proper habits that will maximize their potential on the instrument. • The principles of good posture are the same, whether the student performs in seated or standing position: balanced, lengthened, centered, and functional (mobile, not static pose) • Priority should be placed on developing control in standing playing position before moving to seated playing position. • Establishing good seated posture requires that students have chairs (or stools, in the case of the bass—see BF 1.2.3—Establish Basic Bass Playing Position) that are stable and well constructed, tall enough (feet should touch ground; upper legs parallel to the ground), with flat seats (no backwards slope; a slight forward slope is acceptable). Chairs with a cushioned seat are preferred. Sequence of Activities—Standing • Standing tall, students stand with arms hanging normally at their sides, one foot under each shoulder and weight balanced on both feet. • The left foot may be slightly forward and turned a little to the left. • Students should practice shifting weight from one foot to the other and then coming back to a centered standing position, so that they understand what a balanced position feels like. Though only violinists, violists, and bassists play in a standing position, this is also an excellent activity for cellists, as a precursor to establish a good sitting position. Sequence of Activities—Sitting • Sit forward on chair • Place feet slightly apart on floor • Student body should be balanced and ready to stand without moving feet or sliding forward in chair	• Posture is lengthened, balanced, and centered • Students demonstrate a posture that is mobile, not posed or *frozen* • Students maintain posture in both seated and standing positions

Standards Links:

Resources and References:

Category 1:	Executive Skills and Knowledge
Content Area:	**1A. Body Format Skills and Knowledge**
Benchmark:	*Students establish a lengthened and balanced posture; support instrument without tension, demonstrate ease of motion; format is adjusted for physiological changes due to growth; control of weight distribution, unilateral movement, bilateral movement, in sitting and standing position.*
Learning Task:	**1.2—Establish Basic Playing Position (violin and viola)**

Learning Sequences & Processes	Indicators of Success
<u>General Information, Prior Knowledge, and Precursors</u> • Posture must be established in both seated and standing positions • Establishing playing position involves a sequence of activities and the development of new muscle groups. Students may become fatigued as they are developing endurance. • The establishment of *rest* and *playing* positions is important at this stage. • Review posture continuously during the establishment of teaching playing position. <u>Sequence of Activities—Rest Position</u> • Option 1—guitar position (see LH 1), if seated or standing, or • Option 2—attention position (seated position only), where the instrument is held vertically on one knee. This is often used for shorter rest periods. <u>Sequence of Activities—Playing Position</u> • Sit forward on chair • Place feet slightly apart on floor • Student body should be balanced and ready to stand without moving feet or sliding forward in chair • A two-handed hold is preferable when learning how to place the instrument in playing position. The left hand holds the instrument by the left upper bout (with the instrument facing away from the player) and the right hand holds the instrument on the right lower bout. • The instrument is raised above the shoulder and lowered into position (this helps establish a balanced and level hold) • The end button is aimed toward the throat. • The instrument is balanced between the left collarbone and the base knuckle of the left hand. • Place scroll at approximate 45 degree angle from imaginary lines drawn out from the nose and left ear (when facing forward)	• Posture is lengthened, balanced, and centered • Students demonstrate a posture that is mobile, not posed or *frozen* • Students maintain posture in both seated and standing positions • The left hand thumb rests gently on the side of the instrument neck. • There should be an open space under the instrument neck between the thumb and the base knuckle of the first finger. • The instrument is parallel to the floor or the scroll is even with the chin height. • The head is turned slightly to the left so the jawbone rests gently on the chinrest. • A shoulder pad or shaped sponge may be used to help provide adequate support. • Students should be able to move their head and maintain a relaxed position. • The left arm should be under the violin and able to move easily. • The left elbow is approximately under the fingerboard. • The left wrist should be relatively straight.

Standards Links:

Resources and References:

Category 1:	Executive Skills and Knowledge
Content Area:	**1A. Body Format Skills and Knowledge**
Benchmark:	*Students establish a lengthened and balanced posture; support instrument without tension, demonstrate ease of motion; format is adjusted for physiological changes due to growth; control of weight distribution, unilateral movement, bilateral movement, in sitting and standing position.*
Learning Task:	**1.3—Establish Basic Playing Position (cello)**

Learning Sequences & Processes	Indicators of Success
General Information, Prior Knowledge, and Precursors • Posture must be established • Establishing playing position involves a sequence of activities and the development of new muscle groups. Students may become fatigued as they are developing endurance. • There is essentially no difference between *rest* and *playing* positions for the cello. The left hand may be placed on the upper bout (left of the fingerboard, when seated). • Review posture continuously during the establishment of teaching playing position. Sequence of Activities • Pull endpin out, adjusting the length so the back of the scroll of the cello is as high as the nose when standing (N.B.—this positioning may range from the chin to the nose, depending on the height of the student). • Once the student is seated, the cello should be held away from the body, using both hands, placed on the upper bouts (shoulders) of the instrument. • Using both hands, bring the cello back into playing position. • The upper back right edge of the cello rests on the body around the lower-1/3 of the sternum (breastbone) • The endpin height allows the cello to be at an angle of 55–65 degrees. Adjust the endpin as necessary. • The C-peg is behind the left ear. For tall students this may be a problem, so the vertical angle of the cello may need to be adjusted by using a longer endpin or moving the neck slightly away from the head. • The inside of both knees gently touch the sides of the cello below the bouts.	• Posture is lengthened, balanced, and centered. • Students demonstrate a posture that is mobile, not posed or *frozen*. • The student should be relaxed, balanced and able to move from side to side. • The left arm is extended straight out and hand forms a relaxed "C" with hand and thumb curved. • The left elbow bends and brings the left hand and aligns fingers with first position. • The left wrist should be relaxed and aligned, not arched or curved backwards. • The pad of the left thumb rests behind the neck under the second finger. • Students should be able to support the cello without using the hands or arms.

Standards Links:

Resources and References:

Category 1:	Executive Skills and Knowledge
Content Area:	**1A. Body Format Skills and Knowledge**
Benchmark:	*Students establish a lengthened and balanced posture; support instrument without tension, demonstrate ease of motion; format is adjusted for physiological changes due to growth; control of weight distribution, unilateral movement, bilateral movement, in sitting and standing position.*
Learning Task:	**1.4—Establish Basic Playing Position (bass)**

Learning Sequences & Processes	Indicators of Success
General Information, Prior Knowledge, and Precursors • Posture must be established in both seated and standing positions • Establishing playing position involves a sequence of activities and the development of new muscle groups. Students may become fatigued as they are developing endurance. • There is essentially no difference between *rest* and *playing* positions for the bass. The left hand may be placed on the upper bout (left of the fingerboard, when seated). • Review posture continuously during the establishment of teaching playing position. Sequence of Activities—Standing Position • Adjust the endpin so the nut is between the forehead and top of the head while standing. • Stand with one foot under each shoulder and weight balanced on both feet. • Using both hands, place the bass at arm's length away from the bass placing the endpin in front of the left foot. Turn the bass slightly to the right so the back right edge is facing the stomach. • Bring the left foot forward and the bass toward the body touching the left side of the stomach. Sequence of Activities—Seated Position • Use a good quality commercial adjustable stool or a standard padded kitchen stool. The height of the stool should be adjusted so that the student can comfortably reach the floor with the heel of the right foot, while having a slight bend in the right knee. • Adjust the endpin so the nut is between the forehead and top of the head while standing. • Sit on the front edge of the bass stool with the right foot on the floor. • The left foot should be placed on a rung of the stool, approximately 8–10 inches off the floor, depending on the size of the student. The legs and knees are far enough apart to accommodate the width of the bass. • Using both hands, place the bass at arm's length with the endpin in front of the left foot. Turn the bass to the students right so the back right edge is facing the stomach. • Bring the bass toward the body so the edge touches the left side of the stomach and the back rests against the inside of the left leg.	• Posture is lengthened, balanced, and centered • Students demonstrate a posture that is mobile, not posed or *frozen* • The student should be relaxed, balanced and able to move from side to side. • The neck of the bass should be close to the neck of the student. • The palm of the right hand should be able to reach the bowing area of the strings. • Balance instrument without hands. • The left arm is extended straight out and hand forms a relaxed "C" with hand and thumb curved. • The left elbow bends and brings the left hand and aligns fingers with first position. • The left wrist should be relaxed and aligned, not arched or curved backwards. • The pad of the left thumb rests behind the neck under the second finger.

Standards Links:

Resources and References:

Category 1:	Executive Skills and Knowledge
Content Area:	1A. Body Format Skills and Knowledge
Benchmark:	*Students establish a lengthened and balanced posture; support instrument without tension, demonstrate ease of motion; format is adjusted for physiological changes due to growth; control of weight distribution, unilateral movement, bilateral movement, in sitting and standing position.*
Learning Task:	2.1—Unilateral Movement

Learning Sequences & Processes	Indicators of Success
<u>General Information, Prior Knowledge, and Precursors</u> • Posture must be established in both seated and standing positions. • Student should be able to support the instrument while maintaining a balanced, lengthened posture without tension. • Good bow hand position is established. Basic bowing is parallel to the bridge. • Unilateral movement is the initial stage of bow arm movement in relation to the body. All elements move in the same direction (e.g., when the bow moves to the right, the body also moves to the right). Unilateral movement leads to bilateral movement (Task 2.2) and ultimately to the development of the sequential bow stroke. <u>Sequence of Activities—Standing Position</u> • Without instruments, students stand with arms to side, balanced equally on both feet. • Starting with 60% of body weight on left side, gradually transfer weight equally to both feet; then transfer 60% of body weight to the right side. (Waist remains flexible.) Practice starting with different levels of weight. Emphasize moving in a free and easy motion, distributing weight back-and-forth between the feet. • Raise right arm into the bowing position (without the bow or the instrument), and practice starting with weight on left leg and bow placed at the imaginary frog. Shift weight in a natural motion to the right leg, while the right arm moves toward the imaginary tip of the bow. • With an instrument—in playing position, set the right-hand on its side (thumb and forefinger side, as if you were pouring out a glass of water). Strum the strings in a down-bow motion while shifting weight from left-to-right and back again. • With instrument in playing position, place bow at frog on G-string. • As student draws a down bow slur (open G-string to open D-string) start with 60% weight on left side and gradually transfer the natural body weight to the right side as the bow approaches the tip. • Starting at the tip, 60% of the body weight starts on the right side of the body and gradually moves to the left side. • This movement is advantageous in long, slow bow strokes. • Practice on different strings and the motion feels different for each of the different string levels. <u>Special Notes for Sitting Position</u> • Body weight is supported by the feet as well as the chair. The weight still shifts from left and right feet and hip bones. The waist is flexible. • In both unilateral and bilateral movements, the player anticipates the change of direction by slightly leaning (from waist) • String bass players require greater mobility due to greater movement of the left hand • The same exercises shown above may be repeated for seated position.	• Posture is lengthened, balanced, and centered • Shoulders, arms, upper body, waist, legs, etc., are all relaxed. • Student moves fluidly during the shift of weight. • Motion is continuous, not broken or hesitant. • Strumming motion should move in an arc-like fashion.

Standards Links:	

Resources and References:	

Category 1: Executive Skills and Knowledge

Content Area:	1A. Body Format Skills and Knowledge
Benchmark:	*Students establish a lengthened and balanced posture; support instrument without tension, demonstrate ease of motion; format is adjusted for physiological changes due to growth; control of weight distribution, unilateral movement, bilateral movement, in sitting and standing position.*
Learning Task:	2.2—Bilateral Movement

Learning Sequences & Processes	Indicators of Success
General Information, Prior Knowledge, and Precursors • See information from 2.1—Unilateral movement. • Unilateral movement must be established. • Bilateral movement is an extension of unilateral movement and leads to the development of the sequential bow stroke. • In unilateral movement, the body moves in the same general direction as the bow. In bilateral movement, the body moves in the opposite direction of the bow. Sequence of Activities • The same exercises used in establishing the unilateral motion may be repeated for the bilateral motion. Simply reverse the starting point for weight distribution. For example, practice starting with weight on the left side, but with the bow at the imaginary tip. Shift weight to the right as the bow moves to the frog. Practice this with and without instruments. • The shift from unilateral to bilateral occurs when the bow speed increases to medium and fast strokes. • Practice with different lengths of bow stroke and emphasizing different portions of the bow (e.g., just the upper-half or just the lower-half). • Practice on each string, as bow levels are different for each string.	• Posture is lengthened, balanced, and centered • Shoulders, arms, upper body, waist, legs, etc., are all relaxed. • Student moves fluidly during the shift of weight. • Motion is continuous, not broken or hesitant. • Strumming motion should move in an arc-like fashion. • Students should feel an opening-and-closing of the body, like an accordion moves.

Standards Links:

Resources and References:

Category 1:	Executive Skills and Knowledge
Content Area:	1A. Body Format Skills and Knowledge
Benchmark:	*Students establish a lengthened and balanced posture; support instrument without tension, demonstrate ease of motion; format is adjusted for physiological changes due to growth; control of weight distribution, unilateral movement, bilateral movement, in sitting and standing position.*
Learning Task:	**2.3—Extension of Technique**

Learning Sequences & Processes	Indicators of Success
General Information, Prior Knowledge, and Precursors • General note: with each of the activities in the prior learning tasks, it is important spending time reinforcing motion and kinesthetic awareness, so that student understandings move from conscious to sub-conscious. There is a danger in introducing new concepts before current concepts have been sufficiently reinforced and mastered. • At the end of each level (i.e., baseline, developing, proficient, and advanced), it is important to create exercises that reinforce and extend the techniques listed above. In this section, we leave room in the learning template for teachers to list their own ideas and exercises from the many resources listed in the resource list. • Any changes in the indicators of success for each element (like those listed to the right) are cues that the student is struggling with a new concept or has developed a bad habit. Teachers need to move backwards through the sequence of skills to determine where the specific problem is occurring. Review should be a part of each day's lesson in any case and the empty space below provides a clear visual reminder of the teacher's need to address the specific needs of the students in their classroom.	• Posture is lengthened, balanced, and centered • Shoulders, arms, upper body, waist, legs, etc., are all relaxed. • Student moves fluidly during the shift of weight. • Motion is continuous, not broken or hesitant. • Students look "natural" as they play.

Standards Links:

Resources and References:

Category 1:	**Executive Skills and Knowledge**
Content Area:	**1A. Body Format Skills and Knowledge**
Benchmark:	*Students establish a lengthened and balanced posture; support instrument without tension, demonstrate ease of motion; format is adjusted for physiological changes due to growth; control of weight distribution, unilateral movement, bilateral movement, in sitting and standing position.*
Learning Task:	**3.1—Extension of Technique**

Learning Sequences & Processes	**Indicators of Success**
<u>General Information, Prior Knowledge, and Precursors</u> • Special Note: As students grow and their physiology changes, it is important to reinforce the basic elements listed above on a regular (perhaps even daily basis). Changes in height and weight, in addition to those changes caused as students physical mature into adult bodies, all dramatically affect basic body format issues. • General note: with each of the activities listed in the prior learning tasks, it is important spending time reinforcing motion and kinesthetic awareness, so that student understandings move from conscious to sub-conscious. There is a danger in introducing new concepts before current concepts have been sufficiently reinforced and mastered. • At the end of each level (i.e., baseline, developing, proficient, and advanced), it is important to create exercises that reinforce and extend the techniques listed above. In this section, we leave room in the learning template for teachers to list their own ideas and exercises from the many resources listed in the resource list. • Any changes in the indicators of success for each element (like those listed to the right) are cues that the student is struggling with a new concept or has developed a bad habit. Teachers need to move backwards through the sequence of skills to determine where the specific problem is occurring. Review should be a part of each day's lesson in any case and the empty space below provides a clear visual reminder of the teacher's need to address the specific needs of the students in their classroom.	• Posture is lengthened, balanced, and centered • Shoulders, arms, upper body, waist, legs, etc., are all relaxed. • Student moves fluidly during the shift of weight. • Motion is continuous, not broken or hesitant. • Students look "natural" as they play.

Standards Links:

Resources and References:

Category 1: Executive Skills and Knowledge

Content Area:	**1A. Body Format Skills and Knowledge**
Benchmark:	*Students establish a lengthened and balanced posture; support instrument without tension, demonstrate ease of motion; format is adjusted for physiological changes due to growth; control of weight distribution, unilateral movement, bilateral movement, in sitting and standing position.*
Learning Task:	**4.1—Extension of Technique**

Learning Sequences & Processes	Indicators of Success
General Information, Prior Knowledge, and Precursors • Special Note: See notes listed for learning tasks 2.3 and 3.1 above. In addition, be aware that the introduction of advanced level repertoire will reveal any flaws in body format that still exist. Teachers need to be sure that students maintain excellent body format as they move into more challenging technical and artistically demanding pieces. • General note: with each of the activities listed in the prior learning tasks, it is important spending time reinforcing motion and kinesthetic awareness, so that student understandings move from conscious to sub-conscious. There is a danger in introducing new concepts before current concepts have been sufficiently reinforced and mastered. • At the end of each level (i.e., baseline, developing, proficient, and advanced), it is important to create exercises that reinforce and extend the techniques listed above. In this section, we leave room in the learning template for teachers to list their own ideas and exercises from the many resources listed in the resource list. • Any changes in the indicators of success for each element (like those listed to the right) are cues that the student is struggling with a new concept or has developed a bad habit. Teachers need to move backwards through the sequence of skills to determine where the specific problem is occurring. Review should be a part of each day's lesson in any case and the empty space below provides a clear visual reminder of the teacher's need to address the specific needs of the students in their classroom.	• Posture is lengthened, balanced, and centered • Shoulders, arms, upper body, waist, legs, etc., are all relaxed. • Student moves fluidly during the shift of weight. • Motion is continuous, not broken or hesitant. • Students look "natural" as they play.

Standards Links:

Resources and References:

Content Area 1B—Left Hand Skills and Knowledge

Students perform with the correct placement and angle of the left arm-wrist-hand-fingers to the instrument; demonstrate position that is balanced and free of tension; play with independence of fingers, ease of motion and control of finger weight; produce characteristic tone, with vibrato (as appropriate); show understanding and ability to apply fingerings, finger patterns, shifting, extensions.

Learning Tasks

1.1   Initial left hand finger placement
1.2   Initial finger patterns
     a.   Violin/Viola
     b.   Cello/Bass
1.3   Lateral finger movement
1.4   Vertical technique
2.1   Extensions
     a.   Violin/Viola
     b.   Cello/Bass
2.2   Introduction of positions
     a.   Violin/Viola
     b.   Cello/Bass
     c.   Half Position
2.3   Refinement of shifting
     a.   Violin/Viola
     b.   Cello
     c.   Bass
2.4   Harmonics
2.5   Finger substitutions
2.6   Simple double stops (e.g., one open string, one fingered string)
2.7   Chromatic alterations (e.g., F–F♯)
2.8   Extension of vertical technique
3.1   Initial vibrato development
3.2   Advanced positions (5th and higher)
3.3   Complex double stops (two fingered strings)
3.4   Advanced finger patterns—Violin/Viola (e.g., augmented and chromatic patterns)
3.5   Extension of vertical technique
4.1   Artistic development and applications of vibrato
4.2   Extension of vertical technique

Category 1: Executive Skills and Knowledge

Content Area:	1B. Left Hand Skills and Knowledge
Benchmark:	*Students perform with the correct placement and angle of the left arm-wrist-hand-fingers to the instrument; demonstrate position that is balanced and free of tension; play with independence of fingers, ease of motion and control of finger weight; produce characteristic tone, with vibrato (as appropriate); show understanding and ability to apply fingerings, finger patterns, shifting, extensions.*
Learning Task:	1.1—Initial Left Hand Finger Placement

Learning Sequences & Processes	Indicators of Success
General Information, Prior Knowledge, and Precursors • Students must be able to perform with a body posture that is balanced, centered, and lengthened. For violins and violas, this includes both sitting and standing positions. • As students begin to play the instrument, it is critical that the left arm and hand remain flexible. Move the hand up and down the fingerboard, tap the neck with the thumb. Observe constantly to be sure no part of the hand and arm is locked into a rigid position. • Many teachers use tapes or dots on the fingerboard to guide intonation in beginning study. (It is recommended that these markers be removed as soon as the student can match pitch in first position.) Though markers can assist in the development of the hand shape, they can actually inhibit the development of audiation and aural skills. Emphasis should be placed on correct finger placement based on aural call-and-response and through the use of solfege or singing. Sequence of Activities • To begin to bring the hand in line with the fingerboard, have students pluck open strings with the left hand 4th finger in approximate 1st to 3rd position locations. • Identify fingers by number (1, 2, 3, 4). • With the instrument well supported, tap each finger on the corresponding marker. For violin and viola—check to be sure the open space between the side of the thumb and the base joint of the first finger is maintained, and that students do not "squeeze" the neck. For cello and bass—be sure that students are not squeezing the neck and that the thumb is relaxed and not collapsed. • Using note names or solfege, sing a major scale pattern from an open string pitch. Explain that, as the length of the vibrating string is shortened by holding it down the pitch is higher. Sing the scale, tapping the corresponding tape/dot for each finger, ascending and descending. • Play (pizzicato or arco) a one-octave major scale from an open string, using only enough finger weight to produce a clear, resonant tone.	• Turn the hand so the knuckles are parallel to the fingerboard. • Fingers move from the base joint. • Stop the string with the fingertip pad. • Use only as much finger weight as is needed to hold the string against the fingerboard. • Keep the fingers curved—no joint should collapse.

Standards Links:

Resources and References:

Category 1:	**Executive Skills and Knowledge**
Content Area:	**1B. Left Hand Skills and Knowledge**
Benchmark:	*Students perform with the correct placement and angle of the left arm-wrist-hand-fingers to the instrument; demonstrate position that is balanced and free of tension; play with independence of fingers, ease of motion and control of finger weight; produce characteristic tone, with vibrato (as appropriate); show understanding and ability to apply fingerings, finger patterns, shifting, extensions.*
Learning Task:	**1.2.a—Initial Finger Patterns (Violin and Viola)**

Learning Sequences & Processes	**Indicators of Success**
General Information, Prior Knowledge, and Precursors • There are four basic finger patterns for violin and viola: 1-2, 2-3, 3-4, open. Fingers are close together for half-steps, spaced apart for whole-steps. Most methods begin with the 2-3 pattern, creating a major scale from the open string. To avoid having the hand "locked" in the 2-3 pattern and to develop the flexibility needed for finger independence, all four patterns should be introduced early in the student's development. Each pattern should be played with consistently good intonation before introducing the next. • Introduce each new pattern both aurally and by physical modeling. Let students practice the pattern both away from the instrument and on the fingerboard before beginning to play it. Keep the left hand and thumb flexible, without excessive tension. Sequence of Activities The 1-2 pattern (low 2) • Using note names or solfege, sing major (high 2) and minor (low 2) tetrachords from the open string. • Play major and minor tetrachords from the open string and let students identify which pattern they hear. • Practice playing scales and simple melodies with 2-3 and 1-2 patterns. • In descending stepwise passages, 3 should be played independently before low 2. The open pattern (low 1) • Open the first finger back to the nut. Avoid leaning the hand back and collapsing the wrist. Play open string to low 1, then to the whole-step position; let students identify which pattern they hear. • Play open string to low 1, then to the whole-step position; let students identify which pattern they hear • Using note names or solfege, alternate singing a half-step or a whole-step from the open string. • Play scales and simple melodies with the open pattern and the 1-2 pattern. The 3-4 pattern (high 3) • Keep the hand balanced so the third finger remains curved and the string is stopped with the fingertip pad. Students may need to move the elbow very slightly forward under the instrument. • Play major (3-4 pattern—high 3) and minor (2-3 pattern) tetrachords from the first finger; let students identify which pattern they hear. • Using note names or solfege, alternate sing major and minor tetrachords from the first finger. • Play scales and simple melodies with the 2-3 and 3-4 patterns.	• The left hand and thumb remain flexible, without excessive tension, allowing ease of movement from one pattern to another. • Students play scales and simple melodies using each pattern with good intonation and maintaining a good left hand position. The open pattern (low 1) • The first finger is opened back without collapsing the wrist The 3-4 pattern (high 3) • The hand is balanced so that the third finger remains curved and the string is stopped with the fingertip pad in the 3-4 pattern.

Standards Links:

Resources and References:

Category 1:	**Executive Skills and Knowledge**
Content Area:	**1B. Left Hand Skills and Knowledge**
Benchmark:	*Students perform with the correct placement and angle of the left arm-wrist-hand-fingers to the instrument; demonstrate position that is balanced and free of tension; play with independence of fingers, ease of motion and control of finger weight; produce characteristic tone, with vibrato (as appropriate); show understanding and ability to apply fingerings, finger patterns, shifting, extensions.*
Learning Task:	**1.2.b—Initial Finger Patterns (Cello and Bass)**

Learning Sequences & Processes	**Indicators of Success**
General Information, Prior Knowledge, and Precursors • There are two basic finger patterns for the cello: Minor (0–1-2–4) and Major (0–1–3-4). On the cello, each finger plays a half step. Whole-steps are created by skipping a finger (e.g., 1st finger to 3rd finger is a whole step), or by using an extended pattern (introduced later). • There are two basic finger patterns for the bass: Minor (0–1-2–0) and (0–1–4-0). On the bass, the third finger is not used (until much higher positions), and the half-steps occur between 1st and 2nd fingers and 2nd and 4th fingers. The whole-step occurs between 1st and 4th fingers. • Introduce each new pattern both aurally and by physical modeling. Let students practice the pattern both away from the instrument and on the fingerboard before beginning to play the notes either pizzicato or arco. Keep the left hand and fingers flexible, without excessive tension. • Other patterns are created by either extending the hand (for the cello) or by changing the position of the hand (shifting). See the corresponding Learning Tasks below. Sequence of Activities • Using note names or solfege, the teacher sings and students echo major and minor tetrachords from one of the open string notes (D is easiest for most students in terms of vocal range). • The teacher plays and students echo major and minor tetrachords from the open string and let students identify which pattern they hear. Practice this pizzicato first, then arco. • Practice playing scales and simple melodies with both patterns.	• The left hand and fingers remain flexible, without excessive tension, allowing ease of movement from one pattern to another. • Students play scales and simple melodies using each pattern with good intonation and maintaining a good left hand position.

Standards Links:

Resources and References:

Category 1:	Executive Skills and Knowledge
Content Area:	1B. Left Hand Skills and Knowledge – Violin/Viola
Benchmark:	*Students perform with the correct placement and angle of the left arm-wrist-hand-fingers to the instrument; demonstrate position that is balanced and free of tension; play with independence of fingers, ease of motion and control of finger weight; produce characteristic tone, with vibrato (as appropriate); show understanding and ability to apply fingerings, finger patterns, shifting, extensions.*
Learning Task:	1.3—Lateral Finger Movement

Learning Sequences & Processes	Indicators of Success
General Information, Prior Knowledge, and Precursor • For a facile left-hand technique, students must be able to move the fingers laterally across the strings as well as up and down each string. • For good intonation across two strings, students should learn to think of half- and whole-step relationships across the strings: i.e., E to F is a half-step on the D-string; B to C is a half-step on the A-string; therefore, in playing E on the D-string to C on the A-string, 1st and 2nd fingers will be close. • To maintain the frame of the hand from the highest to the lowest string, the left arm must be able to move freely to balance the hand over each string. • As is true in all left hand actions, excessive tension hinders free movement. Sequence of Activities • Demonstrate and have students finger a "Geminiani chord"—first finger on the lowest string, 2nd on the next string, 3rd on the next, and 4th on the highest string. Holding the first finger down, tap the other three. • Demonstrate and have students practice "elbow harps"—with the fingers held curved over the lowest string, swing the left elbow under the instrument, causing the fingers to pluck across the four strings. • Demonstrate, explain and have students play examples of half- and whole-step relationships across two strings. • Point out and practice lateral finger movement in literature being studied.	• The left hand and thumb remain flexible, without excessive tension, allowing ease of movement from one pattern to another. • Students demonstrate the ability to play excerpts requiring lateral finger movement without excessive tension in the left hand, and with good intonation.

Standards Links:

Resources and References:

Level:	Baseline

Category 1: Executive Skills and Knowledge

Content Area:	1B. Left Hand Skills and Knowledge – Violin/Viola
Benchmark:	*Students perform with the correct placement and angle of the left arm-wrist-hand-fingers to the instrument; demonstrate position that is balanced and free of tension; play with independence of fingers, ease of motion and control of finger weight; produce characteristic tone, with vibrato (as appropriate); show understanding and ability to apply fingerings, finger patterns, shifting, extensions.*
Learning Task:	1.4—Vertical Technique

Learning Sequences & Processes	Indicators of Success
General Information, Prior Knowledge, and Precursor • The goal is for students to develop control over stages of weight into the string with left-hand fingers Sequence of Activities This series of exercises is done without the bow: • Teacher invites students to choose their favorite finger, string, and spot on the string (pitch is not important to this exercise) • Teacher asks students to barely touch the surface of the string with that finger • Teacher labels this degree of weight as 0% • Teacher invites students to use the weight of the finger to gradually lower the string to the finger board • Teacher labels this degree of weight as 100% • Teacher invites students to find 0% again, then 25%, 50%, 75%, and the lightest 100% they can find • Repeat this series with each of the other three fingers.	• The left hand and thumb remain flexible, without excessive tension, allowing ease of movement from one pattern to another. • Students perceive the string pressed down to the fingerboard as a graduated event rather than a single level of weight • Students learn to think vertically on the fingerboard • Students control left-hand fingering technique adjusting for downward weight and release. • Students can modify left-hand weight at will by adjusting the specific amount of weight in each finger.

Standards Links:

Resources and References:

Category 1:	Executive Skills and Knowledge
Content Area:	**1B. Left Hand Skills and Knowledge**
Benchmark:	*Students perform with the correct placement and angle of the left arm-wrist-hand-fingers to the instrument; demonstrate position that is balanced and free of tension; play with independence of fingers, ease of motion and control of finger weight; produce characteristic tone, with vibrato (as appropriate); show understanding and ability to apply fingerings, finger patterns, shifting, extensions.*
Learning Task:	**2.1.a—Violin/Viola Extensions**

Learning Sequences & Processes	Indicators of Success
General Information, Prior Knowledge and Precursors	Students will perform tonal patterns, simple melodies, and scales involving upward and downward extensions with:

General Information, Prior Knowledge and Precursors

- Extensions enable the player to reach outside the frame of the hand without shifting. In upward (forward) extensions, the fourth finger moves a half-step higher (i.e., from E to F on the A-string). In downward (backward) extensions, the first finger moves a half-step lower (i.e., from B to B♭ on the A-string).

- In playing extensions, the position of the hand on the neck does not change (i.e., in the extensions described above, the hand stays in first position); however, moving the thumb slightly toward the center of the hand may facilitate the downward extension. Excessive tension between the thumb and the base joint of the index finger on the neck makes it difficult to open the fingers forward or back.

Sequence of Activities

- Demonstrate and explain the use of extensions.

- Working without the bow, have students place all four fingers on the string in the 1-2 pattern, then "open the first finger back" by sliding it toward the nut, then back to the 1-2 placement. The wrist should not collapse, and the position of the 2nd, 3rd, and 4th fingers should not change. Repeat, beginning with other finger patterns.

- Have students place all four fingers on the string in the 2-3 pattern and slide the 4th finger up approximately a half-step back. The 1st, 2nd, and 3rd fingers should stay in place. Repeat, beginning with other finger patterns.

- For violists, depending on the size and strength of the hand, a half-position shift may be a better choice than an extension.

- Avoid excessive tension by having students tap the side of the thumb against the neck at intervals during this exercise.

- Demonstrate and have students pluck, then bow, the first finger note and the downward extension alternately.

- Demonstrate and have students pluck, then bow, the fourth finger note and the upward extension alternately.

- Play a variety of scale patterns and melodies using upward and downward extensions.

Indicators of Success

Students will perform tonal patterns, simple melodies, and scales involving upward and downward extensions with:

- a good hand position
- flexible fingers, without excessive tension between the thumb and base joint of index finger on the neck
- good intonation

Standards Links:

Resources and References:

| Level: | **Baseline** |

| **Category 1:** | **Executive Skills and Knowledge** |

| **Content Area:** | **1B. Left Hand Skills and Knowledge** |

| **Benchmark:** | *Students perform with the correct placement and angle of the left arm-wrist-hand-fingers to the instrument; demonstrate position that is balanced and free of tension; play with independence of fingers, ease of motion and control of finger weight; produce characteristic tone, with vibrato (as appropriate); show understanding and ability to apply fingerings, finger patterns, shifting, extensions.* |

| **Learning Task:** | **2.1.b—Cello Extensions** |

Learning Sequences & Processes	**Indicators of Success**
General Information, Prior Knowledge and Precursors • Students must have a relaxed left-hand position, with correct placement of the thumb, and the ability to make firm contact with the strings without collapsing the wrist or fingers. • As with the violin and viola, extensions enable the player to reach outside the frame of the hand without shifting. For the cello, extensions are required as soon as students must perform notes that are either a half-step above the open string (such as E♭ on the D-string) or when there are two consecutive whole-steps above the first finger (such as E–F♯–G♯ or E♭–F–G on the D-string). • In the backward (downward) extension, the first finger reaches back by a half-step, creating a whole-step between the first and second finger. The rest of the hand should not twist or otherwise collapse in order to accomplish this. • In the forward (upward) extension, the first finger remains in position, but the remaining fingers and thumb all move downward, while the first finger serves as a pivot point for the hand to open up, again creating a whole-step between the first and second fingers. Sequence of Activities • Demonstrate and explain the use of extensions. • Working without the bow, have students place all four fingers on the D-string, then "open the first finger back" by reaching back towards the nut, then back to the normal, non-extended position. The wrist should not collapse, and the position of the 2nd, 3rd, and 4th fingers should not change. Repeat, beginning with other finger patterns. • Have students place all four fingers on the D-string. Keeping the first finger in place, release the 2nd, 3rd, 4th fingers and thumb, allowing the hand to open up between the 1st and 2nd fingers (creating a whole step between those fingers). The 2nd, 3rd, and 4th fingers should now be placed respectively on the notes F♯–G–G♯. The first finger should be pointing upwards towards the nut, as it does for the backward extension (not curved with the middle knuckle pointing toward the nut). The thumb should move with the 2nd finger, and the 2nd, 3rd, and 4th fingers should be curved and relaxed. • Avoid excessive tension by having students tap the side of the thumb against the neck at intervals during this exercise. • Demonstrate and have students pluck, then bow, the first finger note and the backward extension alternately. Repeat with the forward extension. • Play a variety of scale patterns and melodies using upward and downward extensions.	Students will perform tonal patterns, simple melodies, and scales involving upward and downward extensions with: • a good hand position • flexible fingers, without excessive tension between the thumb and neck • good intonation • correct finger placement (especially the angle of the 1st finger and the placement of the thumb, corresponding to the 2nd finger)

Standards Links:

Resources and References:

Category 1: Executive Skills and Knowledge

Content Area:	**1B. Left Hand Skills and Knowledge**
Benchmark:	*Students perform with the correct placement and angle of the left arm-wrist-hand-fingers to the instrument; demonstrate position that is balanced and free of tension; play with independence of fingers, ease of motion and control of finger weight; produce characteristic tone, with vibrato (as appropriate); show understanding and ability to apply fingerings, finger patterns, shifting, extensions.*
Learning Task:	**2.2.a—Introduction of Positions (Violin and Viola)**

Learning Sequences & Processes	Indicators of Success

<u>General Information, Prior Knowledge and Precursors</u>
 	
• From the first lessons, students should practice moving the arm and hand freely up and down the fingerboard
• Students should play in first position with consistently good intonation, maintaining an acceptable hand position, before moving to higher positions
• Positions are numbered according to the number of note letter names from the open string, i.e., on D, first finger plays E♭ or E in first position, F or F♯ in second position, G or G♯ in third position, etc.
• In every position, the fingers play notes in stepwise sequence—i.e., if the first finger plays G, 2nd plays A, 3rd plays B, and 4th plays C, etc.
• As the hand moves into higher positions, the physical distance between the fingers becomes slightly smaller with each new position. The thumb should shift with the hand.
• From 1st to 4th position, the frame of the hand stays the same; beginning in 5th position, the upper arm swings toward the center of the violin/viola, the pad of the thumb comes under the neck and the hand is extended around the instrument
• Shifting is the technique of moving the hand from one position to another
• Learning familiar songs in new positions is an important introductory and transition exercise for students to develop the aural skills that correspond with playing in tune in positions.
 	
<u>Sequence of Activities</u>
• Demonstrate and explain the use of extensions.
• Third position is usually the first higher position introduced.
• Students play simple melodies by ear in the new position.
• Students learn to read and sing letter names of the notes in third position on the highest string, then play in third position.
• Working from printed music, students
    1) sing the example,
    2) play it in first position (except on the highest string), and
    3) play it again in third position.
• This activity sequence can be followed as each new position is introduced. In the higher positions, students will sing the example an octave lower; and fewer examples can be played in first position.
	Students will perform tonal patterns, simple melodies, and scales involving upward and downward shifts with:
	
	• a good hand position
	• flexible fingers, without excessive tension between the thumb and base joint of the index finger on the neck
	• good intonation

Standards Links:

Resources and References:

Category 1:	**Executive Skills and Knowledge**
Content Area:	**1B. Left Hand Skills and Knowledge**
Benchmark:	*Students perform with the correct placement and angle of the left arm-wrist-hand-fingers to the instrument; demonstrate position that is balanced and free of tension; play with independence of fingers, ease of motion and control of finger weight; produce characteristic tone, with vibrato (as appropriate); show understanding and ability to apply fingerings, finger patterns, shifting, extensions.*
Learning Task:	**2.2.b—Introduction of Positions (Cello and Bass)**

Learning Sequences & Processes	**Indicators of Success**

General Information, Prior Knowledge and Precursors
 	
• From the first lessons, students should practice moving the arm and hand freely up and down the fingerboard
 	
• Students should play in first position with consistently good intonation, maintaining an acceptable hand position, before moving to higher positions
 	
• Positions are numbered according to the number of note letter names from the open string, i.e., on D, first finger plays E♭ or E in first position, F or F♯ in second position, G or G♯ in third position, etc.
 	
• As the hand moves into higher positions, the physical distance between the fingers becomes slightly smaller with each new position
 	
• Shifting is the technique of moving the hand from one position to another
 	
• Learning familiar songs in new positions is an important introductory and transition exercise for students to develop the aural skills that correspond with playing in tune in positions.
 	
Sequence of Activities
 	
• Demonstrate and explain the use of extensions.
 	
• Third position is usually the first higher position introduced.
 	
• Students play simple melodies by ear in the new position.
 	
• Students learn to read and sing letter names of the notes in third position on the highest string, then play in third position.
 	
• Working from printed music, students
    1) sing the example,
    2) play it in first position (except on the highest string), and
    3) play it again in third position.
 	
• This activity sequence can be followed as each new position is introduced. In the higher positions, students will sing the example an octave lower; and fewer examples can be played in first position
	Students will perform tonal patterns, simple melodies, and scales involving upward and downward shifts with:
	
	• a good hand position
	
	• flexible fingers, without excessive tension between the thumb and the neck
	
	• good intonation

Standards Links:

Resources and References:

Category 1: Executive Skills and Knowledge

Content Area:	1B. Left Hand Skills and Knowledge
Benchmark:	*Students perform with the correct placement and angle of the left arm-wrist-hand-fingers to the instrument; demonstrate position that is balanced and free of tension; play with independence of fingers, ease of motion and control of finger weight; produce characteristic tone, with vibrato (as appropriate); show understanding and ability to apply fingerings, finger patterns, shifting, extensions.*
Learning Task:	2.2.c—Introduction of Positions—Half Position

Learning Sequences & Processes	Indicators of Success
General Information, Prior Knowledge and Precursors • Half position is essentially when the first finger plays the note that is a half-step above the open string (alt., a half-step below the first finger in first position). For example, for the violin and viola on the D-string, the 1st finger plays D♯/E♭, 2nd finger plays E, 3rd finger plays F♯, and 4th finger plays G♯. • Half position can be used to avoid staying in first position and extending the 1st finger backwards, and to perform some double stops. For the cellos this is the same as a backward extension. • Half position is especially helpful for viola in playing intervals that require uncomfortable stretches in first position. • On the bass, the whole hand shifts back in half position. So, on the D-string, the 1st finger plays D♯/E♭, the 2nd finger plays E♮, and 4th finger plays F♮. Sequence of Activities • Demonstrate and explain half position. Use aural patterns first before visual models. • Demonstrate and have students play stepwise half position patterns on each string. • Let students practice exercises/etudes in half position. • Point out and practice half position sequences in literature being studied. • Similar activities may be used as those described in Learning Tasks 2.2.a and 2.2.b above.	As students play in half position they should demonstrate: • a good hand position • flexible fingers, without excessive tension between the thumb and neck • good intonation Additional: • It is essential that the hand position not be compromised in ½ position. For violin/viola, the wrist should not collapse. This is especially common on the highest strings. • For the cello, the wrist should not twist. • For the bass, the entire arm should shift back into half position.

Standards Links:

Resources and References:

Category 1:	Executive Skills and Knowledge
Content Area:	**1B. Left Hand Skills and Knowledge**
Benchmark:	*Students perform with the correct placement and angle of the left arm-wrist-hand-fingers to the instrument; demonstrate position that is balanced and free of tension; play with independence of fingers, ease of motion and control of finger weight; produce characteristic tone, with vibrato (as appropriate); show understanding and ability to apply fingerings, finger patterns, shifting, extensions.*
Learning Task:	**2.3.a—Refinement of Shifting (Violin and Viola)**

Learning Sequences & Processes	Indicators of Success

General Information, Prior Knowledge and Precursors
 	
• Music for students at this level will most often require 1st, 2nd, and 3rd positions. However, to ensure that students develop freedom of movement without excessive tension as they learn to shift, continue large, non-pitch-specific shifting movement—i.e., moving from the elbow, with fingers lightly touching the two middle strings, move the hand up and down the entire length of the fingerboard. Between fourth and fifth positions, the upper arm should swing forward, bringing the pad of the thumb into the curve of the neck and the hand around the bout. With the same motion, but with the fingers curved slightly above the strings, drop the fingers on a string to play indeterminate pitches up and down the fingerboard.
 	
• Shifting exercises should continue to emphasize and aural and kinesthetic awareness over visual references and awareness.
 	
Sequence of Activities
 	
• Model playing in 1st, 2nd, and 3rd positions, explain, and have students demonstrate that:
 	
  • shifting is an arm movement, rather than a hand movement—the arm carries the hand
 	
  • with the exception of shifts executed while playing an open string, the shift is accomplished by slightly releasing the weight of the finger on the string, and sliding on the "old" finger—i.e., the finger stopping the note immediately before the shift
 	
  • the shift is made on the "old bow," i.e. during the bow change—if the bow is changed before the shift is completed, the "slide" will be audible (this technique is sometimes deliberately used to make an "expressive" shift
 	
• Practice shifts from the finger that is down to the same finger in different position, then from the finger that is down to a pitch played by a different finger—i.e., first finger B on the A-string to second finger E on the A-string. The principal of shifting on the "old" finger holds in both kinds of shifts. Picking the fingers up and "jumping" to the new position almost insures faulty intonation.
 	
• Have students play scales, etudes, and pieces using shifts between 1st, 2nd, and 3rd positions.
	Students will perform pieces requiring shifting between 1st, 2nd, and 3rd positions, demonstrating:
	
	• fluid arm movement, with the shifting finger remaining on the string
	
	• correct left hand formation
	
	• good intonation

Standards Links:

Resources and References:

Category 1:	Executive Skills and Knowledge
Content Area:	**1B. Left Hand Skills and Knowledge**
Benchmark:	*Students perform with the correct placement and angle of the left arm-wrist-hand-fingers to the instrument; demonstrate position that is balanced and free of tension; play with independence of fingers, ease of motion and control of finger weight; produce characteristic tone, with vibrato (as appropriate); show understanding and ability to apply fingerings, finger patterns, shifting, extensions.*
Learning Task:	**2.3.b—Refinement of Shifting (Cello)**

Learning Sequences & Processes	Indicators of Success

<u>General Information, Prior Knowledge and Precursors</u>
 	
• Music for students at this level will most often require 1st, 3rd and 4th positions. However, to ensure that students develop freedom of movement without excessive tension as they learn to shift, continue large-motion, non-pitch-specific shifting movement—i.e., moving from the elbow, with fingers lightly touching the two middle strings, move the hand up and down the entire length of the fingerboard. Between 4th and 5th positions, the upper arm should swing forward, bringing the side of the thumb up on top of the strings (preparatory for thumb position), while the fingers remain curved and over the strings. The angle of the fingers changes as the thumb moves over the top of the fingerboard, generally becoming more curved, with the fingers making contact with the strings closer to the tip of the finger.
 	
• Shifting exercises should continue to emphasize and aural and kinesthetic awareness over visual references and awareness.
 	
<u>Sequence of Activities</u>
 	
• Practice the "Ski Jump" exercise, where students slide up and down the fingerboard from the nut to the end of the fingerboard, hooking the left-hand ring finger under the string and then releasing the string with a pizzicato as the hand "jumps" off the end of the fingerboard in the same way a ski jumper would.
 	
• Model playing in 1st, 3rd, and 4th positions, explain, and have students demonstrate that:
 	
   • shifting is an arm movement, rather than a hand movement—the arm carries the hand
 	
   • with the exception of shifts executed while playing an open string, the shift is accomplished by slightly releasing the weight of the finger on the string, and sliding on the "old" finger—i.e., the finger stopping the note immediately before the shift
 	
   • the shift is made on the "old bow," i.e. during the bow change—if the bow is changed before the shift is completed, the "slide" will be audible (this technique is sometimes deliberately used to make an "expressive" shift
 	
• Practice shifts from the finger that is down to the same finger in different position, then from the finger that is down to a pitch played by a different finger—i.e., 1st finger E on the D-string to 2nd finger B-flat on the D-string (in 4th position). The principal of shifting on the "old" finger holds in both kinds of shifts. Picking the fingers up and "jumping" to the new position almost guarantees faulty intonation.
 	
• Have students play scales, etudes, and pieces using shifts between 1st, 3rd and 4th positions.
	Students will perform pieces requiring shifting between 1st, 3rd and 4th positions, demonstrating:
	
	• fluid arm movement, with the shifting finger remaining on the string
	
	• correct left hand formation
	
	• good intonation

Standards Links:

Resources and References:

Category 1:	**Executive Skills and Knowledge**
Content Area:	**1B. Left Hand Skills and Knowledge**
Benchmark:	*Students perform with the correct placement and angle of the left arm-wrist-hand-fingers to the instrument; demonstrate position that is balanced and free of tension; play with independence of fingers, ease of motion and control of finger weight; produce characteristic tone, with vibrato (as appropriate); show understanding and ability to apply fingerings, finger patterns, shifting, extensions.*
Learning Task:	**2.3.c—Refinement of Shifting (Bass)**

Learning Sequences & Processes	**Indicators of Success**

General Information, Prior Knowledge and Precursors
 	
• Music for students at this level will most often require 1st, 2nd, 3rd and 4th positions. However, to ensure that students develop freedom of movement without excessive tension as they learn to shift, continue large, non-pitch-specific shifting movement—i.e., moving from the elbow, with fingers lightly touching the two middle strings, move the hand up and down the entire length of the fingerboard. Between 4th and 5th positions, the upper arm should swing forward, bringing the side of the thumb up on top of the strings (preparatory for thumb position), while the fingers remain curved and over the strings. The angle of the fingers changes as the thumb moves over the top of the fingerboard, generally becoming more curved, with the fingers making contact with the strings closer to the tip of the finger.
 	
• Shifting exercises should continue to emphasize and aural and kinesthetic awareness over visual references and awareness.
 	
Sequence of Activities
 	
• Practice the "Ski Jump" exercise, where students slide up and down the fingerboard from the nut to the end of the fingerboard, hooking the left-hand ring finger under the string and then releasing the string with a pizzicato as the hand "jumps" off the end of the fingerboard in the same way a ski jumper would.
 	
• Model playing in 1st, 2nd, 3rd, and 4th positions, explain, and have students demonstrate that:
 	
  • shifting is an arm movement, rather than a hand movement—the arm carries the hand
 	
  • with the exception of shifts executed while playing an open string, the shift is accomplished by slightly releasing the weight of the finger on the string, and sliding on the "old" finger—i.e., the finger stopping the note immediately before the shift
 	
  • the shift is made on the "old bow," i.e. during the bow change—if the bow is changed before the shift is completed, the "slide" will be audible (this technique is sometimes deliberately used to make an "expressive" shift
 	
• Practice shifts from the finger that is down to the same finger in different position, then from the finger that is down to a pitch played by a different finger—i.e., 1st finger E on the D-string to 2nd finger B-flat on the D-string (in 4th position). The principal of shifting on the "old" finger holds in both kinds of shifts. Picking the fingers up and "jumping" to the new position almost guarantees faulty intonation.
 	
• Have students play scales, etudes, and pieces using shifts between 1st, 2nd, 3rd and 4th positions.
	Students will perform pieces requiring shifting between 1st, 2nd, 3rd and 4th positions, demonstrating:
	
	• fluid arm movement, with the shifting finger remaining on the string
	
	• correct left hand formation
	
	• good intonation

Standards Links:

Resources and References:

Category 1:	**Executive Skills and Knowledge**
Content Area:	**1B. Left Hand Skills and Knowledge**
Benchmark:	*Students perform with the correct placement and angle of the left arm-wrist-hand-fingers to the instrument; demonstrate position that is balanced and free of tension; play with independence of fingers, ease of motion and control of finger weight; produce characteristic tone, with vibrato (as appropriate); show understanding and ability to apply fingerings, finger patterns, shifting, extensions.*
Learning Task:	**2.4—Harmonics**

Learning Sequences & Processes	Indicators of Success
<u>General Information, Prior Knowledge and Precursors</u> Harmonics are tones produced on string instruments by touching the string lightly, rather than stopping it against the fingerboard, at a node, causing the string to vibrate in segments and producing a clear, flute-like sound. • The second harmonic, produced by touching the string at the octave, causes the string to vibrate in two segments, sounding an octave higher than the open string. • The third harmonic, produced by touching the string at the fifth, causes the string to vibrate in three segments, sounding an octave plus a fifth higher than the open string. • The fourth harmonic, produced by touching the string at the fourth, causes the string to vibrate in four segments, sounding two octaves higher than the open string. • The fifth harmonic, produced by touching the string at a major sixth, causes the string to vibrate in five segments, sounding two octaves plus a major third higher than the open string. • The 3rd, 4th, and 5th harmonics will have multiple touch points. • Harmonics are indicated in the music by diamond shaped notes, or by a small circle over a note that would be fingered. • Harmonics are used to provide contrasting tone quality, and sometimes to facilitate fingering in the higher positions. <u>Sequence of Activities—Learning New Positions</u> • Working without the bow, have students lightly slide one finger up and down each string, from 1st position through 5th position and as high as they can reach. • Repeat, using the bow. Young students enjoy thinking of this as the "ghost game'—especially if it comes around Halloween! Find at least five harmonics on each string. • Play the harmonics separately. • Working from printed music, play short melodies and/or scales using harmonics.	Students will demonstrate understanding of harmonics by: • playing the second, third, fourth and fifth harmonics with a clear tone • identifying the notation/symbols which indicate harmonics • reading and playing simple melodies which include harmonics accurately and with good tone quality

Standards Links:

Resources and References:

Category 1:	Executive Skills and Knowledge
Content Area:	**1B. Left Hand Skills and Knowledge**
Benchmark:	*Students perform with the correct placement and angle of the left arm-wrist-hand-fingers to the instrument; demonstrate position that is balanced and free of tension; play with independence of fingers, ease of motion and control of finger weight; produce characteristic tone, with vibrato (as appropriate); show understanding and ability to apply fingerings, finger patterns, shifting, extensions.*
Learning Task:	**2.5—Finger Substitutions (Violin/Viola)**

Learning Sequences & Processes	Indicators of Success

General Information, Prior Knowledge and Precursors
 	
• Finger substitutions are needed in playing: double stops, or a smooth melodic line, when the notes on two adjacent strings are an augmented fourth (Aug4), augmented fifth (Aug5), or a diminished fifth (dim5) apart; chromatic scales; half shifts through an extension (more often on viola than on violin).
 	
• In playing notes that are an Aug4 or a dim5 apart—i.e., C♮ on the A-string and F♯ on the D-string—C♮ would be played with the second finger on A, and F♯ would be played with the third finger on D. An example of an augmented fifth is playing F♮ on the D-string and C♯ on the A-string; F♮ would be played with the 2nd finger and C♯ with the third. This principle is applicable in playing any Aug4, Aug5, or dim5 on adjacent strings.
 	
• The most common chromatic scale fingering is open, 1-1, 2-2, 3-4—i.e., open D-string, 1st finger E♭–E, 2nd finger F–F♯, 3rd finger G, 4th finger G♯, open A-string, etc.
 	
• In some instances, it is desirable to shift through an extension, especially on viola. This is much more likely in the higher positions, where the distances on the fingerboard are shorter. An example might be in a scale passage in third position, 1st finger plays D on the A-string, 2nd extends to F—with 2nd finger as a pivot, the hand then moves to 4th position; 3rd and 4th fingers play G and A.
 	
Sequence of Activities
 	
• Playing notes an Aug4 or dim5 apart:
  • have students play a scale sequence which includes the two notes; observe the placement of the targeted finger on each string
  • play the two notes alternately, using the same finger demonstrate and explain the use of finger substitution for the interval; play the two notes alternately, using the finger substitution; practice the finger substitution, both melodically and as a double stop; perform pieces that use finger substitution
• Playing chromatic scales:
  • introduce, explain, and demonstrate chromatic scales; have students play the chromatic scale fingering on each string
  • play the chromatic scale in first position from the open G-string to 4th finger B on the E-string (violin), or the open C-string to 4th finger E on the A-string (viola)
• Playing a half shift through an extension:
  • demonstrate and explain the fingering; have student play the passage with an actual shift, then with a half shift through alternate fingering; repeat until the passage can be played smoothly with good intonation
	• Given a piece of music at the student's performance level requiring finger substitution, the student will identify the passage and the appropriate finger substitution.
	
	• The student will play augmented fourths and/or diminished fifths, using finger substitutions appropriately, with a good left hand position, good intonation, and resonant tone quality.
	
	• The student will play a chromatic scale in first position with a good left hand position and intonation.
	
	• The student will demonstrate shifting through an extension with flexibility in the left hand and arm and good intonation.

Standards Links:

Resources and References:

Category 1:	Executive Skills and Knowledge
Content Area:	**1B. Left Hand Skills and Knowledge**
Benchmark:	*Students perform with the correct placement and angle of the left arm-wrist-hand-fingers to the instrument; demonstrate position that is balanced and free of tension; play with independence of fingers, ease of motion and control of finger weight; produce characteristic tone, with vibrato (as appropriate); show understanding and ability to apply fingerings, finger patterns, shifting, extensions.*
Learning Task:	**2.6—Simple Double Stops**

Learning Sequences & Processes	Indicators of Success
General Information, Prior Knowledge and Precursors <ul><li>Double stops are played by sounding two adjacent strings together. Simple double stops consist of playing a fingered note on one string with the adjacent higher or lower open string.</li><li>Double stops can be plucked or bowed. The technique for bowing double stops is addressed in "Right Hand Skills and Knowledge."</li><li>In ensemble, double stops are frequently played *divisi*, with the outside player assigned the upper note and the inside player assigned the lower note.</li><li>In playing simple double stops, the finger should touch the string slightly to the side away from the open string—i.e., in playing a double stop with a fingered note on A and open D, the finger should be placed slightly on the E-string side of the A-string, so that it does not touch the D-string.</li><li>In playing double stops, avoid using excessive finger pressure, which can create tension in the thumb and the whole hand.</li><li>Simple double-stops may also be used as a teaching tool for helping reinforce correct left-hand position. Exercises such as *tunneling*, where one finger is placed on a string (such as the D-string) while the next highest open string (such as the A-string for violin, viola, and cello) is plucked or bowed, help students to develop correct hand position and finger placement.</li></ul> Sequence of Activities <ul><li>Demonstrate and explain simple double stops.</li><li>Have students play a tetrachord (or other melodic patterns) on the D-string; repeat, playing a double-stop with the open A-string. Then, play a tetrachord on the A-string; repeat, playing a double stop with the open D.</li><li>Continue, working in the same way with each pair of adjacent strings.</li><li>Introduce pieces that include simple double stops. Fiddle tunes (e.g., "Bile 'em Cabbage Down") are excellent teaching tools for learning simple double-stops.</li></ul>	<ul><li>Students will perform simple double stops with a clear tone, good intonation, and a good left hand position.</li><li>Both strings should sound clearly while the double-stop is performed</li></ul>

Standards Links:

Resources and References:

Category 1: Executive Skills and Knowledge

Content Area:	**1B. Left Hand Skills and Knowledge – Violin/Viola**
Benchmark:	*Students perform with the correct placement and angle of the left arm-wrist-hand-fingers to the instrument; demonstrate position that is balanced and free of tension; play with independence of fingers, ease of motion and control of finger weight; produce characteristic tone, with vibrato (as appropriate); show understanding and ability to apply fingerings, finger patterns, shifting, extensions.*
Learning Task:	**2.7—Chromatic Alterations**

Learning Sequences & Processes	Indicators of Success
General Information, Prior Knowledge, and Precursors • Chromatic alterations occur when the music involves accidentals that require the player to change finger patterns on the same string within a piece. • In playing chromatic alterations, particular attention should be given to maintaining a good hand position, making the alteration with finger movement, rather than collapsing or extending the wrist. As is true in all left hand skills, gripping the neck of the instrument with the thumb and the base joint will prohibit ease of movement. Sequence of Activities • Check to be sure students understand sharps, flats, and naturals, and the direction of the chromatic alterations to be played. • Place all fingers on the string. Next, slide one finger along the string until its tip touches the next fingertip. The sliding finger is lightened, but remains in contact with the string. For example, holding 1st finger E, 3rd finger G, and 4th finger A down on the D-string, slide the 2nd finger from F♮ to F♯ and back. Repeat several times. • Repeat, sliding each finger higher or lower while holding the remaining three down. • Play simple melodies that include accidentals. • Stress the importance of "finger before bow"—to avoid a "smear," the finger must be in place for the chromatic alteration before the bow is changed.	The student will respond to accidentals by playing chromatic alterations with: • a good left hand position, free of excessive tension • correct technical execution of the alterations by sliding the finger along the string, rather than lifting the finger between notes. • clear articulation • accurate intonation

Standards Links:

Resources and References:

Category 1: Executive Skills and Knowledge

Content Area:	**1B. Left Hand Skills and Knowledge – Violin/Viola**
Benchmark:	*Students perform with the correct placement and angle of the left arm-wrist-hand-fingers to the instrument; demonstrate position that is balanced and free of tension; play with independence of fingers, ease of motion and control of finger weight; produce characteristic tone, with vibrato (as appropriate); show understanding and ability to apply fingerings, finger patterns, shifting, extensions.*
Learning Task:	**2.8—Extension of Vertical Technique**

Learning Sequences & Processes	Indicators of Success
General Information, Prior Knowledge, and Precursor • The goal is for students to develop control over stages of weight into the string with left-hand fingers. Sequence of Activities This series of exercises is done without the bow: • Teacher invites students to choose their favorite finger on a specific pitch • Teacher asks students to barely touch the surface of the string with that finger • Teacher labels this degree of weight as 0% • Teacher invites students to use the weight of the finger to gradually lower the string to the fingerboard • Teacher labels this degree of weight as 100% • Teacher invites students to find 0% again, then 25%, 50%, 75%, and the lightest 100% they can find • Teacher invites students to notice how their bow arm responds, almost mirroring the left-hand weight	• The left hand and thumb remain flexible, without excessive tension, allowing ease of movement from one pattern to another. • Students perceive the string pressed down to the fingerboard as a graduated event rather than a single level of weight • Students learn to think vertically on the fingerboard • Students control left-hand fingering technique adjusting for downward weight and release. • Students can modify left-hand weight at will by adjusting the specific amount of weight in each finger. • Students learn to distinguish between the tone produced via full weight and tone produced with graduated weight • Students learn that full weight can actually be lighter than they originally thought

Standards Links:

Resources and References:

Category 1:	**Executive Skills and Knowledge**
Content Area:	**1B. Left Hand Skills and Knowledge**
Benchmark:	*Students perform with the correct placement and angle of the left arm-wrist-hand-fingers to the instrument; demonstrate position that is balanced and free of tension; play with independence of fingers, ease of motion and control of finger weight; produce characteristic tone, with vibrato (as appropriate); show understanding and ability to apply fingerings, finger patterns, shifting, extensions.*
Learning Task:	**3.1—Initial Vibrato Development**

Learning Sequences & Processes	Indicators of Success
General Information, Prior Knowledge and Precursors • Vibrato is an expressive technique created by rolling the fingertip <u>below</u> the pitch and back. • Preparation for vibrato begins from the first lesson, when correct and relaxed posture, instrument position, and left-hand position are introduced and developed. Any deficiencies or tension in technique will quickly be revealed during the vibrato development process. Students who do not support the instrument correctly or have excess tension will experience problems developing vibrato. • Students should play with a balanced left hand position, free of excessive tension, and with consistently good intonation before beginning vibrato study. • Play one-finger one-octave scales from open strings shifting the weight of the hand from one finger to the next. • Vibrato is sometimes characterized as initiated by the finger, wrist, or arm. To perform any of these vibratos, the shoulder, elbow, wrist, thumb and finger joints must be free of excessive tension. • Two common impediments to vibrato are squeezing the neck between the thumb and the base joint of the first finger (or, for cello and bass, between the thumb and the neck), and excessive pressure on the finger making the pitch on the fingerboard. • Students should listen to examples of good vibrato to learn characteristic sound. Sequence of Activities • The first four activities can be done in guitar, then playing, position (vln/vla only). • Vibrato activities should move from large muscle activities to more refined motions. • In high position with pad of the left thumb resting in the curve of the neck, moving hand from the wrist and forearm, have students wave "goodbye" to themselves; tap fingers on top of instrument just left of the fingerboard. Cello/bass may start with the thumb on top of the fingerboard (on resting on the top of the instrument) and practice moving the arm up-and-down, while the thumb stays in position. • Lightly touch all four fingers simultaneously on string and "polish" the string by sliding back and forth in a smooth waving motion. The position of the wrist remains constant; avoid bending the wrist in toward the neck. • Move the hand back to 1st position. Vln/vla: release the base joint of the first finger, leaving a "feather space" between the base joint and the neck. Cello/bass: keep 2nd finger relaxed, not gripping the neck. • Beginning with the 2nd or 3rd finger, roll the fingertip below the pitch and back, keeping all knuckles soft and flexible. The wrist should not bend inward toward the neck. • Working with each finger on each string, play vibrato keeping a steady 8th note pulse in a moderate tempo, then in triplets and in other rhythms. • Gradually increase speed, always keeping the arm, hand, and fingers flexible.	• Students will demonstrate an even vibrato at moderate speed, maintaining a good left hand position and good intonation. • Instrument is correctly supported during performance • Left-arm is free of tension • All parts of the vibrato mechanism (i.e., shoulder, upper arm, elbow, forearm, wrist, hand, and fingers) remain loose and mobile throughout the activity

Standards Links:

Resources and References:

Category 1: Executive Skills and Knowledge

Content Area:	1B. Left Hand Skills and Knowledge
Benchmark:	*Students perform with the correct placement and angle of the left arm-wrist-hand-fingers to the instrument; demonstrate position that is balanced and free of tension; play with independence of fingers, ease of motion and control of finger weight; produce characteristic tone, with vibrato (as appropriate); show understanding and ability to apply fingerings, finger patterns, shifting, extensions.*
Learning Task:	3.2—Advanced Positions (5th and higher)

Learning Sequences & Processes	Indicators of Success
General Information, Prior Knowledge and Precursors • As students move into the higher positions, continue the movements up and down the fingerboard (as introduced in Level 1). Throughout the study of shifting, the left hand and arm must remain flexible. • For most students, the shape of the hand is the same in 1st through 4th positions. Depending on the size of the hand and the shape of the instrument, adjustments may need to be made in the angle of the left wrist and forearm in order to keep the fingers over the fingerboard. • Vln/vla: between 4th and 5th positions, the upper arm should swing forward toward the center of the body, bringing the pad of the thumb into the curve of the neck and the hand around the bout. (Some violists may need to bring the thumb tip to the side of the fingerboard.) Cello/bass: between 4th and 6th positions the thumb generally stays near the curve at the base of the neck; in higher positions, the thumb moves to the top of the strings (thumb position), where it serves an additional function for playing notes. • As previously explained, shifting is an arm movement, rather than a hand movement— *the arm carries the hand.* The thumb moves with the hand. • With the exception of shifts executed while playing an open string, shifting is accomplished by slightly releasing the weight of the finger on the string, and sliding on the "old" finger—i.e., the finger stopping the note immediately before the shift. • Vln/Vla: In 5th position, the fingers play the same notes as in first position, but on the next lower string, i.e., 1st finger plays the same B in 1st position on the A-string and on the D-string in 5th position. In positions above the 5th, the thumb remains in the curve of the neck, and the hand is opened to reach higher on the fingerboard. • The shift is made on the "old bow," i.e., during the bow change. If the bow is changed before the shift is completed, the "slide" will be audible (this technique is sometimes deliberately used to make an "expressive" shift). Sequence of Activities • The first four activities can be done in guitar position, then in playing position (Vln/Vla). • With all four fingers resting lightly on the string, slide up and down the fingerboard, swinging the arm slightly forward between 4th and 5th positions, and bringing the thumb into the curve of the neck • Play one-finger one-octave scales from open strings shifting the weight of the hand from one finger to the next. • Play simple, familiar melodies with one finger. • Have students play scales, exercises, and/or pieces that include shifts to and from 5th and higher positions.	The student will shift to and from fifth and higher positions in the context of scales, etudes, and pieces being studied, demonstrating: • Correct instrument position, supported without tension. • Relaxed and balanced motion in the left arm during the shifting process • Correct left-hand position during the shift (maintaining the correct position even as the hand moves past the base of the neck and over the bout) • An elongated and balanced posture, not compressing or "clutching" as they shift • Accurate intonation

Standards Links:

Resources and References:

Category 1:	**Executive Skills and Knowledge**
Content Area:	**1B. Left Hand Skills and Knowledge**
Benchmark:	*Students perform with the correct placement and angle of the left arm-wrist-hand-fingers to the instrument; demonstrate position that is balanced and free of tension; play with independence of fingers, ease of motion and control of finger weight; produce characteristic tone, with vibrato (as appropriate); show understanding and ability to apply fingerings, finger patterns, shifting, extensions.*
Learning Task:	**3.3—Complex Double Stops**

Learning Sequences & Processes	**Indicators of Success**
<u>General Information, Prior Knowledge and Precursors</u> • Complex double stops are created by playing fingered notes on two adjacent strings. • Double stops can be plucked or bowed. The technique for bowing double stops is addressed in "Right Hand Skills and Knowledge." • In ensemble, double stops are frequently played *divisi*, with the outside player assigned the upper note and the inside player assigned the lower note. • In playing double stops, avoid using excessive finger pressure, which can create tension in the thumb and the whole hand. • For Vln/Vla: In playing fingered double stops, special attention must be given to the half-/whole-step placement of the fingers on the two strings—i.e., in playing the double stop E on the D-string and C♮ on the A-string, first and second fingers will be in a half-step (i.e., the 1-2 pattern) placement; in playing E on the D-string and C♯ on the A-string, first and second fingers will be in a whole-step (i.e., the 2-3 pattern) placement. This principle applies to all intervals across two strings. • To play fingered double stops with good intonation, the player must listen to both harmonic (vertical) and melodic (horizontal) tonal relationships. <u>Sequence of Activities</u> • Play each note separately (bow changes strings). • Next, finger both notes, bowing first the lower note, then tuning—adding—the upper note to it. Gradually shorten the length of time spent on the lower note alone until it is played merely as a slight grace-note anticipation. • Finally, play both notes of the double stop together, in tune and with perfect synchronization and dynamic balance." (See Barnes, 2005, 48) • Have students play a variety of pieces—solo and ensemble—that contain complex double stops.	Students will demonstrate an understanding of complex double stops by: • describing the half- and whole-step finger placement across two strings for double stops in the music they are studying • performing complex double stops with a good left hand position, free of excessive tension • performing complex double stops with accurate intonation and characteristic tone quality

Standards Links:

Resources and References:

	Level:	**Proficient**

Category 1:	**Executive Skills and Knowledge**
Content Area:	**1B. Left Hand Skills and Knowledge**
Benchmark:	*Students perform with the correct placement and angle of the left arm-wrist-hand-fingers to the instrument; demonstrate position that is balanced and free of tension; play with independence of fingers, ease of motion and control of finger weight; produce characteristic tone, with vibrato (as appropriate); show understanding and ability to apply fingerings, finger patterns, shifting, extensions.*
Learning Task:	**3.4—Advanced Finger Patterns—Violin/Viola**

Learning Sequences & Processes	**Indicators of Success**
General Information, Prior Knowledge, and Precursors • The four basic finger patterns introduced in Level 1 are based on patterns of whole- and half-steps. When playing half-steps, adjacent fingers are close together; when playing whole-steps, there is a space between them. More advanced patterns occur when three half-steps come together, there is a distance of more than a step between two adjacent fingers, etc. Therefore, students must have an adequate working knowledge of half and whole-steps to understand these more advanced patterns. • Advanced finger patterns are more often found in more advanced literature, which often requires students to play in higher positions. Because the physical distance between the fingers becomes smaller as students play in higher positions, half-step sequences may require that the fingers be almost on top of each other, especially for students with large hands. • To play advanced patterns with good intonation, the student must have developed the ability to accurately discriminate half and whole-steps aurally. Sequence of Activities • Demonstrate, explain and let students sing and play a one-octave chromatic scale. (Most scale books suggest the following fingering from each open string: open-1-2-1-2-3-4, with a half-step between each pair of adjacent fingers.) Point out that there are twelve half-steps in an octave. • Demonstrate, explain and let students sing and play augmented seconds. • Introduce passages involving advanced finger patterns in literature appropriate for the students' level of study. Lead students to analyze the patterns, determine how they should be fingered, and sing and play them. • Challenge students to improvise or write short phrases with advanced finger patterns.	Students will demonstrate an understanding of advanced finger patterns by: • Analyzing a new passage or piece of music in to determine various fingering options. • Describing the benefits or challenges of a particular fingering choice. • Apply fingering choices to literature appropriate for their current level of skill.

Standards Links:

Resources and References:

Category 1:	**Executive Skills and Knowledge**

Content Area:	**1B. Left Hand Skills and Knowledge**
Benchmark:	*Students perform with the correct placement and angle of the left arm-wrist-hand-fingers to the instrument; demonstrate position that is balanced and free of tension; play with independence of fingers, ease of motion and control of finger weight; produce characteristic tone, with vibrato (as appropriate); show understanding and ability to apply fingerings, finger patterns, shifting, extensions.*
Learning Task:	**3.5—Extension of Vertical Technique**

Learning Sequences & Processes	Indicators of Success
General Information, Prior Knowledge, and Precursors • The goal is for students to develop control over stages of weight into the string with left-hand fingers. Sequence of Activities This series of exercises is done *with* the bow: • The goal is for students to develop control over stages of weight into the string with left-hand fingers. • Teacher chooses a familiar scale, pattern, or easy song • Teacher asks students to bounce each finger three times per note from 0% to 100% back to 0% weight • Students use all four fingers rather than open strings for this exercise • 0% should sound like airy and light ("fairy dust") • Students should demonstrate various tonal differences on a scale or other simple exercises, while experimenting with various vertical weights.	• The left hand and thumb remain flexible, without excessive tension, allowing ease of movement from one pattern to another. • Students perceive the string pressed down to the fingerboard as a graduated event rather than a single level of weight • Students learn to think vertically on the fingerboard • Students control left-hand fingering technique adjusting for downward weight and release. • Students can modify left-hand weight at will by adjusting the specific amount of weight in each finger. • Students learn to distinguish between the tone produced via full weight and tone produced with graduated weight. • Students understand that full weight can actually be lighter than they originally thought. • Students are able to modify left-hand weight intentionally to control tone color and quality.

Standards Links:

Resources and References:

Category 1: Executive Skills and Knowledge

Content Area:	**1B. Left Hand Skills and Knowledge**
Benchmark:	*Students perform with the correct placement and angle of the left arm-wrist-hand-fingers to the instrument; demonstrate position that is balanced and free of tension; play with independence of fingers, ease of motion and control of finger weight; produce characteristic tone, with vibrato (as appropriate); show understanding and ability to apply fingerings, finger patterns, shifting, extensions.*
Learning Task:	**4.1—Artistic Development and Application of Vibrato**

Learning Sequences & Processes	Indicators of Success

General Knowledge, Prior Learning, and Precursors
 	
• As students grow toward musical independence, they begin to vary the amplitude and speed of vibrato to create a wide palette of tone coloration, guided by stylistic understandings and individual artistic instinct.
 	
• When playing *forte*, the vibrato should be faster and wider; when playing *piano*, it should be narrower and less fast. The speed of the vibrato should fit the context of the music.
 	
• To enable the variation in amplitude and speed to create an expressive vibrato, the finger, wrist, and arm must be free of excessive tension.
 	
• Students can gain an aural concept of expressive vibrato by listening to recordings by various artists and comparing their use of vibrato.
 	
Sequence of Activities
 	
• For an artistic vibrato, it is necessary that the joint of the finger nearest the tip be flexible. An exercise that is helpful in developing this is to flex each finger against the thumb, bending and flattening the joint near the tip. (This is primarily true for violin/viola, though all finger joints for all instruments must be flexible in order to perform with a good vibrato.)
 	
• To develop the ability to vary the speed of the vibrato, work with a metronome, increasing the number of oscillations on each beat, maintaining evenness.
 	
• As an exercise, work to gain control by playing single notes with a vibrato that is:
  • wide and slow (as an exercise only)
  • wide and fast
  • narrow and slow
  • narrow and fast
 	
• Begin varying the amplitude and speed of the vibrato with pieces the student knows, and which stimulate expressive playing.
 	
• Students should practice maintaining the vibrato as they switch between fingers, so that the tone is unbroken and consistent.
	Students will demonstrate the ability to vary the amplitude and speed of vibrato, with the following elements:
	
	• The left hand and thumb remain flexible, without excessive tension, allowing ease of movement from one pattern to another.
	
	• Standards of musical practice for a particular period or style
	
	• Making informed choices about tone color and personal interpretation

Standards Links:

Resources and References:

Category 1:	Executive Skills and Knowledge
Content Area:	**1B. Left Hand Skills and Knowledge**
Benchmark:	*Students perform with the correct placement and angle of the left arm-wrist-hand-fingers to the instrument; demonstrate position that is balanced and free of tension; play with independence of fingers, ease of motion and control of finger weight; produce characteristic tone, with vibrato (as appropriate); show understanding and ability to apply fingerings, finger patterns, shifting, extensions.*
Learning Task:	**4.2—Extension of Vertical Technique**

Learning Sequences & Processes	Indicators of Success
General Information, Prior Knowledge, and Precursors • The goal is for students to develop control over stages of weight into the string with left-hand fingers. Sequence of Activities This series of exercises is done *with* the bow: • Teacher chooses a familiar scale, pattern, or easy song • Teacher asks students to bounce each finger three times per note from 0% to 100% back to 0% weight • Students use all four fingers rather than open strings for this exercise • 0% should sound like airy and light ("fairy dust") • Students should demonstrate various tonal differences on a selected piece of appropriate solo or ensemble repertoire.	• The left hand and thumb remain flexible, without excessive tension, allowing ease of movement from one pattern to another. • Students perceive the string pressed down to the fingerboard as a graduated event rather than a single level of weight • Students learn to think vertically on the fingerboard • Students control left-hand fingering technique adjusting for downward weight and release. • Students can modify left-hand weight at will by adjusting the specific amount of weight in each finger. • Students learn to distinguish between the tone produced via full weight and tone produced with graduated weight. • Students understand that full weight can actually be lighter than they originally thought. • Students are able to modify left-hand weight intentionally to control tone color and quality.

Standards Links:

Resources and References:

Content Area 1C—Right Hand Skills and Knowledge

Students perform with fluent bowing motion, control of variables (weight, angle, speed, and placement), in a variety of bowing techniques and articulations, with characteristic tone.

Learning Tasks

1.1 Perform pizzicato in guitar position—Violin/Viola

1.2 Perform pizzicato in playing position
   a. Violin/Viola
   b. Cello/Bass

1.3 Establishing the initial bow hold
   a. Violin/Viola
   b. Cello/Bass (French bow)
   c. Bass (German bow)

1.4 Perform pre-bowing exercises
   a. Violin/Viola
   b. Cello/Bass (French bow)
   c. Bass (German bow)

1.5 Perform with simple connected (détaché) bow strokes
   a. Violin/Viola
   b. Cello/Bass (French bow)
   c. Bass (German bow)

1.6 Perform with simple separated (staccato) bow strokes

1.7 Direction changes

1.8 Short slurs

1.9 String Crossings

1.10 Basic bow distribution

1.11 Introduction to weight, angle, speed, and placement (including contact point and part of the bow)

2.1 Extending the détaché bow stroke

2.2 On-the-string strokes
   a. Martelé
   b. Slurred staccato
   c. Hooked bowings
   d. Longer slurs
   e. Accented détaché

2.3 Off-the-string strokes
   a. Brush stroke

2.4 Simple double stops (bowing portion)

2.5. Extension of technique related to control of bowing variables

3.1 More advanced détaché bowings
   a. Louré
   b. Détaché lance
   c. Portato
   d. Rapid détaché
   e. Tremolo

3.2 Off-the-string strokes
   a. Spiccato

3.3 Special effect bowings
   a. Flautando
   b. Sul ponticello
   c. Sul tasto
   d. Col legno

3.4 Chords

3.5 Extension of technique related to control of bowing variables

4.1 Ricochet bowing

4.2 Sautillé

4.3 Flying spiccato

4.4 Extension of technique related to control of bowing variables

Category 1:	Executive Skills and Knowledge
Content Area:	**1C. Right Hand Skills and Knowledge**
Benchmark:	*Students perform with fluent bowing motion, control of variables (weight, angle, speed, and placement), in a variety of bowing techniques and articulations, with characteristic tone.*
Learning Task:	**1.1—Perform pizzicato in guitar position (violin and viola only)**

Learning Sequences & Processes	Indicators of Success
Prior Knowledge & Precursors • Knowledge of instrument parts and string names Sequence of Activities • Teacher models guitar position and students imitate. • Teacher demonstrates plucking motion using the thumb. • Using guitar position is an option that some teachers may not use. Some current textbooks start violin and viola students using guitar position to get the left hand set before placing it on the shoulder. Additional Information • Guitar position may be used to prevent fatigue as students are learning to hold the instruments in playing position. • Initial fingering patterns and beginning songs may be performed with the instrument in guitar position. • Be sure that students maintain a correct left hand position relative to the neck of the instrument while in guitar position. • Initial vibrato activities may also be performed in guitar position.	• Scroll is at shoulder height. • Back of instrument is against stomach. • Right elbow is draped over chinrest freeing right hand and thumb. • Left-hand is gently holding the left bout with the wrist in a straight line (for open strings) • Students pluck the string close to the end of the fingerboard using the pad of the thumb using a downward motion. • The thumb is plucking over the fingerboard. • Listen for a ringing tone

Standards Links:

Resources and References:

Category 1:	Executive Skills and Knowledge
Content Area:	**1C. Right Hand Skills and Knowledge**
Benchmark:	*Students perform with fluent bowing motion, control of variables (weight, angle, speed, and placement), in a variety of bowing techniques and articulations, with characteristic tone.*
Learning Task:	**1.2.a—Perform pizzicato in playing position (violin and viola only)**

Learning Sequences & Processes	Indicators of Success
Precursors • Instrument is placed in correct playing position. Sequence of Activities • Shake right hand out to relieve tension. • Using the right hand, form a gentle fist. Raise the thumb so it points upward. • Bring thumb to the fingerboard on the high-string side and place the tip under the edge of the right side of the fingerboard close to the end. • Using the fatty pad of the index finger gently pull the string to the right. Additional Information • The shape of the right arm and hand should be curved and relaxed; this assists in preparation of the arm mechanism (muscles and movement) for initial bowing activities. • Pizzicato activities should include both right-hand alone activities and also activities that combine right- and left-hand activities.	• Tip of thumb is under the fingerboard. • The pad of the index finger is contacting the string and using a gentle pulling motion. • Open strings being plucked should have a clear, ringing tone. • The right arm should remain relaxed and in good position throughout performance.

Standards Links:

Resources and References:

Category 1:	**Executive Skills and Knowledge**
Content Area:	**1C. Right Hand Skills and Knowledge**
Benchmark:	*Students perform with fluent bowing motion, control of variables (weight, angle, speed, and placement), in a variety of bowing techniques and articulations, with characteristic tone.*
Learning Task:	**1.2.b—Perform pizzicato in playing position (cello and bass)**

Learning Sequences & Processes	**Indicators of Success**
Precursors • Instrument is placed in correct playing position. Sequence of Activities • Shake right hand out to relieve tension. • Turn (pronate) the right hand (like emptying a glass of water) so that the index finger is closest to the ground. • Bring thumb to the fingerboard on the low-string side and place the tip on the edge of the right side of the fingerboard, approximately 8–10 inches from the lower end of the fingerboard. Using the fatty pad of the index finger gently pull the string to the right. Additional Information • The shape of the right arm and hand should be curved and relaxed; this assists in preparation of the arm mechanism (muscles and movement) for initial bowing activities. • Pizzicato activities should include both right-hand alone activities and also activities that combine right- and left-hand activities.	• Tip of thumb is under the fingerboard. • The pad of the index finger is contacting the string and using a gentle pulling motion. • Open strings being plucked should have a clear, ringing tone. • The right arm should remain relaxed and in good position throughout performance.

Standards Links:

Resources and References:

Category 1:	**Executive Skills and Knowledge**
Content Area:	**1C. Right Hand Skills and Knowledge**
Benchmark:	*Students perform with fluent bowing motion, control of variables (weight, angle, speed, and placement), in a variety of bowing techniques and articulations, with characteristic tone.*
Learning Task:	**1.3.a—Establishing the Initial Bow Hold (violin and viola)**

Learning Sequences & Processes	**Indicators of Success**
Prior Knowledge and Precursors • Bow hand shape without bow, pencil or straw • Use straw or pencil to establish basic bow hand shape before introducing the actual bow. Students should have good control of fingers and balanced and relaxed bow hand before moving to the dowel rod or bow. • Repeat exercises performed on the straw or pencil, but using a dowel rod.* Practice holding dowel in middle and at the end. Use exercises such as bunny/fox, rock/roll, et al, to develop flexibility and kinesthetic awareness of balance and relaxed bow hand. • Specific positions of fingers will vary based on the specific shape and size of student's hand. General principles include thumb across from middle two fingers; index finger lying on side, contacting stick between top two knuckles; pinky rests on top of stick. Sequence of Activities • Hand-to-bow, rather than bow-to-hand. The hand serves as a bow guide, rather than exerting extensive pressure or "grip." • Use mobility exercises (see resources below) to develop awareness of hand relaxation and motion. • Teach bow hand upside-down or support bow with two hands. • Bow hand should be taught independently from left hand skills during beginning stages. *Wooden dowel rods may be purchased at home improvement stores in 4-foot lengths, which should then be cut in half (2-foot lengths). Use a 1/4" diameter for violin/viola, 3/8" for cello, and 5/16" for bass.*	• All fingers are curved, thumb is curved • Bow hand is relaxed and flexible • Arm, wrist, hand, and fingers are free of tension • Position of fingers will vary based on shape and size of hand. • Students can "flex" bow hand, while maintaining control of stick

Standards Links:

Resources and References:

Category 1:	Executive Skills and Knowledge
Content Area:	**1C. Right Hand Skills and Knowledge**
Benchmark:	*Students perform with fluent bowing motion, control of variables (weight, angle, speed, and placement), in a variety of bowing techniques and articulations, with characteristic tone.*
Learning Task:	**1.3.b—Establishing the Initial Bow Hold (cello and bass—French bow)**

Learning Sequences & Processes	Indicators of Success
Precursors • Students can maintain bow hand shape without bow, pencil or straw • Use straw or pencil to establish basic bow hand shape before introducing the actual bow. Students should have good control of fingers and balanced and relaxed bow hand before moving to the dowel rod or bow. • Repeat exercises performed on the straw or pencil, but using a dowel rod.* Practice holding dowel in middle and at the end. Use exercises such as bunny/fox, rock/roll, et al, to develop flexibility and kinesthetic awareness of balance and relaxed bow hand. • Specific positions of fingers will vary based on the specific shape and size of student's hand. General principles include thumb across from middle two fingers; index finger lying on side, contacting stick between top two knuckles; pinky rests on side (French bass bow). Sequence • Hand-to-bow, rather than bow-to-hand. The hand serves as a bow guide, rather than exerting extensive pressure or "grip." • Use mobility exercises (see resources below) to develop awareness of hand relaxation and motion. • Teach bow hand upside-down or support bow with two hands. • Bow hand should be taught independently from left hand skills during beginning stages. *Wooden dowel rods may be purchased at home improvement stores in 4-foot lengths, which should then be cut in half (2-foot lengths). Use a 1/4" diameter for violin/viola, 3/8" for cello, and 5/16" for bass.*	• All fingers are curved, thumb is curved • Bow hand is relaxed and flexible • Arm, wrist, hand, and fingers are free of tension • Position of fingers will vary based on shape and size of hand. • Students can "flex" bow hand, while maintaining control of stick

Standards Links:	

Resources and References:	

Category 1: Executive Skills and Knowledge

Content Area:	**1C. Right Hand Skills and Knowledge**
Benchmark:	*Students perform with fluent bowing motion, control of variables (weight, angle, speed, and placement), in a variety of bowing techniques and articulations, with characteristic tone.*
Learning Task:	**1.3.c—Establishing the Initial Bow Hold (bass—German bow)**

Learning Sequences & Processes	Indicators of Success
Precursors • Students should have a relaxed right arm, and be able to play pizzicato with a warm-sound. • Students should be able to support the bass in either seated or standing position (as the teacher directs), without having to use either the right- or left-hand to support the instrument. • The German bass bow is frequently used in jazz playing, as well as classical playing. Therefore, many students learn to play with both types of bows, but typically not until the high school or collegiate levels. Sequence • Students should perform several exercises to help them develop the bow hand shape, such as "Waving a Magic Wand," where students practice gently waving the arm in the air, as if they had a magic wand in their hand. The hand should be relaxed and fingers should easily flex as they do this exercise. • The pizzicato placement of the right hand can also help prepare students for the bow hold. Students should lay their hand upside-down (as if they have just poured out a glass of water) on the top of the strings. Using a gentle strumming motion, students should move their arms across the strings, returning to the "set" position in an arco motion. • "Super Glue"—students should imagine that a drop of super glue has been placed on the tip of their thumb and on the first and middle finger-tips. Without the bow, they should practice waving their hands (fingers "stuck" together) vertically and horizontally, so that they develop a sense of how the fingers open and close as the hand and arm change direction. • Before using the bow itself, teachers may use a pencil or straw to help students gain a kinesthetic awareness of how to hold the bow, without putting too much pressure on the bow itself. • With the bow: The thumb, first finger, and middle finger form the shape of a flattened "C," with the end screw of the bow resting in the fleshy webbing of the skin in between the thumb and first finger. The thumb touches the stick across from the first and second fingers. The third finger relaxes inside the frog (does not touch any part of the frog), while the pinky is curved and placed on the bottom of the frog, providing a counter-balance to the rest of the hand. • The bow should be supported by the left-hand and placed into the right-hand (the teacher may also place the bow in the student's hand), rather than grabbing the bow with the right-hand. • Students tend to want to grab the bow immediately, so a good intermediate step is to hold the bow with the tip pointing to the ground, gently raising and lowering the arm, so that students have a sense of how the hand reacts to and guides the bow.	• All fingers are curved, thumb is curved • Bow hand is relaxed and flexible • Arm, wrist, hand, and fingers are free of tension • Position of fingers will vary based on shape and size of hand. • Students can "flex" bow hand, while maintaining control of stick

Standards Links:

Resources and References:

Category 1:	Executive Skills and Knowledge
Content Area:	**1C. Right Hand Skills and Knowledge**
Benchmark:	*Students perform with fluent bowing motion, control of variables (weight, angle, speed, and placement), in a variety of bowing techniques and articulations, with characteristic tone.*
Learning Task:	**1.4.a—Perform pre-bowing exercises (violin and viola)**

Learning Sequences & Processes	Indicators of Success
Prior Knowledge & Precursors • Student can demonstrate a relaxed, correct bow hold using a pencil, straw and/or dowel rod. • Students know the terms and correct directions for down- and up-bow. Sequence of Activities • Have all students practice finger taps to a CD in common time. • Smiley face thumb—have students turn their right hand to the right and look for a curved thumb that looks like a smile. • Open/close the door—with right arm parallel to the floor at face level, place left index finger in the elbow and open and close the gate door to imitate bowing motion. Chant names of classmates and move arm in rhythm. • Form bow hold on the bow either at the balance point or at the frog depending on teacher preference. Have all students practice down- and up-bows by vertically air bowing. • Put the bow on a cake of rosin and practice the bowing motion while saying down and up. • Going tubing!—Use a toilet paper tube, paper towel tube (or for longer lasting usage, use PVC tubing, cut to 6" lengths) and practice bowing through it. Hold the tube slightly above the left shoulder.	• Students using a straw will bend the straw if they are using too much pressure or squeezing. • Relaxed fingers will be able to tap in rhythm with a smooth motion. • A curved thumb will look as if it is smiling, • Open/close the gate—violin and viola students will use their forearm. • Students will move their right arm to the right for a down-bow and to the left for an up-bow. • Right arms will imitate the correct bowing motion as they play down and up bows on the rosin. • Students using tubes should be able to move their arms as described above. Movement will be smooth. • All fingers should be curved and relaxed.

Standards Links:

Resources and References:

Level:	Baseline

Category 1: Executive Skills and Knowledge

Content Area:	1C. Right Hand Skills and Knowledge
Benchmark:	*Students perform with fluent bowing motion, control of variables (weight, angle, speed, and placement), in a variety of bowing techniques and articulations, with characteristic tone.*
Learning Task:	**1.4.b—Perform pre-bowing exercises (cello and bass—French bow)**

Learning Sequences & Processes	Indicators of Success
<u>Prior Knowledge & Precursors</u> • Student can demonstrate a relaxed, correct bow hold using a pencil, straw and/or dowel rod. • Students know the terms and correct directions for down- and up-bow. <u>Sequence of Activities</u> • Have all students practice finger taps to a CD in common time. • Smiley face thumb—have students turn their right hand to the right and look for a curved thumb that looks like a smile. • Open/close the door—with right arm parallel to the floor at face level, place left index finger in the elbow and open and close the gate door to imitate bowing motion. Chant names of classmates and move arm in rhythm. • Form bow hold on the bow either at the balance point or at the frog depending on teacher preference. Have all students practice down- and up-bows by vertically air bowing. • Put the bow on a cake of rosin and practice the bowing motion while saying down and up. • Going tubing!—Use a toilet paper tube, paper towel tube (or for longer lasting usage, use pvc tubing, cut to 6" lengths) and practice bowing through it. Hold the tube slightly above the left shoulder.	• Students using a straw will bend the straw if they are using too much pressure or squeezing. • Relaxed fingers will be able to tap in rhythm with a smooth motion. • A curved thumb will look as if it is smiling, • Open/close the gate—violin and viola students will use their forearm. • Students will move their right arm to the right for a down-bow and to the left for an up-bow. • Right arms will imitate the correct bowing motion as they play down and up bows on the rosin. • Students using tubes should be able to move their arms as described above. Movement will be smooth. • All fingers should be curved and relaxed.

Standards Links:	

Resources and References:	

Category 1: Executive Skills and Knowledge

Content Area:	**1C. Right Hand Skills and Knowledge**
Benchmark:	*Students perform with fluent bowing motion, control of variables (weight, angle, speed, and placement), in a variety of bowing techniques and articulations, with characteristic tone.*
Learning Task:	**1.4.c—Perform pre-bowing exercises (bass—German bow)**

Learning Sequences & Processes	Indicators of Success
<u>Precursors</u> • Body posture should be well established and students should be able to play simple melodies (pizzicato). The instrument should be supported correctly in sitting or standing position (as the teacher directs). <u>Sequence</u> • Relax the right arm (hanging down by the student's side), so that the student is able to easily swing the arm back-and-forth like the trunk of an elephant. • Without the bow, students should practice moving their right arm in a horizontal motion, as if they are painting a wall. The hand should be relaxed and move easily back-and-forth. Students should do this at eye-level and then also at the level of the strings on the bass. Note that the horizontal motion changes direction based on which string the students are playing. • See other exercises from 1.3.c above • Once the student is relaxed and moves in a fluid motion, the bow hold should be re-established. • Using two hands, or with teacher help, the student places the bow on the strings, so that the bow is parallel to the ground. Many students struggle with this motion and end up bowing at a severe angle to the string, with the bow pointed towards the ground. This is an unacceptable position and will lead to long-term bad habits and poor playing technique.	• All fingers are curved, thumb is curved • Bow hand is relaxed and flexible • Arm, wrist, hand, and fingers are free of tension • Position of fingers will vary based on shape and size of hand. • Students can "flex" bow hand, while maintaining control of stick

Standards Links:
Resources and References:

Category 1:	Executive Skills and Knowledge
Content Area:	1C. Right Hand Skills and Knowledge
Benchmark:	*Students perform with fluent bowing motion, control of variables (weight, angle, speed, and placement), in a variety of bowing techniques and articulations, with characteristic tone.*
Learning Task:	**1.5.a—Perform with simple connected (détaché) bow strokes (violin and viola)**

Learning Sequences & Processes	Indicators of Success
Prior Knowledge and Precursors • Relaxed bow hold, preferably held at the balance point in the beginning stages • Student is able to successfully demonstrate the pre-bowing exercises • Student can define and demonstrate (vertical air-bow) down- and up-bows Sequence of Activities • The instrument is in correct playing position with the left hand fingers on the bout and the thumb cradling the neck. • Bow exercises on the open string, such as Lift-set, Silent Rock-n-Roll, Teeter-Totter • The teacher models the next sequence and students describe the tone. • Follow the leader and place the bow on the D-string midway between the bridge and the fingerboard. Open and close the door as you draw the bow on the open D (The teacher may place the bow for the first time and get the arm motion started). • Slightly lower the elbow and right arm and roll the bow over to the A-string and open and close the door, watching that the bow remains on the A-string and parallel to the bridge. • Play simple rhythms on the A- and D-strings. • Lift-set-bow. Students will approach the string from above—set the bow on the string and immediately move it. Coming from above should add a little more of the natural weight from the arm.	• Students place the bow near the frog and then lift and replace the bow near the tip with a steady motion. • Students place the bow in the middle of the stick and silently rock from the G to the E (C to A for viola) string using the correct arm level for each string. • The bow is midway between the bridge and the fingerboard with the bow parallel to the bridge. Looking down the fingerboard, the bow hair is only contacting the D-string. • The forearm will open and close without excess shoulder motion and the bow will remain parallel to the bridge. • Students demonstrate a characteristic tone using open strings.

Standards Links:

Resources and References:

Category 1:	Executive Skills and Knowledge
Content Area:	**1C. Right Hand Skills and Knowledge**
Benchmark:	*Students perform with fluent bowing motion, control of variables (weight, angle, speed, and placement), in a variety of bowing techniques and articulations, with characteristic tone.*
Learning Task:	**1.5.b—Perform with simple connected (détaché) bow strokes (cello)**

Learning Sequences & Processes	Indicators of Success
<u>Prior Knowledge and Precursors</u> • Relaxed bow hold, preferably held at the balance point in the beginning stages • Student successfully demonstrates the pre-bowing exercises • Student defines and demonstrates (air-bow) down and up bows <u>Sequence of Activities</u> • The instrument is in correct playing position. • Bow exercises on the open string, such as Lift-set, Silent Rock-n-Roll, Teeter-Totter • The teacher models the next sequence and students describe the tone. • Follow the leader and place the bow on the D-string midway between the bridge and the fingerboard. Open and close the door with the elbow leading as you draw the bow on the open D-string (The teacher may place the bow for the first time and get the arm motion started). • Slightly raise the elbow and right arm and roll the bow to the A-string and open and close the door, watching that the bow remains on the A-string and parallel to the bridge. • Play simple rhythms on the A- and D-strings. • Lift-set-bow. Students will approach the string from above—set the bow on the string and immediately move it. Coming from above should add a little more of the natural weight from the arm.	• Students place the bow near the frog and then lift and replace the bow near the tip with a steady motion. • Students place the bow in the middle of the stick and silently rock from the C- to the A-string using the correct arm level for each string. • The bow is midway between the bridge and the fingerboard with the bow parallel to the bridge. Looking down the fingerboard, the bow hair is only contacting the D-string. • The forearm will open and close without excess shoulder motion and the bow will remain parallel to the bridge. • Students demonstrate a characteristic tone using open strings.

Standards Links:

Resources and References:

Category 1:	**Executive Skills and Knowledge**
Content Area:	**1C. Right Hand Skills and Knowledge**
Benchmark:	*Students perform with fluent bowing motion, control of variables (weight, angle, speed, and placement), in a variety of bowing techniques and articulations, with characteristic tone.*
Learning Task:	**1.5.c—Perform with simple connected (détaché) bow strokes (bass)**

Learning Sequences & Processes	**Indicators of Success**
Precursors • Relaxed bow hold, preferably held at the balance point in the beginning stages • Student successfully demonstrates the pre-bowing exercises • Student defines and demonstrates (air-bow) down- and up-bows Sequence • The instrument is in correct playing position. • Bow exercises on the open string, such as Lift-set, Silent Rock-n-Roll, Teeter-Totter • Students should perform shorter bow strokes first, in the middle 1/3 of the bow, before trying to attempt long, legato bow strokes, which require much greater control. • The teacher models the next sequence and students describe the tone. • Follow the leader and place the bow on the D-string about two-thirds of the way down to the bridge. Swing the arm in a "pendulum" like motion from the shoulder. As you pull the bow on the open D-string (The teacher may place the bow for the first time and get the arm motion started). • Slightly lower the elbow and right arm and roll the bow down to the A-string. Move the arm away from the body, watching that the bow remains on the A-string and parallel to the bridge. The frog should remain parallel to the floor. • Play simple rhythms on the A- and D-strings. • Lift-set-bow. Students will approach the string from above—set the bow on the string and immediately move it. Coming from above should add a little more of the natural weight from the arm.	• Students place the bow near the frog and then lift and replace the bow near the tip with a steady motion. • Students place the bow in the about 2 inches past the winding and silently rock from the E to the G-string using the correct arm level for each string. • The bow contacts the string two-thirds of the way down to the bridge with the bow parallel to the floor. Looking down the fingerboard, the bow hair is only contacting the D-string. • The arm gently swings from the shoulder the bow will remain parallel to the floor. • Students demonstrate a characteristic tone using open strings.

Standards Links:

Resources and References:

Category 1:	**Executive Skills and Knowledge**
Content Area:	**1C. Right Hand Skills and Knowledge**
Benchmark:	*Students perform with fluent bowing motion, control of variables (weight, angle, speed, and placement), in a variety of bowing techniques and articulations, with characteristic tone.*
Learning Task:	**1.6—Perform with simple separated (staccato) bow strokes.**

Learning Sequences & Processes	**Indicators of Success**
General Information, Prior Knowledge and Precursors • Student can perform with the correct bow hold and is able to play with a controlled détaché bow stroke. • Staccato or martelé? The term staccato can be confusing. As a musical term, staccato refers to performing notes in a separated manner. Some of the beginning method books introduce staccato in book one while others use the term martelé. Martelé is one of several bowing techniques used to achieve a separated or staccato sound. The difference between the two is that a martelé stroke requires preparation as the bow sinks into the string, moves forward with an immediate release producing a louder, stronger tone. A basic staccato stroke stays on the string with a definite stop between notes. The martelé bow stroke will be discussed in more detail in section 2.2a of the right-hand technique portion of the curriculum. Sequence of Activities • Demonstrate a scale using separated-style bowing. Ask students to describe what they hear. Show students the symbol for staccato. • Have students put their bows on the D-string. Tell them to pinch the beginning of each note using their index finger. Try bowing 4 open D's. • Have half of the class bow a D-major scale using short, stopped bow strokes. Have the other half pluck the scale. • Explain that a staccato quarter note will sound like an eighth note because of the stop and space between notes. • Find the martelé or staccato section of the class method book and work on the pieces using such a bowing.	• Bow will stop after each note. Bow stays on the string and there is no accent. • The pizzicato and staccato note lengths should match. • Bow comes to an "easy" and controlled stop. There is no crunching sound when the bow stops moving.

Standards Links:	

Resources and References:	

Category 1:	Executive Skills and Knowledge
Content Area:	**1C. Right Hand Skills and Knowledge**
Benchmark:	*Students perform with fluent bowing motion, control of variables (weight, angle, speed, and placement), in a variety of bowing techniques and articulations, with characteristic tone.*
Learning Task:	**1.7—Direction Changes**

Learning Sequences & Processes	Indicators of Success

General Information, Prior Knowledge and Precursors
 	
• The ability to make smooth, consistent, and controlled direction changes requires several elements:
  • A body posture that is balanced, lengthened and mobile.
  • An instrument that is correctly supported.
  • A bow hand that is relaxed, with fingers that are correctly positioned and are mobile, rather than posed or tense.
• Though direction changes are placed at this point in the sequence of technique, the teacher should emphasize an excellent direction change motion from the first stages of bow-hand development.
 	
Sequence of Activities
 	
• The development of a fluid bow direction change motion begins before the bow is actually used. Students should practice exercises for changing directions first without the bow, beginning with just the hand movement, then adding a straw, pencil, or dowel rod.
• The bow arm moves in anticipation of the actual bow change. So, exercises should emphasize all elements of the bow arm working in unison rather than in isolation.
• Practice moving the arm in a vertical "paint brush" motion so that the hand and fingers follow the motion of the upper arm and shoulder. The bow arm mechanism should move in a sequential motion that is not stiff or jerky. Practice the same motion horizontally, similar to a motion like treading water.
• Practice direction changes first in the middle portion of the bow before moving to the tip or the frog.
• Add the pencil or dowel, and then finally the bow, as students gain confidence and skill.
• Move to the string, but be sure that students maintain a good contact point with the string. As they bow, the sound should be even. Practice shorter, medium-speed bow strokes first before moving to rapid or extremely slow bows.
• In the middle of the bow, the majority of the bow direction change motion will be visible in the forearm, wrist, hand, and fingers. As you move toward the ends of the bow, the upper arm and shoulder will have greater function.
	• All joints and muscles remain relaxed throughout the motion
	• Students maintain functionality and mobility throughout the bow direction changes.
	• The arm and body remain balanced throughout the motion.

Standards Links:

Resources and References:

Category 1:	Executive Skills and Knowledge
Content Area:	**1C. Right Hand Skills and Knowledge**
Benchmark:	*Students perform with fluent bowing motion, control of variables (weight, angle, speed, and placement), in a variety of bowing techniques and articulations, with characteristic tone.*
Learning Task:	**1.8—Short Slurs**

Learning Sequences & Processes	Indicators of Success
<u>General Information, Prior Knowledge and Precursors</u> • Students perform with the correct bow hold and are able to play with a controlled détaché bow stroke. • The right arm remains relaxed during the entire détaché bow stroke. • Students know the terms and correct directions for down- and up-bows. • Simple slurs require some mechanical sophistication and coordination on the part of the students. At the beginning students associate a single note with a single bow stroke. Keeping the bow moving one direction while the left-hand fingers change notes can be confusing for some students. The ability to have the right and left arms operate independently and move in opposite directions is not a natural activity and must be trained. Younger children may struggle with this activity at the beginning. <u>Sequence of Activities</u> • Students perform a single down-bow stroke while saying "down-bow." Repeat with the up-bow stroke, saying "up-bow." • Students air bow saying the bow direction (i.e., up- or down-bow) with the bow in a vertical position. • Students play and say "down-bow, up-bow." • Teacher models a down-bow slur using an easy finger pattern such as open D, then 1st finger E on the D-string. (N.B. Some teachers may start teaching slurs using open strings before introducing one-string slurs. This is left to the discretion of the teacher. Either way, this should be done as a rote activity several weeks before introducing slurs on the written page.) • A variation to this could be: D, rest, E, rest, stopping the bow between each note. • While air bowing in the vertical position, students do a down-bow, saying "D– E." • Students with some coordination difficulties can try saying "do–wn" (one part of the word on the first note, the second part of the word on the second note) to become more conscious of the bow direction. • Put the bow on a cake of rosin and practice the slur while saying "D–E." • Put the bow on the string and practice down-bow slurs. • Repeat the process (if necessary) for up- bows and later open string crossings. • Introduce slur symbol and slurs in the music after students have mastered this rote exercise.	• Bowing directions are accurately played. • In the vertical position, students can use a single downwards motion while saying two different note names. • Students can demonstrate two-note slurs with a characteristic tone.

Standards Links:

Resources and References:

Category 1:	**Executive Skills and Knowledge**
Content Area:	**1C. Right Hand Skills and Knowledge**
Benchmark:	*Students perform with fluent bowing motion, control of variables (weight, angle, speed, and placement), in a variety of bowing techniques and articulations, with characteristic tone.*
Learning Task:	**1.9—String Crossings**

Learning Sequences & Processes	**Indicators of Success**
General Information, Prior Knowledge and Precursors • Student can perform with the correct bow hold and is able to play with a controlled détaché bow stroke. Sequence of Activities • Demonstrate a scale using separated-style bowing. Ask students to describe what they hear. Show students the symbol for staccato. • Have violin, viola, and cello students place the bow hair on the bridge and rock-n-roll between the lowest to the highest string. Have bass students place bow on the E-string and "rock-n-roll" from the E-string to the G-string. Ask students to watch what happens to their right arm. • Have students place their bow on their lowest string and try a silent rock-n-roll. Say, "Freeze!" and have students look down their fingerboard to see that the bow is only touching the specified string. • Demonstrate on a violin and cello going from open D-string to the A-string. Tell students to watch as you anticipate the string crossing and ease the bow towards the A-string before actually making the string crossing. • Have students try playing from the D-string to the A-string (fingered A for bass). Repeat several times. Violinists and violists should start on a down-bow. Cello/bass students start on an up-bow. • Have students alternate going from an open D-string to B on the A-string (G-string for bass). • The teacher should work on this by rote before reading the notes. Try some echo patterns using just open strings, and then gradually add more fingered pitches. Note: Consult any of the technique books in the resource list for descriptions of arcs, circles and figure eights that the right hand makes during string crossings.	• No excess tension in the bow hand and the bow remains parallel to the bridge. This means that the bow does not move directly up-and-down (especially for cello/bass) but follows the arc of the bridge. • The right arm on the violin and viola will lower as the students move towards their highest string. Cello/bass arms will raise and move out as they move from low to high strings. • Violin will start with a down-bow and the cello with an up-bow. Towards the end of the first bow stroke, the bow will begin to almost lean into the A right before the change. • The finger on the higher string will stay down.

Standards Links:

Resources and References:

Category 1: Executive Skills and Knowledge

Content Area:	1C. Right Hand Skills and Knowledge
Benchmark:	*Students perform with fluent bowing motion, control of variables (weight, angle, speed, and placement), in a variety of bowing techniques and articulations, with characteristic tone.*
Learning Task:	1.10—Basic Bow Distribution (upper half, lower half, etc.)

Learning Sequences & Processes	Indicators of Success
General Information, Prior Knowledge and Precursors • Student can perform with the correct bow hold and is able to play with a controlled détaché bow stroke. • Violinists and violists generally start in the upper-half or two-thirds of the bow, so extending bow distribution moves them into the lower-half or two-thirds of the bow. Cellists and bassists generally start in the middle part of the bow, so extending the bow stroke will move them into the upper- and lower-third of the bow. • There is common misunderstanding that bow speed increases when the value of a note decreases (for example, move the bow twice as fast to play eighth-notes compared to quarter notes). The result is bow speed that is too fast and makes an unfocused or glassy sound. In reality, bow length is the primary determining factor in relationship to rhythms. Eighth notes will use less bow than quarter notes, and so on. Weight, placement, and angle are also important factors and interrelated to bow speed. For the beginning student, speed and length are the two easiest concepts to understand. (See the next curriculum item, *1.10—Introduction of contact point, weight, speed, and angle*, for more information). Sequence of Activities • Review parts of the bow with students as well as bow lifts and down and up-bows. • Demonstrate playing in the UH (upper half), LH (lower half), using a WB (whole bow) and playing at the tip or frog. • Play lift-set and follow the leader. The leader will move the bow to various parts of the bow and the students will imitate. • Place bow at the frog and bow to the middle. • Discuss and demonstrate lower half (LH) bowing and show the symbol. Do the same for the UH and M (middle). Have students try playing in each location. • Demonstrate using a whole bow (WB). Play 2 half notes and then a whole note. Have students describe the difference. • Try playing a down-bow whole note. Lift and make a big full moon motion to start another down-bow. Play a scale using a half note and two quarters on each pitch. Say whole bow, upper-half; whole bow, lower-half while playing. • Find examples in the music currently being studied where students can apply bow distribution.	• Bow is parallel to the bridge and free of excess tension. Violin and viola students use their bow in the middle to upper half and cello/bass use the lower half. • Students will be able to move rapidly between various parts of the bow. • Bows remain parallel to the bridge at all locations. • Bow will be used but the bow speed will increase for the half notes. • The half note will get a WB and the quarters will be in the corresponding half of the bow.

Standards Links:

Resources and References:

100

Category 1:	**Executive Skills and Knowledge**
Content Area:	**1C. Right Hand Skills and Knowledge**
Benchmark:	*Students perform with fluent bowing motion, control of variables (weight, angle, speed, and placement), in a variety of bowing techniques and articulations, with characteristic tone.*
Learning Task:	**1.11—Introduction of weight, angle, speed, and placement (contact point and part of bow)**

Learning Sequences & Processes	**Indicators of Success**
<u>Prior Knowledge and Precursors</u> • Correct bow hold at the frog, ability to demonstrate a very basic détaché stroke. <u>Definitions</u> • Weight—the amount of weight coming through the bow arm and transferring to the stick via the fingers (purposeful flexion) • Angle—the correct angle of the bow in relation to the string (generally parallel to the bridge) • Speed—the speed at which the bow moves on the string • Placement—includes both the contact point (point on the string where the bow contacts the string) and the part of the bow used to achieve the bow stroke. <u>Sequence of Activities—General</u> • Using lift-set, place the bow at varying contact points. • Use the lane concept for teaching contact point. Lane 1 would be closest to the fingerboard with Lane 5, closest to the bridge. Most beginning textbooks have students bowing in lanes 2–4. <u>Sequence of Activities—Weight</u> • While weight is not the first thing beginners need to worry about, many students unknowingly will apply too much pressure in the beginning so it should be addressed. • Experiment by adding five, ten, and twenty pounds to the bow. <u>Sequence of Activities—Speed</u> • Keeping an even speed will be the most important skill for the beginning student. • Demonstrate using several different speeds and ask the students to describe using miles per hour, cars (standard car vs. a race car), walking speeds, etc. This becomes increasingly more important as students learn a variety of note lengths. <u>Sequence of Activities—Angle</u> • Practice "rock-and-row." First, keeping the bow still at one point, have the student move the bow in a rowing motion, making sure that the wrist and elbow are flexible. This helps loosen the bow arm mechanism. • Elevators—Practice moving from string to string, with a smooth motion, having the arm/elbow height adjust according to string height. Note that the angle of string change should follow the shape of the bridge (vertical for violin/viola, more horizontal with cello/bass)	• Students identify lanes 1–5 and can demonstrate a simple détaché in lane 3. • The characteristic tone of a simple détaché stroke clear, even, and focused, resulting from a bow arm that is free of excess tension. • Students are able to manipulate all four elements (weight, angle, speed, and placement) to adjust basic tone.

Standards Links:

Resources and References:

Category 1:	**Executive Skills and Knowledge**
Content Area:	**1C. Right Hand Skills and Knowledge**
Benchmark:	*Students perform with fluent bowing motion, control of variables (weight, angle, speed, and placement), in a variety of bowing techniques and articulations, with characteristic tone.*
Learning Task:	**2.1—Extending the Détaché Bow Stroke (Sequential Bow Stroke)**

Learning Sequences & Processes	**Indicators of Success**
General Information, Prior Knowledge and Precursors • Students perform with the correct bow hold and play with a controlled détaché bow stroke. • Basic direction change motions are comfortable, fluid, and controlled, and lead to the development of the sequential bow stroke. • The sequential bow stroke involves the coordinated movement of the body from lower body to the upper body, through the arms, into the hands and fingers, to the bow, in anticipation and response to the bow stroke. Though it is easier to show than describe, the sequential bow stroke generally has a naturally wavy shape, rather than angular, or simply having the body move in the opposite direction of the bow. • The initial bow strokes generally take place in the middle part of the bow. Therefore, extending the bow stroke emphasizes working the extreme upper (upper 1/3 to tip) and lower parts of the bow (lower 1/3 to frog). Sequence of Activities • As a warm-up, the teacher demonstrates rote rhythm patterns using the simple détaché bow stroke, in the middle part of the bow. • The students play repeated eighth- or quarter-note patterns (medium speed) slowly moving towards the tip of the bow. The teacher directs the students to note the difference in the arm motion (what parts of the arm are moving) and to pay attention to changes in WASP as they play. (For example, the students will need to add bow weight towards the tip in order to maintain the same tone as they had in the middle of the bow.) • The same exercise is used, but this time moving towards the bottom part of the bow. • A variety of rhythm patterns may be used to work either end of the bow. It's good to mix both symmetrical patterns and asymmetrical patterns (such as repeated eighth-sixteenth-sixteenth patterns). • Once students are comfortable at the ends of the bow, the teacher should use a variety of note patterns and bow lengths, working both ends of the bow, moving back and forth between upper, middle, and lower portions of the bow. • As students gain confidence, the teacher should emphasize rhythm patterns that reinforce bowing in various parts of the bow (e.g., whole bow, upper-half, lower half, upper third, middle third, lower third, tip, frog, and various combinations of those).	• Students control WASP at all parts of the bow • Students maintain a fluid and consistent bow stroke motion. • Tone remains consistent throughout the bow stroke. • The bow arm mechanism is flexible and balanced.

Standards Links:

Resources and References:

Category 1: Executive Skills and Knowledge

Content Area:	**1C. Right Hand Skills and Knowledge**
Benchmark:	*Students perform with fluent bowing motion, control of variables (weight, angle, speed, and placement), in a variety of bowing techniques and articulations, with characteristic tone.*
Learning Task:	**2.2.a—Martelé**

Learning Sequences & Processes	Indicators of Success
General Information, Prior Knowledge and Precursors • Student can perform with the correct bow hold and is able to play with a controlled détaché bow stroke. • Martelé is generally performed in the middle or upper-third of the bow. It is an accented staccato stroke, ranging from a slightly weighted articulation at the beginning of the stroke to a heavier, sharply accented bow stroke, depending on stylistic and period considerations. • Martelé may be marked with a staccato or wedge articulation marking, but this is not universally the case. Sequence of Activities • Teacher demonstrates both a détaché and martelé bow stroke. Ask students to identify the differences both in sound and visual appearance of the stroke. • Form bow hold on a pencil or dowel rod and transfer/apply weight to the index finger to visualize what will happen on the bow. Release the weight immediately. • Place the bow on the D-string. Slightly lean the bow hand into the bow stick (directing the stick of the bow towards the hair). Pinch or depress the string, pull the bow quickly and release the pressure immediately. Stop the bow and then continue doing some martelé strokes. As the bow begins to move, listen for a small popping sound. The bow should stay straight. In the early stages, try using a quarter of the bow in the upper third of the bow. • Choose a selection in the textbook and play using the martelé stroke. • Vary the length and weight of the stroke in order to achieve different effects.	• Students will respond that there is a physical stop in between notes with the martelé stroke, an accent at the beginning and the bow stays on the string. • Pencil or dowel rod will dip downwards. As weight is released, the stick will come back up. • Vln./vla—Leverage comes from a curved thumb thrusting upward and pressure from the first finger on the stick. • Cello/bass—Thumb is not as curved as vln. and pushes forward with index finger resisting by pressing towards the string. (Green, p. 71) • Bow will remain on the string with an accented start and a non-accented release at the end of the stroke.

Standards Links:

Resources and References:

Category 1: Executive Skills and Knowledge

Content Area:	**1C. Right Hand Skills and Knowledge**
Benchmark:	*Students perform with fluent bowing motion, control of variables (weight, angle, speed, and placement), in a variety of bowing techniques and articulations, with characteristic tone.*
Learning Task:	**2.2.b—Slurred Staccato**

Learning Sequences & Processes	Indicators of Success
General Information, Prior Knowledge and Precursors • Student can perform with the correct bow hold and is able to play with a controlled détaché bow stroke. • Students can perform basic two-note slurs with good control of tone. • Students can accurately perform rhythm patterns containing dotted-notes followed by shorter notes, such as dotted-eighth/sixteenth or dotted-quarter/eighth. • Slurred staccato and hooked martelé are related, but also distinctly different bowings. Slurred staccato is a symmetrical bowing, where the double up-bow uses two basically equal bow lengths. The hooked bowing is asymmetrical, where the short note connects to the long note as an upbeat in a single rebound motion in the right hand. Sequence of Activities • Teacher models both a down- and up-bow slur using two quarter notes per bow. Students copy. Begin with open strings then practice by changing pitches at the beginning of the slur, and then during the slur itself. • Teacher models a slurred staccato using two quarter notes (same or different pitch), asking students to describe the bowing. • Teacher holds bow vertically and air bows two staccato down bows saying, "Down-stop-down." Students imitate. Repeat using "Up-stop-up." • Place bow on the string and have students try a down-bow staccato using 2 quarter notes, then repeat using an up-bow. • Play a down-bow half note followed with a 4 note slurred staccato bowing. • Students should practice setting the weight of the bow, as they would for a martelé stroke, between the slurred staccato notes. This will help ensure a clean start and articulation to the note.	• Students perform with a relaxed bow arm, relaxed and curved fingers, and control of bow speed. • Students indicate that the bow physically stops before continuing to the second note. • Students will be able to coordinate the down-bow slur with the stop. • The bow will physically stop on the string before continuing to the next note within the slur. • Mastery level—Students should master slurred, symmetrical staccato before preceding with non-symmetrical hooked bowing.

Standards Links:

Resources and References:

Category 1: Executive Skills and Knowledge

Content Area:	**1C. Right Hand Skills and Knowledge**
Benchmark:	*Students perform with fluent bowing motion, control of variables (weight, angle, speed, and placement), in a variety of bowing techniques and articulations, with characteristic tone.*
Learning Task:	**2.2.c—Hooked Bowing**

Learning Sequences & Processes	Indicators of Success
General Information, Prior Knowledge and Precursors • Student can perform with the correct bow hold and is able to play with a controlled détaché bow stroke. • Students can perform basic two-note slurs, with good control of tone. • Students can perform the slurred staccato with control and a relaxed bow arm. • Students can accurately perform rhythm patterns containing dotted-notes followed by shorter notes, such as dotted-eighth/sixteenth or dotted-quarter/eighth. • Slurred staccato and hooked martelé are related, but also distinctly different bowings. Slurred staccato is a symmetrical bowing, where the double up-bow uses two basically equal bow lengths. Hooked bowing is a descriptive term for asymmetrical notes that occur in one bow stroke, where the short note connects to the long note as an upbeat in a single rebound motion in the right hand. Most often applied to dotted rhythms, the bow continues in the same directions and it can be either legato or staccato. • The hooked bowing can be a fatiguing bowing to perform if students do not learn to play the bowing with a relaxed bow hand and arm from the beginning. The bowing also requires good control of the ends of the bow, as developed during the détaché process. Sequence of Activities • Students vertically air bow and speak/sing the rhythm accurately before playing it on the string. The motion of the hook is important to teach away from the instrument before moving to the instrument. Slower bowings will likely be easier than faster hooked bowing patterns. • Teacher models both a down and up-bow hooked bowing using two quarter notes per bow. Students copy. Begin with open strings then practice by changing pitches at the beginning of the slur, and then during the slur itself. • Teacher models a hooked bowing using a long note, stop-bow, followed by a short-long combination (the hook), asking students to describe the bowing. • Teacher holds bow vertically and air bows the hooked bowing, both beginning down bow and up bow, saying, "Down, stop, down-up" Students imitate. Repeat using "Up, stop, up-down." • Place bow on the string and have students try a down-bow hooked bowing using 2 quarter notes, then repeat using an up-bow. • Students should practice setting the weight of the bow, as they would for a martelé stroke, between the long and short notes. This will help ensure a clean start and articulation to the note.	• Students perform with a relaxed bow arm, relaxed and curved fingers, and control of bow speed. • Students indicate that the bow physically stops before continuing to the second note. • The bow will physically stop on the string before continuing to the short-note that begins the hooked bowing.

Standards Links:

Resources and References:

Category 1: Executive Skills and Knowledge

Content Area:	**1C. Right Hand Skills and Knowledge**
Benchmark:	*Students perform with fluent bowing motion, control of variables (weight, angle, speed, and placement), in a variety of bowing techniques and articulations, with characteristic tone.*
Learning Task:	**2.2.d—Longer slurs (3 or more notes)**

Learning Sequences & Processes	Indicators of Success
General Information, Prior Knowledge and Precursors • Student can perform with the correct bow hold and is able to play with a controlled détaché bow stroke.. • Students can perform basic two-note slurs, with good control of tone. • Students should understand the basic principles of bow distribution, especially if music contains both longer slurs and shorter rhythm patterns. Sequence of Activities • Teacher models a three-note slur. Ask students to describe the slur, the bowing motion, and the quality of the sound. • Have students try a three-note slur stopping the bow after each note. • Remove the stopped bows and play a three-note legato slur. • Increase multiple note slurs by using four notes, etc. Try doing an "Add-a-Note Scale." Play a down-bow with the note D. Play another down-bow and play D, E. Add another note with each bow. • Have students practice producing an even sound, which may require adding weight towards the end of the slur on an up-bow and reducing weight as the bow moves back to the frog. • Once students can perform the slurs with control, have the students identify and practice long slurs in music. • Practice selections on an open string, so students understand what the bow is doing in relation to the piece; specifically, that the rhythm of bow changes is different from the actual rhythm of the piece. For example a passage may contain four quarter-notes, but the bow actually performs a single whole-note because of the four-note slur.	• Students perform with a relaxed bow arm, relaxed and curved fingers, and control of bow speed. • Students will respond that there were three notes in the bow and the teacher used about a third of the bow for each note • Students will use appropriate amounts of bow for each note in the slur (e.g., at the most basic level, 1/3 of the bow for each note of a three-note slur). • Students will perform with accurate bow distribution and control of weight and speed in relation to the length of the slur and part of the bow being used.

Standards Links:
Resources and References:

Category 1:	Executive Skills and Knowledge
Content Area:	**1C. Right Hand Skills and Knowledge**
Benchmark:	*Students perform with fluent bowing motion, control of variables (weight, angle, speed, and placement), in a variety of bowing techniques and articulations, with characteristic tone.*
Learning Task:	**2.2.e—Accented Détaché**

Learning Sequences & Processes	Indicators of Success
General Information, Prior Knowledge and Precursors • Students can perform with the correct, relaxed bow hold and to play a détaché stroke with control. • Students can perform détaché and martelé bow strokes with characteristic tone and control of basic tone production elements (weight, angle, speed, and placement) • Accented Détaché is essentially a "percussive attack, produced by great initial bow speed and pressure. It is basically a non-staccato articulation and can be performed at greater speeds than martelé." (Berman, Jackson & Sarch, 18) Accented détaché does not have the characteristic space between notes that the martelé bow stroke has. Sequence of Activities • Teacher models détaché and martelé bow strokes. Students imitate, experimenting with manipulation of weight and speed to produce desired sound. • Teacher plays a D major scale using three quarter notes per pitch, accenting beat one. Students describe what they hear, and echo teacher demonstration. • Students try adding weight by applying pressure (less for cello/bass) with the index finger and slightly increasing bow speed at the initiation of the bow stroke. • Students practice adding accents on both up- and down-bows. • Draw the symbol (>) for accented notes. Ask students to find examples of accented notes in their music.	• Students perform with a relaxed bow arm, relaxed and curved fingers, and control of bow speed. • Students will perform with accurate bow distribution and control of weight and speed in relation to the weight of the accent and part of the bow being used. • Bow does not stop between notes.

Standards Links:

Resources and References:

Category 1:	**Executive Skills and Knowledge**
Content Area:	**1C. Right Hand Skills and Knowledge**
Benchmark:	*Students perform with fluent bowing motion, control of variables (weight, angle, speed, and placement), in a variety of bowing techniques and articulations, with characteristic tone.*
Learning Task:	**2.3.a—Brush Stroke (Beginning Spiccato)**

Learning Sequences & Processes	**Indicators of Success**
General Information, Prior Knowledge and Precursors • Students can perform with the correct, relaxed bow hold and play a détaché stroke with control. Any incorrect finger placement (such as straightened or tense fingers, a thumb that is not placed correctly or has no bend in it, or a tight/straight pinky) will inhibit the bow stroke. It is essential that students have a well-formed and relaxed bow hand before moving to the spiccato or brush strokes. • Students can perform détaché and martelé bow strokes with characteristic tone and control of basic tone production elements (weight, angle, speed, and placement) • Off-the-string strokes are sometimes called "from-the-string" strokes as they also start on the string, but then the stroke continues bouncing or brushing the string. Off-string strokes really occur on a spectrum ranging from extremely short (with a crisp, more vertical stroke) to longer (less vertical, more horizontal stroke). With students at this level, the goal is to develop the basic bouncing motion while maintaining a relaxed bow hand with curved fingers, moving in a motion that is natural and uses the flexion of the bow to help accomplish the stroke. • Once students are able to perform with a natural motion, the stroke may be refined depending on the desired length and crispness of the staccato, or for stylistic considerations. • Berman, Jackson, and Sarch call the brush stroke, "a type of spiccato bowing in which the horizontal motion is emphasized so that the bow drags or brushes the string and is lifted." (p. 16) Also described as a beginning spiccato stroke. Sequence of Activities • Find the balance point on the bow. Initially, form bow hold on the stick at the balance point. As students become more comfortable with the natural rebound of the bow, they may also perform these beginning motions with the bow held at the frog. • While maintaining a correct bow hold, direct students to freely drop the bow (moving from a vertical to a horizontal bow position, like a windshield wiper) on an open string near the tip of the bow, in order to gain a sense of the natural rebound motion of the bow. Let the bow rebound naturally until it comes to a stop. Have students keep their hand relaxed so that they feel the response of the bow. Practice dropping the bow near the tip, mid-point, and balance point of the bow, so students can feel how the bow responds differently at each location. • Repeat the above, but this time, have the students sustain the bouncing of the bow, using just a small bit of right hand pivot or rotation to continue the bouncing motion. The bow should be moving bouncing vertically, with no horizontal or side-to-side motion. • Slowly add more horizontal movement, experimenting with varying levels of vertical and horizontal motion. • Have students try bouncing the bow closer to the balance point using eighth notes. Find an example of this bow stroke in the music being studied. Describe the symbol (.) used to notate spiccato.	• Students perform with a relaxed bow arm, relaxed and curved fingers, and control of bow speed. • Students will perform with accurate bow distribution and control of weight and speed in relation to the weight of the accent and part of the bow being used. • Bow does not stop between notes. It should rebound naturally and stay in motion. • Fingers and thumb remain relaxed and curved during process.

Standards Links:

Resources and References:

Category 1:	Executive Skills and Knowledge
Content Area:	**1C. Right Hand Skills and Knowledge**
Benchmark:	*Students perform with fluent bowing motion, control of variables (weight, angle, speed, and placement), in a variety of bowing techniques and articulations, with characteristic tone.*
Learning Task:	**2.4—Simple Double Stops (Bowing Portion)**

Learning Sequences & Processes	Indicators of Success
General Information, Prior Knowledge and Precursors • Double stops are played by sounding two adjacent strings together. Simple double stops consist of playing a fingered note on one string with the adjacent higher or lower open string. • Double stops can be plucked or bowed. The technique for fingering double stops is addressed in Content Area 2B Learning Task 2.6 Simple Double Stops. • In ensemble, double stops are frequently played *divisi*, with the outside player assigned the upper note and the inside player assigned the lower note. • In playing simple double stops, the weight of the bow should generally be even distributed on both strings, but a performer may choose to emphasize one of the two strengths for artistic purposes. • In playing double stops, avoid using excessive bow weight or pressure, which can create tension in the bow hand and also prevent the instrument from producing a full sound. • Simple double-stops may also be used as a teaching tool for helping reinforce correct right-hand position. By maintaining an even sound on both strings during the full bow-stroke, students must be able to control the weight of the bow and the angle of the bow stroke. • This exercise is also a precursor to develop the skills necessary to tune the instrument in fifths. Sequence of Activities • Demonstrate and explain simple double stops. • Practice the following open-string patterns: D-D-A-A (or similar on another string), then A-A-D-D. Alternate bowing patterns D-D-D-A, A-D-D-D-, so that students are also comfortable with the string change. Then, practice the following patterns: D-D/A (together)-D/A-A, then repeat going from the A back to the D. • Have students play a tetrachord (or other melodic patterns) on the D-string; repeat, playing a double-stop with the open A-string. Then, play a tetrachord on the A-string; repeat, playing a double stop with the open D. • Continue, working in the same way with each pair of adjacent strings. • Introduce pieces that include simple double stops. Fiddle tunes (e.g., "Bile 'em Cabbage Down") are excellent teaching tools for learning simple double-stops.	• Students perform with a relaxed bow arm, relaxed and curved fingers, and control of bow speed. • Students maintain an even sound as they switch strings or move to double-stops.

Standards Links:

Resources and References:

Category 1: Executive Skills and Knowledge

Content Area:	**1C. Right Hand Skills and Knowledge**
Benchmark:	*Students perform with fluent bowing motion, control of variables (weight, angle, speed, and placement), in a variety of bowing techniques and articulations, with characteristic tone.*
Learning Task:	**2.5—Extension of technique for control bowing variables (weight, angle, speed, placement)**

Learning Sequences & Processes	Indicators of Success

General Information, Prior Knowledge and Precursors
 	
• Students can perform with the correct, relaxed bow hold and play a détaché stroke with control. Students demonstrate basic control of weight, angle, speed (WASP), and placement and understand how these relate to each other.
 	
• Understanding of basic rhythm values—whole, half, quarter, and eighth notes.
 	
• As students develop better control of the bow at the frog and tip, they should be able to compensate for issues related to WASP elements. This is crucial as students begin to perform literature containing longer phrases, slurs, ties, etc.
 	
• An important consideration and common error: shorter note values do not result in faster bow movement. In other words, the principle isn't that the students use the whole bow for every note, but that the proper amount of bow is determined by the desired tone and rhythmic values. In other words, all things being equal (i.e., weight, angle, speed, and placement), a whole note will use four times as much bow as a quarter note.
 	
Sequence of Activities
 	
• Present the following scenarios to students and ask them to experiment with bow weight, angle, speed, and placement:
 	
  1. Try playing a whole note exclusively in the upper half of the bow. Analyze results, looking for student understanding of challenges related to sustaining the tone, maintaining bow weight, even sound, etc.
  2. Try a whole note using a very fast bow speed.
  3. Play a whole note starting at the frog using a quarter of the bow for each beat.
  4. Using a whole note, try it close to the fingerboard, close to the bridge and then mid-way. Which bow lane or highway worked best?
  5. Play a whole note close to the bridge with 50 pounds of weight. What happened? Experiment with weight and speed.
  6. Repeat above exercises varying the rhythm patterns.
  7. Play a scale using one beat for note one, two beats for the second note and so forth.
	• Students perform with a relaxed bow arm, relaxed and curved fingers, and control of bow speed.
	
	• Students will perform with accurate bow distribution and control of weight and speed in relation to the weight of the accent and part of the bow being used.
	
	• Students by trial and error will discover what works in terms of bow placement, speed and weight.
	
	• Each instrument (vln, vla, vcl, and bass) is slightly different, so it is difficult to give a hard-and-fast rule about where to place the bow. But in general, students should understand the following principles:
	
	  • As bow speed increases and bow weight decreases, and distance from the bridge also increases.
	
	  • As bow speed decreases and bow weight increases, the distance from the bridge decreases.

Standards Links:

Resources and References:

Category 1:	Executive Skills and Knowledge
Content Area:	**1C. Right Hand Skills and Knowledge**
Benchmark:	*Students perform with fluent bowing motion, control of variables (weight, angle, speed, and placement), in a variety of bowing techniques and articulations, with characteristic tone.*
Learning Task:	**3.1.a, 3.1.b, and 3.1.c—More Advanced Détaché Bowings—Détaché Lancé, Détaché Porté, and Portato (Louré)**

Learning Sequences & Processes	Indicators of Success

General Information, Prior Knowledge and Precursors
 	
• Students can perform with the correct, relaxed bow hold and play a détaché stroke with control. Students demonstrate basic control of weight, angle, speed, and placement and understand how these relate to each other.
 	
• The détaché "family" includes a range of bowings with various degrees of separation, nuance of accent, and amount of weight, emphasis or slur.
 	
• There is not universal agreement on a specific definition for each of the following bowings, but generally three other détaché bowings are found:
  a. *Détaché lancé*—is a gentle bow stroke, which effects a slight space between each note as the bow changes direction. Usually no marking is shown in the score, although some scores will indicate a line and a dot over or under the note head (Rabin). Characteristically a short unaccented détaché bow-stroke with some staccato separation of strokes (Berman, Jackson, and Sarch).
  b. *Détaché porte*—This détaché stoke begins with a slight swelling. Pressure is applied after horizontal motion begins and peak volume is reached shortly after soft initial attack. (Berman, Jackson & Sarch) p. 19. A common marking used to indicate this articulation is the single line (–) over a note.
  c. *Portato* or *louré*—A series of notes in a single bow direction. There is not generally separation between the notes, but instead a general pulsing, where the tone continues without pause. Generally used in accompaniment passages, where the dynamic level is piano.
 	
Sequence of Activities
 	
• As with many of the bowing activities described to this point, modeling and demonstration are the most effective means of helping students understand the nuances of the bowing.
 	
• Teacher describes and demonstrates the various bowings. Recorded examples (especially video examples) will be excellent showing the variations between the strokes.
 	
• Show the symbols most often used for each bowing.
 	
• Find examples of the bowings in the music being studied.
	• Students perform with a relaxed bow arm, relaxed and curved fingers, and control of bow speed.
	
	• Students will perform with accurate bow distribution and control of weight and speed in relation to the weight of the accent and part of the bow being used.
	
	• *Détaché Lancé*—the speed slows slightly towards the end of the stroke.
	
	• *Détaché porté* and *portato (louré)*—the bow speed is faster using the bow closer to the fingerboard. The bow does not stop between notes, which will have a special emphasis sounding like a pulse.

Standards Links:

Resources and References:

Category 1:	Executive Skills and Knowledge
Content Area:	1C. Right Hand Skills and Knowledge
Benchmark:	*Students perform with fluent bowing motion, control of variables (weight, angle, speed, and placement), in a variety of bowing techniques and articulations, with characteristic tone.*
Learning Task:	**3.1.d, 3.1.e—More Advanced Détaché Bowings—Rapid Détaché and Tremolo**

Learning Sequences & Processes	Indicators of Success
General Information, Prior Knowledge and Precursors • Students can perform with the correct, relaxed bow hold and play a détaché stroke with control. Students demonstrate basic control of weight, angle, speed, and placement and understand how these relate to each other. • The détaché "family" includes a range of bowings with various degrees of separation, nuance of accent, and amount of weight, emphasis or slur. • There is not universal agreement on a specific definition for each of the following bowings, but generally two other détaché bowings are found: d. *Rapid détaché*—is played in the middle or slightly above the middle of the bow when used for a series of repeated short notes. When a precise number of strokes per beat are indicated, the patterns are termed 'measured tremolo.' The bow may bounce through its own elasticity and momentum and the stroke is effective over a wide range of dynamics. Rapid détaché and sautillé bowings are related in practice (Rabin). Measured tremolo is indicated when there are one or two lines through the note stem. One line would indicate to play eighth notes and two lines; sixteenth notes. e. *Tremolo*—is typically a very fast, generally unmeasured bowing (see *Rapid Détaché*, above, for a description of measured tremolo) played between the middle and tip, depending on dynamic level. Unmeasured tremolo is indicated when the note stem has three lines through it. Sequence of Activities • As with many of the bowing activities described to this point, modeling and demonstration are the most effective means of helping students understand the nuances of the bowing. • Teacher describes and demonstrates the various bowings. Recorded examples (especially video examples) will be excellent showing the variations between the strokes. • Show the symbols most often used for each bowing. • Find examples of the bowings in the music being studied.	• Students perform with a relaxed bow arm, relaxed and curved fingers, and control of bow speed. • Students will perform with accurate bow distribution and control of weight and speed in relation to the weight of the accent and part of the bow being used. • *Tremolo* and *rapid détaché*—the bow arm remains relaxed and moves easily throughout the bow strokes. • The bowing motion is typically initiated in the hand using fast and small motions. The bow does not stop when changing pitch. • The stroke should be louder with longer bow strokes towards the middle of the bow. The bow stroke will also be performed more slowly on lower instruments and pitches.

Standards Links:	

Resources and References:	

Category 1:	**Executive Skills and Knowledge**
Content Area:	**1C. Right Hand Skills and Knowledge**
Benchmark:	*Students perform with fluent bowing motion, control of variables (weight, angle, speed, and placement), in a variety of bowing techniques and articulations, with characteristic tone.*
Learning Task:	**3.2—Spiccato**

Learning Sequences & Processes	Indicators of Success
General Information, Prior Knowledge and Precursors • Students can perform with the correct, relaxed bow hold and play a détaché stroke with control. Students demonstrate basic control of weight, angle, speed, and placement and understand how these relate to each other. • Students can perform basic brush stroke. • *Spiccato* refers to a slow to moderate speed bouncing stroke. Every degree of crispness is possible in the spiccato from gently brushed to percussively dry. (Berman, Jackson & Sarch, p. 46). It is generally achieved by a controlled dropping and rebounding of the bow. It has both vertical and horizontal components. Variations in shortness are achieved through changing and manipulating which part of the bow is used. Heavy staccato is played in the lower half, while lighter staccato is played in the middle or even upper part of the bow. Spiccato bowing is rarely done above the camber point of the bow. • Note that spiccato is often performed even when there is no specific marking for staccato. The teacher or conductor needs to be aware of performance practice and historical tradition when determining when the spiccato bow stroke is to be used. Sequence of Activities • As with many of the bowing activities described to this point, modeling and demonstration are the most effective means of helping students understand the nuances of the bowing. The activities used to develop the brush stroke may also be used to develop the spiccato bow stroke. • Teacher describes and demonstrates the difference between the brush stroke and the spiccato stroke. • Using a relaxed bow hold, have students drop bow onto string and let it rebound (use bouncing ball image) to get the idea of resiliency. Gradually bounce in a slow eighth note pattern. • Visualize making the letter U or an arc so when the bow drops it is an arc-like motion. The bow hits the string in the bottom of the U or the flat part of the arc. • Add the down and up-bow motion to the bounce using the same rhythm. • Find an example of this bow stroke in the music being studied. Describe the symbol (.) frequently used to notate spiccato.	• Students perform with a relaxed bow arm, relaxed and curved fingers, and control of bow speed. • Students will perform with accurate bow distribution and control of weight and speed in relation to the weight of the accent and part of the bow being used. • Brush stroke should have longer horizontal contact with the string and is played at the balance point. The horizontal movement will give the tone more sound. • Spiccato starts on the string and then becomes a synchronized dropping and rebounding of the bow. The more vertical motion will give spiccato a crisper sound. • The arm and wrist should start off in a slightly higher position to achieve the bounce. As the spiccato gets faster, more hand and finger movement will be needed. • Watch that the rebound is not too high off the string. • Slightly roll the stick towards the fingerboard to improve the stroke.

Standards Links:

Resources and References:

Category 1:	Executive Skills and Knowledge
Content Area:	**1C. Right Hand Skills and Knowledge**
Benchmark:	*Students perform with fluent bowing motion, control of variables (weight, angle, speed, and placement), in a variety of bowing techniques and articulations, with characteristic tone.*
Learning Task:	**3.3.a., 3.3.b., 3.3.c., and 3.3.d—Special Effect Bowings—Col legno, Flautando, Sul Ponticello, and Sul Tasto**

Learning Sequences & Processes	Indicators of Success

General Information, Prior Knowledge and Precursors
 	
• Students can perform with the correct, relaxed bow hold and play a détaché stroke with control. Students demonstrate basic control of weight, angle, speed, and placement and understand how these relate to each other.
 	
   a. *Col legno*—with the wood of the bow; to either draw the bow stick across the string or tap the string with the bow stick. In pure *col legno*, the bow hair is not used, but the edge of the hair can be allowed to contact the string along with the wood so that a more discernable pitch can be heard in the *col legno* tone color. *Col legno battuto*—hitting or tapping the string with the wood of the bow stick—a percussive effect. Often used in conjunction with the *ricochet* bowing below.
 	
   b. *Flautando*—Literally "fluting or flute-like." An airy and breathy tone color obtained on a string instrument by drawing the bow lightly (light bow pressure ratio to bow speed) over the strings. (BJS, p. 22)
 	
   c. *Sul ponticello*—On or upon the bridge. A special tone color…produced by bowing very close to or upon the bridge, so that the pitch becomes weak or even unrecognizable and the raspy, nasal upper partials tend to dominate. Produces shimmer, glassy tone colors. (BJS, p. 38)
 	
   d. *Sul tasto*—Refers to bow placement over the fingerboard to obtain a soft, distant light tone quality. (BJS, p. 53)
 	
Sequence of Activities
 	
• As with many of the bowing activities described to this point, modeling and demonstration are the most effective means of helping students understand the nuances of the bowing. Discuss the many special effects, demonstrate, and play recordings. Most teachers would introduce these effects as they were called for in repertoire being studied but they can be introduced just for fun.
 	
• Demonstrate *sul tasto* and *flautando* and explain that *flautando* while usually played over the fingerboard can be played elsewhere as long as it is a light bow stroke. Have students try playing *sul tasto*.
 	
• Demonstrate *sul ponticello* and explain the similarities between it and *sul tasto*. Have students try it with the bow on the bridge and right next to the bridge.
 	
• Have students experiment using more weight and different bow speeds both on the bridge and over the fingerboard.
 	
• Demonstrate *col legno* and have students practice going from arco to *col legno* silently.
 	
• Add some previously learned effects such as tremolo and glissando and have students make stories using these effects.
 	
• Find special effects used in the music being studied.
	• Students perform with a relaxed bow arm, relaxed and curved fingers, and control of bow speed.
	
	• Students will perform with accurate bow distribution and control of weight and speed in relation to the weight of the accent and part of the bow being used.

Standards Links:

Resources and References:

Category 1:	Executive Skills and Knowledge
Content Area:	1C. Right Hand Skills and Knowledge
Benchmark:	*Students perform with fluent bowing motion, control of variables (weight, angle, speed, and placement), in a variety of bowing techniques and articulations, with characteristic tone.*
Learning Task:	3.4—Chords

Learning Sequences & Processes	Indicators of Success

General Information, Prior Knowledge and Precursors
 	
 • This learning tasks deals with chords of three or more notes (sometimes called triple stops or quadruple stops).
 	
 • See Content Area 1B Learning Task 2.6 and Content Area 1C Learning Task 2.4 for preparation information related to performing simple double stops.
 	
 • See Content Area 1B Learning Task 3.3 for information related to performing complex double stops.
 	
 • Chords have several functions in string playing. One is harmonic (such as performing chords to provide a tonal context for an unaccompanied work, like the Bach Cello Suites). A second function is ornamental (providing additional colors or richness to a passage). Another function is timbral, such as when a sections in a string orchestra perform multiple parts at once, adding to the richness and sonority of the ensemble.
 	
 • Chords are generally played two ways:
 	
    • Blocked—dividing a chord into two smaller simple double stops, where one part of the section plays the top notes and the other part of the section plays the bottom notes; or, in solo music, where a quadruple stop is divided into two double stops, played from bottom-to-top, nearly simultaneously, almost like a grace note.
 	
    • Rolled or arpeggiated—in this case the chord is played from lowest note to the highest note, and each note is placed in quick succession.
 	
 • In orchestral music, most chords are performed as blocked chords. Performance practice, convention, and technical requirements will guide the decision about how to divide the chords.
 	
 Sequence of Activities
 	
 • Because chords are in essence two simple or complex double stops played in quick succession, the techniques for learning to play chords is nearly the same as for learning those two skills. The primary differences include 1) the need to finger three or for strings simultaneously and 2) the need to shift with the bow between one or two lower strings and one or two higher strings.
 	
 • As with the simple double stops, practice exercises where the bow moves between sets of strings, using the middle (or shared) string (in the case of a triple stop) as the pivot string. Practice the bowing motion required to execute the specific chord separately from fingering (in other words, practice just on open strings).
 	
 • Add the fingers to each string separately. Strumming the chords pizzicato will also help reinforce the need to keep all fingers in firm contact with the strings, as the notes will not ring if fingers are not placed correctly.
 	
 • For repeated chords, the fingers generally stay on all of the chordal notes. For individual chords (especially when arpeggiated) the fingers on the bottom string will release. This also allows the use of vibrato on the top notes of the chord, especially when those notes are sustained.
	• Students maintain a full sound that is evenly distributed between the chordal notes.
	
	 • Tone is clear and rings when chords are strummed.
	
	 • Students control WASP variables throughout the chord.
	
	 • Students adjust individual chord tones for intonation.

Standards Links:

Resources and References:

Category 1:	Executive Skills and Knowledge
Content Area:	**1C. Right Hand Skills and Knowledge**
Benchmark:	*Students perform with fluent bowing motion, control of variables (weight, angle, speed, and placement), in a variety of bowing techniques and articulations, with characteristic tone.*
Learning Task:	**3.5—Extension of technique related to control of bowing variables (weight, angle, speed, and placement)**

Learning Sequences & Processes	Indicators of Success
<u>General Information, Prior Knowledge and Precursors</u> • See Content Area 1C Learning Tasks 1.11 and 2.5 for information about developing initial control of bowing variables. • At this point students should be able to use the four bowing variable elements to make adjustments in dynamics, intensity, and to produce and consistent and characteristic tone. • At the proficient level students are introduced to the concept of using WASP variables for musical and artistic effect, such as performing with an ensemble sound that is blended and consistent in terms of timbre, volume, and balance, or for changing the emotional affect of a piece, such as increasing the intensity of the tone, performing with different tonal colors, and so on. • The emphasis in this activity is to focus student attention on the other performers around them, and to learn to adjust the small nuances of their own performance in order to play as an ensemble. If the teacher directs every aspect of bow control (i.e., what part of the bow to use, how much bow to use, and where to place the bow) students will learn to execute exactly as the teacher wants, but will not learn to determine themselves how to the subtle adjustments necessary to perform at a more advanced level. Ultimately, the goal is to develop student's ability to aurally discriminate and to play with sensitivity and understanding. <u>Sequence of Activities</u> • Using an excerpt from music currently being performed by the ensemble (or using a simple rote piece), have the students practice experimenting on the effect that changing each one of the WASP variables has on tone or timbre. • Next, the teacher (or another student) models a different tone on a sustained note for the students. The students must then determine what to change in order to match exactly the new tone color. Have different students practice modeling different tone colors or timbral effects, with the orchestra adjusting the WASP variables each time until the tone matches exactly. • If recordings are available, the teacher may ask the students to compare different recordings of the same piece. This can be particularly effective when comparing examples of pieces performed on modern versus period instruments. • It can be particularly effective to have students perform these exercises with their eyes closed, as they learn how to adjust WASP variables to achieve the desired tonal result. The ears are better guides than the eyes are for this exercise. • Practice an assigned piece with possible tonal or timbral options. Ask the students to evaluate the quality of each and to determine the specific performance interpretation for the assigned piece.	• Students perform with a relaxed bow arm, relaxed and curved fingers, and control of bow speed. • Students will perform with accurate bow distribution and control of weight and speed in relation to the weight of the accent and part of the bow being used. • Students by trial and error will discover what works in terms of bow placement, speed and weight. • Students make informed decisions about what variables to adjust in order to perform the assigned work with the expected tonal outcome. • Students are able to make adjustments to WASP variables in performance.

Standards Links:

Resources and References:

Category 1: Executive Skills and Knowledge

Content Area:	**1C. Right Hand Skills and Knowledge**
Benchmark:	*Students perform with fluent bowing motion, control of variables (weight, angle, speed, and placement), in a variety of bowing techniques and articulations, with characteristic tone.*
Learning Task:	**4.1—Ricochet**

Learning Sequences & Processes	Indicators of Success
<u>General Information, Prior Knowledge and Precursors</u> • Students can perform with the correct, relaxed bow hold and play a détaché stroke with control. Students demonstrate basic control of weight, angle, speed, and placement and understand how these relate to each other. • *Ricochet* (alt., *Saltando* or *jeté*)—A series of two or more slurred and, characteristically very fast bounces, usually performed in upper-half and performed down-bow. The bow is dropped upon the string so that the initial impetus and natural elasticity of the bow gives rise to a spontaneous series of successive bounces. (BJS, p. 40) • *Ricochet* is frequently performed in conjunction with the *col legno* bowing. <u>Sequence of Activities</u> • As with many of the bowing activities described to this point, modeling and demonstration are the most effective means of helping students understand the nuances of the bowing. • As with the development of the brush stroke and spiccato bow stroke, the ricochet requires a relaxed hand. The bowing motion can be taught beginning by dropping the bow hair on the string and controlling the rebound motion. Unlike the brush and spiccato strokes, the ricochet is typically two bounces in a single direction (down-bow). • Students will place their bows in the upper half of the stick using flat bow hair. Ask them to quickly throw the bow against the string and the natural spring of the stick will aid the bounce. • Practice performing a double down-bow followed by a single up-bow stroke. • Find special effects used in the music being studied.	• Students perform with a relaxed bow arm, relaxed and curved fingers, and control of bow speed. • Students will perform with accurate bow distribution and control of weight and speed in relation to the weight of the accent and part of the bow being used.

Standards Links:

Resources and References:

Category 1:	Executive Skills and Knowledge
Content Area:	**1C. Right Hand Skills and Knowledge**
Benchmark:	*Students perform with fluent bowing motion, control of variables (weight, angle, speed, and placement), in a variety of bowing techniques and articulations, with characteristic tone.*
Learning Task:	**4.2—Sautillé**

Learning Sequences & Processes	Indicators of Success
<u>General Information, Prior Knowledge and Precursors</u> • Sautillé is an advanced bowing technique that cannot be accurately executed if students do not have a completely relaxed bow hold with mobility in each joint and an understanding of the bowing variables. • Sautillé is frequently misunderstood and interpreted as an uncontrolled tremolo, where the bow simply jumps off of the string. Sautillé is a measured bow stroke that is performed *from-the-string* (rather than off-the-string) and happens when balance is achieved between the weight of the bow hand and the rebound of the bow vertically together with the horizontal motion of the bow hand and the speed of the repeated bow stroke. Sautillé only happens at rapid tempos. • It is generally not possible to execute the sautillé bow stroke with an inferior quality bow or a bow that is not in good working order. <u>Sequence of Activities</u> • Practice the rapid détaché bow stroke and a single note, making sure that students are performing with a relaxed bow arm. The bow stroke should be executed near the camber point of the bow (located just above the middle part of the bow). • Focus the student's attention on the down-stroke (the up-stroke is an automatic rebound motion), and not on trying to play both down and up. In other words, the idea is down (up)-down (up)-down (up)-down (up) rather than down-up-down-up-down-up-down-up. • Start with light weight and slow speed, then gradually add weight and speed until the bow begins to jump off of the string (like the sizzle of bacon as it hits a hot frying pan). Adjust weight and speed until students begin to accomplish the sautillé. Any arm fatigue is a sign that there is tension somewhere in the bow arm mechanism (or even another part of the body). • Once students can play sautillé on a single note or open string, practice switching notes after every four strokes, then two strokes, etc., until the students can switch notes on every stroke.	• Students perform with a relaxed bow arm, relaxed and curved fingers, and control of bow speed. • Students will perform with accurate bow distribution and control of weight and speed in relation to the weight of the accent and part of the bow being used. • The sautillé is natural and not forced. Students are able to play sautillé for an extended period of time without experiencing bow-arm fatigue. • The bow stays close to the string throughout the passage. The motion is controlled and not exaggerated or ragged.

Standards Links:

Resources and References:

Category 1: Executive Skills and Knowledge

Content Area:	**1C. Right Hand Skills and Knowledge**
Benchmark:	*Students perform with fluent bowing motion, control of variables (weight, angle, speed, and placement), in a variety of bowing techniques and articulations, with characteristic tone.*
Learning Task:	**4.3—Flying Spiccato**

Learning Sequences & Processes	Indicators of Success
<u>General Information, Prior Knowledge and Precursors</u> • Students can perform with the correct, relaxed bow hold and play a détaché stroke with control. Students demonstrate basic control of weight, angle, speed, and placement and understand how these relate to each other. • Students should be able to perform the slurred staccato, brush, and spiccato bow strokes with control. • *Flying spiccato* is a form of linked (slurred) *spiccato* used to prepare down-bow landings and to adjust bow distribution closer to the frog. The first note usually starts on the string and comes off. (Kjelland, p. 66). In terms of execution, the *flying spiccato* is a series of collé motions in a single bow stroke, always done up-bow. <u>Sequence of Activities</u> • As with many of the bowing activities described to this point, modeling and demonstration are the most effective means of helping students understand the nuances of the bowing. • The bowing may be learned by performing individual up-bows using the *collé* bow stroke. Add to the length of the strokes by one each time (two, then three, and so on). Increase the speed of execution, while making sure the bow hand is balanced and relaxed throughout the stroke. • Find an example of flying spiccato in the music being studied. Discuss the purpose of flying spiccato.	• Students perform with a relaxed bow arm, relaxed and curved fingers, and control of bow speed. • The fingers remain curved and the bow stays close to the string throughout the stroke.

Standards Links:

Resources and References:

Category 1:	**Executive Skills and Knowledge**
Content Area:	**1C. Right Hand Skills and Knowledge**
Benchmark:	*Students perform with fluent bowing motion, control of variables (weight, angle, speed, and placement), in a variety of bowing techniques and articulations, with characteristic tone.*
Learning Task:	**4.4—Extension of technique for control bowing variables (weight, angle, speed, placement)**

Learning Sequences & Processes	Indicators of Success
General Information, Prior Knowledge and Precursors • See Content Area 1C Learning Tasks 1.11, 2.5, and 3.5 for information about developing control of bowing variables. • Students should understand how to control the four bowing variables in order to achieve changes in tone quality, color, and timbre. • At this advanced benchmark level, the students should be expected to make subtle adjustments in the WASP variables (combined with adjustments in vibrato) in order to achieve high-level musical and artistic outcomes. • Many teachers spend a lot of time rehearsing just the notes and rhythms and do not get to this level of subtlety in performance. As a result, students miss out on the opportunity to learn how to perform at an advanced artistic level. Teachers should plan to have the notes and rhythms of a piece learned well enough in advance of the concert in order to spend time on artistic elements. Sequence of Activities • See Learning Task 3.5 for sequences that may be used again here, but with more advanced literature. • Using an advanced level piece, such as one that requires a large range of dynamics or has high technical demands, play through the piece first making no changes in WASP. Ask the students to evaluate their performance and then propose possible technical and stylistic interpretations for the piece. Specific examples of outcomes could include differences between the brush stroke and the spiccato bow stroke (or the wide range of options in between those two), the use of the bowing channels very close to the bridge versus very close to the fingerboard, or where there are extreme dynamic ranges. • Using the brush stroke/spiccato stroke example, ask students to evaluate the differences in articulation, attack, and decay for the specific passage. Ask them to change weight, angle, speed, or placement and then determine what elements should be adjusted to achieve the desired sound. Practice the bow stroke at *piano* and *forte* levels. What part of the bow should be used? What amount of weight should be used? Are there differences in placement and weight between the violins, violas, cellos, and basses? What are the differences between playing on a high string (such as the E-string on the violin) and a lower string? • Because ensembles frequently perform in a variety of acoustical conditions, take the group to different rooms and halls to practice how to adjust tone production and bowing variables in order to accommodate specific acoustical requirements. Make recordings of the ensemble in each location to show the students what happens in a large hall versus a small room.	• Students perform with a relaxed bow arm, relaxed and curved fingers, and control of bow speed. • Students will perform with accurate bow distribution and control of weight and speed in relation to the weight of the accent and part of the bow being used. • Students by trial and error will discover what works in terms of bow placement, speed and weight. • Students make informed decisions about what variables to adjust in order to perform the assigned work with the expected tonal outcome. • Students are able to make subtle adjustments to WASP variables in performance. • Students understand the effects of acoustics and how to adjust tone production in order to effectively perform in multiple performance venues.

Standards Links:

Resources and References:

Content Area 2A—Tonal Aural Skills and Ear Training

Students demonstrate the following abilities: matching and manipulating pitch, playing with a sense of tonality, tonal-melodic and tonal-harmonic function (i.e., the horizontal and vertical relationships/functions of tonality), ear-to-hand skills, aural and kinesthetic awareness of pitch accuracy and intonation, including and related to improvisation.

General Discussion about Tonal Aural Skills and Ear Training

Before moving into the Learning Tasks related to Tonal Aural Skills, we believe it is essential to state the following:

- Tonal aural skills are as integrally tied to successful string playing as they are to successfully communicating in language (listening, speaking, reading, and writing). It is essential that string teachers place strong emphasis on the development of aural skills in the earliest stages of instruction.

- The foundation for strong tonal aural skills, including the ability to play in-tune; echo tonal patterns, melodies, and accompaniments; and improvise melodies and accompaniments, is closely tied to students' abilities to sing patterns and melodies and translate what is heard to the instrument (ear-to-hand skills).

- Students should develop a tonal *vocabulary* that includes an understanding of tonal melodies and harmonies in major *and* minor tonalities.

- The use of solfege provides a strong basis for understanding the relationship between pitches and greatly enhances the ability to translate what is heard to what is performed.

- Students should develop a rich repertoire of songs at the beginning level, including songs in major and minor tonalities, duple and triple meter. These songs will serve as the foundation for music literacy. Tonal patterns derived from these songs may be used to teach basic ear-to-hand skills and beginning pitch notation.

- Strong tonal aural skills lead to greater comprehension of written notation.

- Initial performance of melodic and tonal patterns should be done vocally, then pizzicato, and then with the bow. In other words, aural skills training is not dependent on technical prowess. Combining new executive skills with new aural skills detracts from initial mastery of either. Teachers should use their best judgment as to when to combine elements, but a general guideline is that students should focus on one new element at a time. If new aural concepts are being introduced, avoid introducing new bowing concepts at the same moment.

Developing tonal aural skills at the outset of instruction is not a complex or difficult activity. Consider the following examples of aural skills activities:

Sequence of Activities—Vocal

- Students echo simple tonal (major and minor) patterns on a neutral syllable
- Students sing simple folk songs in major and minor tonalities; both the melody and the bass line should be taught. The bass line is particularly important in helping students develop a sense of tonality and harmony. In addition, many beginning songs have a simple harmonic structure (I, IV, V, etc.) that may be easily plucked on open strings while students sing the melody on solfege or using the words.
- Students alter folk songs in major tonality into minor and vice versa
- Students improvise basic melodic patterns (e.g., single-note, using two or three notes, or longer melodies)

Sequence of Activities—On the Instrument

Note: Depending on the individual student or class progress on executive skills, these following activities may be performed in guitar position, playing position, pizzicato, or with the bow. For example, if students do not yet have the ability to hold the instrument in playing position for a long period of time, basic patterns may be performed in guitar position. Likewise, when a student has developed a good posture, playing position, and basic bow hold, new aural skills may be taught already in playing position.

- Students echo single-note patterns on an open string (pizzicato)
- Students echo single-note patterns on a fingered note (pizzicato)
- Students echo simple melodic and harmonic patterns (pizzicato); patterns may be derived from the songs that will be taught, but should also include patterns not found in the songs, so that students develop the ability to *discriminate* aurally.

- Students perform simple folk songs in major and minor tonalities; as above, both the melody and the bass line should be taught.
- Students alter folk songs in major tonality into minor and vice versa
- Students improvise basic melodic patterns (e.g., single-note, using two or three notes, or longer melodies)

Learning Tasks

1.1   Students perform, by ear, *melodic* tonal patterns (simple patterns and melodies within a tetrachord), in major and minor tonalities (vocally, pizzicato, and/or arco; neutral syllable, then solfege).

1.2   Students identify whether two performed *melodic* tonal patterns are same or different.

1.3   Students correctly associate the words *high* and *low* with relative pitch differences.

1.4   Students correctly identify direction of *melodic* motion (within a tetrachord).

1.5   Students perform, by ear, primary (tonic and dominant) *harmonic* tonal patterns (vocally, pizzicato, and/or arco; neutral syllable, then solfege).

1.6   Students alter melodies and harmonies (major-to-minor, minor-to-major)

1.7   Students improvise (vocally, pizzicato, and/or arco) *melodic* tonal patterns (within a tetrachord; neutral syllable, then solfege).

2.1   Students perform, by ear, *melodic* tonal patterns (patterns and melodies within a one-octave range) in major and minor tonalities (vocally, pizzicato, and/or arco; neutral syllable, then solfege).

2.2   Students manipulate single pitches to adjust intonation and listen for "ringing tones" (resonance, sympathetic vibrations).

2.3   Students perform, by ear, primary (tonic, dominant, and subdominant) *harmonic* tonal patterns (vocally, pizzicato, and/or arco; neutral syllable, then solfege).

2.4   Students improvise (vocally, pizzicato, and/or arco) *melodic* tonal patterns (within an octave)

2.5   Students improvise (vocally, pizzicato, and/or arco) *harmonic* tonal patterns (vocally, pizzicato, and/or arco; neutral syllable, then solfege).

2.6   Students alter melodies and harmonies (major to minor and vice versa).

2.7   Students use fine tuners to adjust strings to match an external tonal reference.

3.1   Students perform, by ear, melodic tonal patterns (patterns and melodies with chromatic alterations) in major and minor tonalities (vocally, pizzicato, and/or arco; neutral syllable, then solfege).

3.2   Students perform primary and secondary (ii, vi, vii) tonal patterns (vocally, pizzicato, and/or arco; neutral syllable, then solfege).

3.3   Students improvise (vocally, pizzicato, and/or arco; neutral syllable, then solfege) melodies and patterns, using chromatic alterations or simple modulations (e.g., major to relative/parallel minor)

3.4   Students improvise (vocally, pizzicato, and/or arco; neutral syllable, then solfege) simple accompaniments to melodies.

3.5   Students use fine tuners and/or pegs to tune strings, in fifths, to an external tonal reference.

4.1   Students perform, by ear, melodies and accompaniments in various modes and scales (e.g., Dorian, Mixolydian, Blues, etc.) and meters.

4.2   Students improvise melodies and accompaniments in various modes and scales (e.g., Dorian, Mixolydian, Blues, etc.) and meters.

Category 2:	**Musicianship Skills and Knowledge**
Content Area:	**2A—Tonal Aural Skills and Ear Training**
Benchmark:	*Students demonstrate the following abilities: matching and manipulating pitch, playing with a sense of tonality, tonal--melodic and tonal--harmonic function (horizontal and vertical relationships/functions of tonality), ear-to-hand skills, aural and kinesthetic awareness of pitch accuracy and intonation, including and related to improvisation.*
Learning Task:	**1.1—Students perform, by ear, *melodic* tonal patterns (within a tetrachord)**

Learning Sequences & Processes	**Indicators of Success**
General Information, Prior Knowledge and Precursors • Students will come into strings class with wide-ranging abilities in terms of aural skills. Long-term success on a string instrument requires the ability to anticipate, listen with comprehension, evaluate, and appropriately remediate tonal patterns, melodies, sequences, harmonies, intonation, etc. • With that in mind, the string teacher will have to determine what the specific aural needs are for *each* student in the class or lesson. In some cases, the strings teacher may need to provide substantial general music training (singing, solfege, etc.) in preparation for the instrument. While aids such as fingerboard tapes may provide a temporary assistance to the teacher, their long-term usage is a crutch for the students and ultimately prevents them from being able to hear well on the instrument. • With that in mind, aural skills training should take place from the very first lesson on a string instrument and, with consistency and intentionality, throughout their entire playing career. • Finally, be sure that students are able to demonstrate all patterns *alone*, as this is the only way you'll know if they really understand. Sequence of Activities • Sing simple melodic tonal patterns, on a neutral syllable (such as bah). Three-note patterns are generally good for beginning-level students. • Play open strings for the students, asking the students to both sing and pluck the demonstrated pitch. *Avoid labeling string names first; start with aural skills and then label.* • Use solfege to demonstrate the same patterns (e.g., mi-re-do). It is helpful if some of the early patterns you use will relate to songs you are later going to play. For example, mi-re-do relates to songs such as *Mary Had a Little Lamb, Hot Cross Buns*, and others. • Teach both major *and* minor patterns, by ear, from the beginning. Students do best when they are required to distinguish, or discriminate (make informed musical choices). The use of parallel minor (such as teaching both the major and minor versions of *Hot Cross Buns* and *Mary Had a Little Lamb*) is an exceptional tool for beginning students. • See Gardner (1999), for examples of basic patterns that are common to beginning string songs.	• Students sing with good tonal control. • Students produce clear pizzicato sound. • Students accurately echo teacher model (alone and as a group). Emphasize both the correct pitches and the quality of the tone produced. • Correct solfege syllables are used with patterns.

Standards Links:

Resources and References:

Category 2:	Musicianship Skills and Knowledge
Content Area:	**2A—Tonal Aural Skills and Ear Training**
Benchmark:	*Students demonstrate the following abilities: matching and manipulating pitch, playing with a sense of tonality, tonal--melodic and tonal--harmonic function (horizontal and vertical relationships/functions of tonality), ear-to-hand skills, aural and kinesthetic awareness of pitch accuracy and intonation, including and related to improvisation.*
Learning Task:	**1.2—Students identify whether two performed *melodic* tonal patterns are the same or different.**

Learning Sequences & Processes	Indicators of Success
General Information, Prior Knowledge and Precursors • To a musician with a trained ear, identifying same and different melodic patterns may seem a very simple task. To an inexperienced or untrained listener, however, the challenge can be considerably greater. While the teacher is focused on the tonal pattern, the student may hear differences in other dimensions—i.e., dynamic level or tempo/ duration. Therefore, it is important that, 1) examples played by the teacher change <u>only</u> the tonal pattern, and, 2) care is taken to insure that students know what they are expected to listen for. • The knowledge of same/different should precede the use of labels such as *high* or *low*, as those can be confusing. Especially when a pitch that is lower on the musical staff is actually physically higher on the instrument (such as a cello or bass). Sequence of Activities After each of the following, ask students to tell whether the two examples are the same or different. If they are different, discuss what the difference is. • Sing simple melodic tonal patterns, on a neutral syllable (such as bah). Three-note patterns are generally good for beginning-level students. • Play a short melodic pattern. Repeat, playing as nearly the same as possible. • Play the same pattern very softly. Repeat, playing very loudly. • Play the same pattern very slowly. Repeat at a much quicker tempo. • Play the same pattern. On the repeat, change some of the pitches. Be sure students listen for differences in the melodic pattern only (not rhythm). • Continue playing other melodic patterns, sometimes repeating and sometimes altering the pattern. When playing patterns that are different, begin with larger pitch alterations. As students become more skilled, the changes should become more subtle. • Challenge students to repeat or change simple melodic tonal patterns in music they know. See if the rest of the class can distinguish same/different from their model. Sample Directions to Students • Raise your hand if the second pattern (or note) is the same. (Be sure students close their eyes, so you know who really is aware.) • Echo my pattern if it was the same/different. • Pluck the note that I changed.	• Students accurately identify when patterns are same/different, verbally (identification) or by playing. • Students should also be able to evaluate their own performance to determine if their patterns were the same or different.

Standards Links:

Resources and References:

Category 2: Musicianship Skills and Knowledge

Content Area:	**2A—Tonal Aural Skills and Ear Training**
Benchmark:	*Students demonstrate the following abilities: matching and manipulating pitch, playing with a sense of tonality, tonal--melodic and tonal--harmonic function (horizontal and vertical relationships/functions of tonality), ear-to-hand skills, aural and kinesthetic awareness of pitch accuracy and intonation, including and related to improvisation.*
Learning Task:	**1.3—Students correctly associate the words *high* and *low* with relative pitch differences.**

Learning Sequences & Processes	Indicators of Success
<u>General Information, Prior Knowledge and Precursors</u> • The words *high* and *low* are ambiguous in English. They are frequently used to mean *loud* and *soft* (volume), *up* or *down* (position), or in relation to intensity. Therefore, students with no previous music study may need to learn to correctly associate the words "high" and "low" with pitch differences. Again, this is particularly confusing when a pitch that is lower on the musical staff is actually physically higher on the instrument (such as a cello or bass). • The most effective learning is multisensory. Using hand and/or body signs in response to higher and lower pitches will make the learning task more concrete and facilitate understanding. Combining hand signs with solfege helps reinforce these concepts. • When students can use the vocabulary *high* and *low* correctly to identify two pitches a large interval apart, use solfege to work with pitches within the scale. <u>Sequence of Activities</u> Some of these activities will be more appropriate for young children than for older students, who may be more self-conscious. The teacher should be sensitive to this in planning instruction. • Ask students to listen as you play open-E, then open-G, on the violin, then tell which is higher or lower. If they respond that G is higher, explain that we often use the word "high" to mean loud, but that in music it means a higher pitch. Continue playing pairs of pitches, making the differences smaller as the students become more skilled. • Have students slide their voices higher and lower like a fire siren. This can also be done on the instrument. Compare what *high* and *low* look like on the instrument with what happens vocally. Do they move the same way or opposite ways? • Teach singing the major scale with solfege. To model higher and lower pitches with body movement, sing the scale as follows (use both hands for movements): *Do*—touch the feet *Fa*—touch the hips *Ti*—touch the head *Re*—touch the ankles *Sol*—touch the waist *Do*—hands above head *Mi*—touch the knees *La*—touch the shoulders Reverse the movements singing the descending scale. • Sing the scale using the Curwen hand signals. (These can be found in Kodály materials or with a search engine on the Internet.) This is helpful when you have limited space. It also is easy to use when students have instruments in their hand. • Continue playing pairs of notes, varying the pitch differences, and have students identify which is higher or lower. • Play an open string and challenge students to play the next higher or lower string.	• Students accurately identify when notes are high/low, verbally (identification) or by playing.

Standards Links:

Resources and References:

Category 2:	**Musicianship Skills and Knowledge**
Content Area:	**2A—Tonal Aural Skills and Ear Training**
Benchmark:	*Students demonstrate the following abilities: matching and manipulating pitch, playing with a sense of tonality, tonal--melodic and tonal--harmonic function (horizontal and vertical relationships/functions of tonality), ear-to-hand skills, aural and kinesthetic awareness of pitch accuracy and intonation, including and related to improvisation.*
Learning Task:	**1.4—Students identify direction of *melodic* motion (within a tetrachord)**

Learning Sequences & Processes	**Indicators of Success**
General Information, Prior Knowledge and Precursors • Review concepts about higher and lower pitches. Be sure students are using the terms "high" and "low" correctly to label pitches relationships. • Solfege and hand signs continue to be helpful in identifying melodic direction. • Because melody direction corresponds to the direction of the notes on the staff, it can be identified both visually and aurally. Sequence of Activities • Play and sing (on neutral syllables or solfege) ascending tetrachords. Let students model the direction in the air with their hands and identify it verbally. • Play and sing descending tetrachords. Again, model the direction physically and identify it verbally. • Play examples of melodies within a tetrachord that change directions. Let students model the direction of the melody physically and describe it verbally. • Compare notation with the sound of melodic examples within a tetrachord. Point out that the direction of the notes on the staff mirrors the direction of the melody played or sung. Play examples of melodies within a tetrachord and let students trace the contour of the melody on the music or draw a line on a blank staff showing the shape of the melody.	After hearing a short melody within a tetrachord, students will accurately describe the melody direction verbally, or, • by drawing a line on a staff showing the direction of the melody, or • by modeling the melody direction in the air with their hands.

Standards Links:

Resources and References:

Category 2: Musicianship Skills and Knowledge

Content Area:	**2A—Tonal Aural Skills and Ear Training**
Benchmark:	*Students demonstrate the following abilities: matching and manipulating pitch, playing with a sense of tonality, tonal--melodic and tonal--harmonic function (horizontal and vertical relationships/functions of tonality), ear-to-hand skills, aural and kinesthetic awareness of pitch accuracy and intonation, including and related to improvisation.*
Learning Task:	**1.5—Students alter melodies and harmonies (major-to-minor, minor-to-major)**

Learning Sequences & Processes	Indicators of Success
General Information, Prior Knowledge and Precursors • This activity is essential in preparing students for future success in improvisation and composition. • The ability to perform simple melodies and harmonies with alternations in tonality (major-to-minor, minor-to-major) also has a strong positive effect on student's ability to play in tune or make adjustments in intonation. • This activity is performed with familiar melodies or songs. Sequence of Activities • Students should sing, by ear and using solfege, a familiar folk song, such as "Mary had a Little Lamb." • Change the melody into the parallel minor, altering the third of the scale (e.g., from *mi* to *me*). The teacher should perform the piano accompaniment (or accompany using a different instrument) while the students sing, so that the change from major to minor tonality is aurally very clear to the students. • The students sing the song in major then in minor, until they are comfortable with the solfege and the alterations. • As the class sings, the teacher switches the harmony from major to minor (and vice versa) in random spots, which requires the students to listen carefully and adjust their solfege syllables accordingly. • This activity should be performed first in familiar keys, but then as soon as possible, students should be given a new starting pitch and required to repeat the song in major and minor from the new key. • Once students are comfortable singing the melody in both major and minor, the activities above should be repeated on the instrument (pizzicato and then arco). • Repeat the activities above with the bass line. • Note: The use of Curwen hand symbols may also aid this particular activity.	• Students accurately sing and perform known melodies in major and are accurately alter the melody to the parallel minor (using solfege and also on the instrument). • Students can perform the songs in multiple key areas.

Standards Links:

Resources and References:

127

Category 2:	Musicianship Skills and Knowledge
Content Area:	2A—Tonal Aural Skills and Ear Training
Benchmark:	*Students demonstrate the following abilities: matching and manipulating pitch, playing with a sense of tonality, tonal--melodic and tonal--harmonic function (horizontal and vertical relationships/functions of tonality), ear-to-hand skills, aural and kinesthetic awareness of pitch accuracy and intonation, including and related to improvisation.*
Learning Task:	**1.6—Students perform, by ear, *primary* (tonic and dominant) harmonic tonal patterns.**

Learning Sequences & Processes	Indicators of Success
<u>General Information, Prior Knowledge and Precursors</u> • Tonal aural skills fluency includes melody *and* harmony. While students are learning melodic tonal skills they need to also learn harmonic tonal skills. • The string instruments are conveniently set-up to access harmonic skills from the first lesson, as the open strings provide both a tonic and dominant reference. • When students learn beginning songs, they should learn *both* the melody and the corresponding bass line. <u>Sequence of Activities</u> • As students learn the solfege syllables, they should learn that *Do* is the resting pitch in major tonality. • Practice singing patterns based on the tonic (Do, Mi, Sol) and dominant VII (Sol, Ti, Re, Fa) chords. Students should be able to discriminate the differences between chords (e.g., tonic does not have *Ti, Re,* or *Fa*). • Teach the bass lines to beginning folk songs. Many beginning songs only use tonic and dominant chords. The teacher can sing the melody while the students play the bass line, and vice versa. (Note: in this case, the bass line is simply the tonic note of each chord in the harmonic progression of the piece). • Divide the class into two sections, have one section play the bass line while the other plays (or sings) the melody. • Create your own "arrangements" by mixing elements: melody, harmony, singing the tune (with and without words), pizzicato, and/or arco, as skill development permits.	• Students correctly change to tonic and dominant chords corresponding to the melody. • Students can verbalize and perform on the instrument tonic and dominant patterns.

Standards Links:

Resources and References:

Category 2: Musicianship Skills and Knowledge

Content Area:	**2A—Tonal Aural Skills and Ear Training**
Benchmark:	*Students demonstrate the following abilities: matching and manipulating pitch, playing with a sense of tonality, tonal--melodic and tonal--harmonic function (horizontal and vertical relationships/functions of tonality), ear-to-hand skills, aural and kinesthetic awareness of pitch accuracy and intonation, including and related to improvisation.*
Learning Task:	**1.7—Students improvise (vocally, pizzicato, and/or arco)** *melodic* **tonal patterns (within a tetrachord; neutral syllable, then solfege)**

Learning Sequences & Processes	Indicators of Success
General Information, Prior Knowledge and Precursors • Improvisation is something that every child does from birth. Children improvise in language, with babble, making up sentences (and words), creating new words, and attempting to communicate in language on many levels. • That same level of creativity found in children in language exists in their musical aptitude as well. And, creativity is an *expected* behavior in language. If individuals cannot "create" in language (i.e., they simply repeat the exact same sentence that is spoken to them, or never have an original thought or conversation), this deficiency is likely to receive remedial attention. • *Why doesn't the same concern exist in music?* • Music is an inherently creative activity—improvising, composing, and arranging are essential skills for musicians to have access to their creative side and be able to explore ideas, emotion, and beyond. For that reason, we have included improvisation as a key part of this curriculum. • Some of the basic echo activities listed previously include improvisatory elements, such as when students make up their own patterns. One of the challenges seen by teachers is that they don't know where to begin. The following sequence provides some basic ideas. There are also excellent resources listed in the resource list at the end of this curriculum. Sequence of Activities • Take known patterns from familiar songs and change one element, such as major to minor. • Provide students with parameters for their improvisation, such as: only three notes. Or, all patterns need to end on the solfege syllable *do*. • Try repeating the same pattern on another string, or another starting pitch (depending on level of student comfort with activity). *For more ideas on improvisation, please see Content Area 2C, which is the primary section where improvisation is addressed in this curriculum.*	• Students are able to create melodies within the framework and structure provided by the teacher.

Standards Links:

Resources and References:

Category 2:	Musicianship Skills and Knowledge
Content Area:	**2A—Tonal Aural Skills and Ear Training**
Benchmark:	*Students demonstrate the following abilities: matching and manipulating pitch, playing with a sense of tonality, tonal--melodic and tonal--harmonic function (horizontal and vertical relationships/functions of tonality), ear-to-hand skills, aural and kinesthetic awareness of pitch accuracy and intonation, including and related to improvisation.*
Learning Task:	**2.1—Students perform, by ear, *melodic* tonal patterns (patterns and melodies within a one-octave range) in major/minor tonalities.**

Learning Sequences & Processes	Indicators of Success
General Information, Prior Knowledge and Precursors • Students should already be able to accurately perform (vocally and on the instrument) melodic patterns within a tetrachord, or even greater intervals. • Overall, this activity is primarily an extension of what takes place at the baseline level. Continue to emphasize these skills regularly (even five minutes as a warm-up at the beginning of a lesson or rehearsal helps activate the listening!). Possible Activities • Take patterns from known songs and have students echo the patterns, attempting to figure out what the original song was. • Have individual students select melodic patterns from songs and perform them for the class, as the model. • Use patterns from songs not yet taught, but as an *anticipatory set* for the students. • Start with neutral syllable, then proceed to solfege, then to the instrument, as students master individual activities.	• Students can both accurately echo and create patterns within a one-octave range. • Emphasize proper tone production, not just correct notes.

Standards Links:

Resources and References:

Category 2:	Musicianship Skills and Knowledge
Content Area:	**2A—Tonal Aural Skills and Ear Training**
Benchmark:	*Students demonstrate the following abilities: matching and manipulating pitch, playing with a sense of tonality, tonal--melodic and tonal--harmonic function (horizontal and vertical relationships/functions of tonality), ear-to-hand skills, aural and kinesthetic awareness of pitch accuracy and intonation, including and related to improvisation.*
Learning Task:	**2.2—Students manipulate single pitches to adjust intonation, while listening for "ringing tones" (resonance, sympathetic vibrations)**

Learning Sequences & Processes	Indicators of Success
General Information, Prior Knowledge and Precursors • Intonation is a fluid concept. Specific intonation for notes changes based on the function of a note within a chord or key. As a result, students need to be prepared in the early stages of training to quickly manipulate pitches. Playing a string instrument with good intonation goes beyond listening for the relative "highness" or "lowness" of a pitch. If notes which match open strings (i.e., have the same letter name) are played perfectly in tune, the corresponding open string will vibrate sympathetically, creating a tone which is more resonant than other fingered notes. These tones are often called "ringing tones." • Ringing tones in first position for violin/viola are: 3rd fingers create octaves with the open string below. 4th fingers create unisons with the open string above. 1st finger on the G- or D-strings (vla, C- or G-string) creates an octave with the open A- or E-string (vla, open D- or A-string). Low 2nd finger on the E-string (vla, open A-string) creates a double octave with the open G-string (vla, open C-string). • Ringing tones in first position for cello are: 4th fingers create octaves with the open string below. 1st finger on the C- or G-string creates an octave with the open D- or A-string. Low 2nd finger on the A-string creates a double octave with the open C-string. • Ringing tones are not as easily accessible on the bass without shifting. For example, 1st fingers create octaves with the second open string below the fingered note. For example, the 1st finger on the G-string, with the open A-string. In 2nd position, the 4th finger creates a unison interval with the open string above. In 3rd position, the 4th finger creates an octave with the open string below. • The ability to produce good ringing tones requires that the instruments are properly tuned and in good repair, with strings in good condition. Sequence of Activities • If a piano is available, tell students you can make a note sound without playing it. First, play the A above middle C; then, silently depress that A and forcefully strike the A two octaves lower. The higher A will sound. As sound waves travel through the air, if they strike another object that matches the speed of the vibrations, that object will vibrate sympathetically. • Demonstrate and explain that, on string instruments, if a note with the same letter name as an open string is played perfectly in tune, you can see and hear the open string vibrate. (This is most easily observed with 3rd finger G- on the D-string on violin/3rd finger C- on the G-string on viola.) • Challenge students to show in first position where ringing tones can be played. For each ringing tone, students should adjust the placement of their fingers until they can see and hear the vibration of the corresponding string. • Identify ringing tones in the scales, etudes, and literature being studied and encourage students to use them as a guide to intonation.	• Students can both accurately echo and create patterns within a one-octave range.

Standards Links:

Resources and References:

Category 2: Musicianship Skills and Knowledge

Content Area:	2A—Tonal Aural Skills and Ear Training

Benchmark:	*Students demonstrate the following abilities: matching and manipulating pitch, playing with a sense of tonality, tonal--melodic and tonal--harmonic function (horizontal and vertical relationships/functions of tonality), ear-to-hand skills, aural and kinesthetic awareness of pitch accuracy and intonation, including and related to improvisation.*

Learning Task:	**2.3—Students perform, by ear, *primary* (tonic, dominant, *and subdominant*) harmonic tonal patterns.**

Learning Sequences & Processes	Indicators of Success
General Information, Prior Knowledge and Precursors • Tonal aural skills fluency includes melody *and* harmony. While students are learning melodic tonal skills they need to also learn harmonic tonal skills. • The string instruments are conveniently set-up to access harmonic skills from the first lesson, as the open strings provide both a tonic and dominant reference. • When students learn beginning songs, they should learn *both* the melody and the corresponding bass line. • This is a continuation activity from Learning Task 1.5 above. Sequence of Activities • As students learn the solfege syllables, they should understand that *Do* is the resting tone (or home note) in major tonalies. • Review singing patterns based on the tonic (Do, Mi, Sol) and dominant VII (Sol, Ti, Re, Fa) chords. Students should be able to discriminate the differences between chords (e.g., tonic does not have *Ti, Re,* or *Fa*). • Add the syllables for the subdominant (*Fa, La,* and *Do*). • Add to the students vocabulary songs that include subdominant chords, together with the tonic and dominant chords. • Use a "discovery" learning strategy, in which students are guided to figure out what the new "mystery" chord is, and where it occurs in the song. • Divide the class into two sections, have one section play the bass line while the other plays (or sings) the melody. • Create your own "arrangements" by mixing elements: melody, harmony, singing the tune (with and without words), pizzicato, and/or arco, as skill development permits. • Have students find songs that include subdominant chords, and ask them to bring them to the next class.	• Students correctly change to tonic and dominant chords corresponding to the melody. • Students can verbalize and perform on the instrument tonic, dominant, and subdominant patterns.

Standards Links:

Resources and References:

Category 2:	**Musicianship Skills and Knowledge**
Content Area:	**2A—Tonal Aural Skills and Ear Training**
Benchmark:	*Students demonstrate the following abilities: matching and manipulating pitch, playing with a sense of tonality, tonal--melodic and tonal--harmonic function (horizontal and vertical relationships/functions of tonality), ear-to-hand skills, aural and kinesthetic awareness of pitch accuracy and intonation, including and related to improvisation.*
Learning Task:	**2.4—Students improvise, by ear, *melodic* tonal patterns (patterns and melodies within a one-octave range) in major/minor tonalities.**

Learning Sequences & Processes	Indicators of Success
General Information, Prior Knowledge and Precursors • This is a continuation activity from Learning Tasks 1.6 and 2.1. • Students should be able to comfortably perform in major and minor tonalities within a one-octave range. • See Content Area 3A, for specific activities.	• Students can both accurately echo and create patterns within a one-octave range. • Emphasize proper tone production, not just correct notes.

Standards Links:

Resources and References:

Category 2:	Musicianship Skills and Knowledge

Content Area:	2A—Tonal Aural Skills and Ear Training
Benchmark:	*Students demonstrate the following abilities: matching and manipulating pitch, playing with a sense of tonality, tonal--melodic and tonal--harmonic function (horizontal and vertical relationships/functions of tonality), ear-to-hand skills, aural and kinesthetic awareness of pitch accuracy and intonation, including and related to improvisation.*
Learning Task:	**2.5—Students improvise, by ear, *harmonic* tonal patterns (tonic, dominant, and subdominant chords).**

Learning Sequences & Processes	Indicators of Success
General Information, Prior Knowledge and Precursors • This is a continuation activity from Learning Tasks 2.3. • Students should be able to comfortably perform in major and minor tonalities within a one-octave range. • Students should be aware of notes/syllables within the primary chords. • See Content Area 3A, for specific activities.	• Students can both accurately echo and create patterns within a one-octave range. • Emphasize proper tone production, not just correct notes.

Standards Links:

Resources and References:

Category 2:	Musicianship Skills and Knowledge
Content Area:	2A—Tonal Aural Skills and Ear Training
Benchmark:	*Students demonstrate the following abilities: matching and manipulating pitch, playing with a sense of tonality, tonal--melodic and tonal--harmonic function (horizontal and vertical relationships/functions of tonality), ear-to-hand skills, aural and kinesthetic awareness of pitch accuracy and intonation, including and related to improvisation.*
Learning Task:	**2.6—Students alter melodies and harmonies (major to minor, modal, and vice versa)**

Learning Sequences & Processes	Indicators of Success
General Information, Prior Knowledge and Precursors • This is a continuation activity of previous improvisation learning tasks. Sequence of Activities • Warm-up with scales in major and relative and parallel minor keys (choose keys based on level of group). • Determine which notes change for each scale. • Perform harmonic patterns for each of the primary chords to be used (determine which notes are altered in the chords for both major and minor keys). • Play song, by ear, in major, then in minor, practicing the melody and harmony separately. • Combine elements. • Have students switch to major and minor "on-cue" from the teacher for whatever part they are playing (melody or harmony). • Practice switching between melody and harmony "on-cue" from the teacher.	• Students accurately perform melodic and harmonic alterations, with fluency and confidence.

Standards Links:

Resources and References:

135

Category 2:	Musicianship Skills and Knowledge
Content Area:	2A—Tonal Aural Skills and Ear Training
Benchmark:	*Students demonstrate the following abilities: matching and manipulating pitch, playing with a sense of tonality, tonal--melodic and tonal--harmonic function (horizontal and vertical relationships/functions of tonality), ear-to-hand skills, aural and kinesthetic awareness of pitch accuracy and intonation, including and related to improvisation.*
Learning Task:	**2.7—Students use fine tuners to adjust strings to match an external tonal reference**

Learning Sequences & Processes	Indicators of Success

General Information, Prior Knowledge and Precursors
 	
• Because string players must find pitches from the open string with minimal visual clues, they must develop a good sense of pitch discrimination from the beginning. It is critical that the open strings be in tune in order for students to practice productively.
 	
• Tuning with the pegs is difficult for beginning students. In addition to the challenge of hearing and matching pitches, the physical finesse required to tune accurately with the pegs is beyond the reach of most beginning players. Also, the pegs on many school instruments are not well adjusted, making tuning even more difficult. Therefore, it is recommended that all instruments be fitted with fine tuners on all four strings.
 	
• Before beginning to tune the instruments, students should demonstrate the ability to discriminate higher and lower pitches and produce a resonant tone on their instruments.
 	
Sequence of Activities
 	
• Demonstrate and explain the mechanics of fine tuners: when the screw is tightened—turned to the right—it pushes against the lever under the tailpiece, increasing tension on the string which then produces a higher tone. When the screw is loosened—turned to the left—the lever releases tension, causing the string to sound lower. Caution students to avoid tightening the screw enough that the lever digs into the top of the instrument.
 	
• Demonstrate and lead students through the following steps in tuning the open strings:
  • LISTEN quietly to the reference tone (may be played on the teacher's instrument, the piano, or an electronic tuner).
  • PLAY (pizzicato or arco) the corresponding open string and determine whether it is the same as or different from the reference tone. (It can be helpful to have students softly hum the reference tone as they work.) If it is the same, move to the next string.
  • IF it is different from the reference tone, determine whether it is higher or lower; then use the tuner to make the necessary adjustment.
  • REPEAT the same sequence for each string.
 	
• Emphasize the importance of listening and remembering the reference tone. Give students repeated guided tuning experiences until they can successfully tune their instruments independently using fine tuners.
	• Students accurately demonstrate the ability to use fine tuners to tune open strings to an external tonal reference.

Standards Links:

Resources and References:

Category 2:	Musicianship Skills and Knowledge
Content Area:	2A—Tonal Aural Skills and Ear Training
Benchmark:	*Students demonstrate the following abilities: matching and manipulating pitch, playing with a sense of tonality, tonal--melodic and tonal--harmonic function (horizontal and vertical relationships/functions of tonality), ear-to-hand skills, aural and kinesthetic awareness of pitch accuracy and intonation, including and related to improvisation.*
Learning Task:	**3.1—Students perform, by ear, melodic tonal patterns and melodies, with chromatic alterations, in major and minor tonalities.**

Learning Sequences & Processes	Indicators of Success
General Information, Prior Knowledge and Precursors • This is a continuation from Learning Task 2.3. • Students should be able to comfortably perform in major and minor tonalities vocally within a one-octave range • Pitch (and rhythm) can be defined as a family of audible spatial or time relationships. Sequence of Activities • Invite students to walk in-place (two steps forward, two steps back). Encourage students to notice the amount of space between their feet as they walk. • Direct students to think of the distance between the two downbeats (when the full foot touches) as equal to the distance between two pitches that are a whole step apart. • Link their walked steps to specific pitches by inviting them to sing the solfege syllable *do* when standing in their start position, then *re* with their first step forward, following by *mi*, then back to *re* and *do*. • Invite students to tap their heel halfway in between that measured space before placing their foot down on the whole step they've just practiced walking, for a few rounds while singing their three pitches up and down. • Introduce the chromatic pitches that correspond to the heeltap by singing or playing them and inviting the students to echo them back. • Challenge students to walk and sing on their own. • Repeat the steps in this exercise using a minor third. • Repeat this entire exercise using a new starting pitch. • Repeat these exercises by linking sung notes to fingered notes using pizzicato.	• Students can accurately sing the first five notes of a chromatic scale when provided with a starting pitch • Students can accurately perform (pizzicato) the first five notes of a chromatic scale when provided with a starting pitch

Standards Links:

Resources and References:

Category 2:	Musicianship Skills and Knowledge
Content Area:	2A—Tonal Aural Skills and Ear Training
Benchmark:	*Students demonstrate the following abilities: matching and manipulating pitch, playing with a sense of tonality, tonal--melodic and tonal--harmonic function (horizontal and vertical relationships/functions of tonality), ear-to-hand skills, aural and kinesthetic awareness of pitch accuracy and intonation, including and related to improvisation.*
Learning Task:	**3.2—Students perform, by ear, primary and secondary (ii, vi, vii)** *harmonic* **tonal patterns**

Learning Sequences & Processes	Indicators of Success
General Information, Prior Knowledge and Precursors • Students can comfortably distinguish the I–IV–V–I chord sequence when played for them and locate these relationships vocally when given a starting pitch. • Students are comfortable using solfege. Sequence of Activities • Following the same sequences as given previously for introducing the primary harmonic patterns (I, IV, V), the teacher may introduce secondary harmonic tonal patterns. Solfege is an excellent way of identifying the root of each chord. For example, do-mi-so are the syllables for the tonic chord; re-fa-la are the syllables for the chord built on the second scale degree. • Sing harmonic patterns starting on each scale degree (as shown above). Practice do-mi-so-mi-do, re-fa-la-fa-re, and so on. • Repeat these patterns on the instrument, first in familiar keys, then in unfamiliar keys. • The teacher may also show, using hand symbols (e.g., one finger for the tonic chord, two fingers for the ii chord, etc.), when to switch between chords, as the class plays arpeggios on each chord. • As students become comfortable with performing the patterns on the instrument, they should perform songs containing ii, vi, or vii chords. Divide the group into two sections. While the first group plays the melody, the second group plays the chords (choosing the root, third, or fifth of the chord). Switch parts and repeat. • If students struggle with playing arpeggiated chords during this exercise, they may first play just the root of each chord, then just the third, the fifth, the seventh (as appropriate) and so on. Then the teacher may add a note (e.g., just the root and third, then the root-third-fifth, etc.) until the students build up confidence. • Play several familiar melodies containing these chords, before moving to improvised accompaniments.	• Students accurately perform pitches from primary and secondary chords. • Students correctly anticipate, identify, and perform chords following teacher hand symbols. • Students are comfortable performing chords in several keys.

Standards Links:

Resources and References:

Category 2:	**Musicianship Skills and Knowledge**

Content Area:	**2A—Tonal Aural Skills and Ear Training**
Benchmark:	*Students demonstrate the following abilities: matching and manipulating pitch, playing with a sense of tonality, tonal--melodic and tonal--harmonic function (horizontal and vertical relationships/functions of tonality), ear-to-hand skills, aural and kinesthetic awareness of pitch accuracy and intonation, including and related to improvisation.*
Learning Task:	**3.3—Students improvise melodies and patterns, using chromatic alterations or simple modulations**

Learning Sequences & Processes	Indicators of Success
General Information, Prior Knowledge and Precursors • In Learning Task 3.1 above, students performed rote patterns and melodies containing chromatic alterations or simple modulations, by ear. In this learning task, students will *improvise* new melodies and patterns using chromatic alterations or simple modulations. • The ability to successfully complete this exercise is dependent on the richness of the student's musical vocabulary. Specifically, this means that the students already know several melodies and songs by ear. They may then draw upon these songs and patterns to create new songs or patterns (or make alterations to those existing songs or patterns). • This improvisation activity is already done by students every day…in their *verbal* conversations. When speaking, students draw upon their knowledge of vocabulary from past conversations to have new conversations in new contexts. Improvising in music is not really that different. The success that students have in terms of language creativity or improvisation relates directly to their preparation in the area of vocabulary, grammar, and past experiences in reading, listening, and writing. Successful improvisation in music requires the same richness of musical understanding and preparation. That is why it is essential that students have a rich aural understanding of musical vocabulary and "grammar" (melodic and tonal structures) in order to ensure success in improvisation. Sequence of Activities • Students select an already familiar melody or tonal pattern. • The teacher directs students to make changes in the existing melody or pattern by altering a single note (to a neighbor note), adding a passing tone, or performing a parallel melody or pattern. This follows the *theme-and-variations* idea introduced in earlier sections. • The bass line is added to the melody. • The teacher directs students to create a new melody over the existing bass line. The melody may be a simple alteration of the known melody, or may be a completely new creation. • Students practice improvising new melodies over the bass line using the call-and-response approach between teacher and student, or between students.	• Students accurately improvise new melodies that relate to the given bass line. • Students are comfortable making mistakes and can recover from their mistakes during the performing. • Students accurately perform passing tones, neighboring tones, ornaments, or variations on the existing melody or tonal pattern.

Standards Links:

Resources and References:

Category 2:	**Musicianship Skills and Knowledge**
Content Area:	**2A—Tonal Aural Skills and Ear Training**
Benchmark:	*Students demonstrate the following abilities: matching and manipulating pitch, playing with a sense of tonality, tonal--melodic and tonal--harmonic function (horizontal and vertical relationships/functions of tonality), ear-to-hand skills, aural and kinesthetic awareness of pitch accuracy and intonation, including and related to improvisation.*
Learning Task:	**3.4—Students improvise simple accompaniments to melodies**

Learning Sequences & Processes	**Indicators of Success**
General Information, Prior Knowledge and Precursors • As discussed earlier, composition and improvisation are closely related activities: in both cases, students are challenged to create their own melodic sequence and/or rhythm patterns. The term "improvise" often inadvertently infers a linear event that does not track and record the player's imagination; whereas the term "compose" describes a tracking process via memorization, and more often, notation. Yet, any great improviser will tell you that the development of tracking capability through memory enables them to build their ideas far more effectively. Sequence of Activities • The teacher selects a melody or invites students to select a melody from their favorite listening or playing material. • The teacher plays the melody of choice and challenges students to find the tonic (the resting note or tonal center) of the piece. • The teacher challenges students to pluck the tonal center and call out the moment that pitch no longer sounds effective against the melody. • The teacher invites students to search for the each "harmonic turning point" in the melody that requires a different pitch to create a successful accompaniment. The class can discuss alternatives, experiment with possibilities, and gradually lock in a sequence of pitches that create a successful accompaniment or bass line. • The teacher challenges students to create rhythm patterns that successfully support the rhythmic feel of the piece, using a predetermined sequence of notes. • The teacher invites students to pluck and play the line that were first sung. Depending on the skill level of the students, they can be challenged to notate their group-developed bass line accompaniment. • Exercise can be repeated on a new melody. • Create variations on this exercise depending on class skill level. For instance, it's also possible to flip-flop this exercise and present a melody and bass line to the class that has a "wrong" note in it, invite them to identify that note, and then challenge them to find a substitute pitch that does work. Or, the teacher may present a melody with a bland bass line and invite them to create rhythm patterns for the bass line that best supports the rhythmic feel of the piece.	• Students accurately anticipate, identify, and perform the chord changes within the bass line (e.g., when tonic switches to dominant, etc.).

Standards Links:

Resources and References:

Category 2:	Musicianship Skills and Knowledge
Content Area:	2A—Tonal Aural Skills and Ear Training
Benchmark:	*Students demonstrate the following abilities: matching and manipulating pitch, playing with a sense of tonality, tonal--melodic and tonal--harmonic function (horizontal and vertical relationships/functions of tonality), ear-to-hand skills, aural and kinesthetic awareness of pitch accuracy and intonation, including and related to improvisation.*
Learning Task:	**3.5—Students use fine tuners and/or pegs to tune strings in 5ths to an external tonal reference.**

Learning Sequences & Processes	Indicators of Success
<u>General Information, Prior Knowledge and Precursors</u> • Once students are comfortable tuning their instruments to a given pitch (e.g., tuning the A-string to another sounding A-string or to a tuner playing the note A), they may begin to tune their instruments in fifths. This process will take time and requires good aural preparation, instruments in good working order, students with the physical coordination to turn a peg or fine tuner while playing their instrument, and the ability to play with good tone production while adjusting the tuners. • It may be best to introduce this activity gradually, for example, tuning three of four strings to the same pitch, and then on a given day, just tuning one of the strings in fifths (such as the D-string against the A-string). • Students should be able to perform long, smooth bow strokes, with control over the whole length of the bow. • Students should already be able to distinguish "same" and "different" sounding pitches in terms of identifying out-of-tune notes. • Students need to be directed to start tuning at the tip of the bow, tune quietly, and to wait two or three seconds to listen carefully to the pitch before tuning their own instruments. <u>Sequence of Activities</u> • A variety of strategies may be used, such as the following: • The teacher demonstrates on an instrument what in-tune and out-of-tune fifths sound like. Students should have their eyes closed and raise their hands when they think that the pitch being adjusted is in- or out-of-tune. This will help the teacher assess which students have good aural understanding and discrimination. • The teacher asks a section (such as the violins) to play an A, while having the other sections tune their D-string against that sounding A. • Depending on the amount of time this takes for a given class, this activity may need to be repeated for several days. Other classes may master the activity quickly. • In subsequent classes, repeat the process with the D- and G-strings, G- and C-strings, and A- and E-strings. • Once students are comfortable tuning against the external reference, they should begin to tune their own instruments in double stops. Because the string bass is tuned in 4ths, the teachers should demonstrate to the basses at this point how to tune their instruments using harmonics (see Content Area 1B—Left Hand Skills & Understandings Learning Task 2.4—Harmonics) • If students have a difficult time hearing whether the pitch is sharp or flat, the teacher directs the students to make the pitch lower (to the point where it's clearly flat) and then bring the pitch back in tune.	• Students accurately identify whether pitch is too high or too low. • Students maintain a long, smooth bow stroke while performing. • Students correctly adjust pitch using fine tuners or pegs.

Standards Links:

Resources and References:

Category 2: Musicianship Skills and Knowledge

Content Area:	2A—Tonal Aural Skills and Ear Training
Benchmark:	*Students demonstrate the following abilities: matching and manipulating pitch, playing with a sense of tonality, tonal--melodic and tonal--harmonic function (horizontal and vertical relationships/functions of tonality), ear-to-hand skills, aural and kinesthetic awareness of pitch accuracy and intonation, including and related to improvisation.*
Learning Task:	**4.1—Students perform, by ear, melodies and accompaniments in various modes and scales (e.g., Dorian, Mixolydian, Blues, etc.) and meters.**

Learning Sequences & Processes	Indicators of Success
General Information, Prior Knowledge and Precursors • In Learning Tasks 3.1–3.4 above, students performed and improvised rote patterns and melodies containing chromatic alterations or simple modulations and primary harmonies (I, IV, and V chords). • The ability to successfully complete this exercise is dependent on the quality of the student's musical vocabulary. Specifically, this means that the students already know several melodies and songs by ear. They may then draw upon these songs and patterns to create new songs or patterns (or make alterations to those existing songs or patterns). For this learning task, students need to listen to songs or larger musical works in various modes. Examples of familiar songs in modes include "Old Joe Clark" (Mixolydian); "Scarborough Fair" (Dorian), by Simon and Garfunkel; "So What" (Dorian), by Miles Davis; "Eleanor Rigby" (Dorian), by the Beatles; and, "Drunken' Sailor" (Dorian). Many folk songs from the British Isles are in Mixolydian and Dorian modes. Examples of blues scales are prevalent in jazz and rock music. Sequence of Activities • Choose a song that uses Dorian, Mixolydian, or Blues. • Practice etudes and/or exercises using the selected scale (such as scale routines, rhythmic variations, scales in thirds, etc.) • Learn the primary accompaniment chords for each mode (Dorian—i, V, III; Mixolydian—I, VI) and the blues scale. • Practice accompanying the scale tones with the appropriate chord. • First sing, then play, the selected song; melody, then bass line. • Practice changing songs in major or minor modes into Dorian, Mixolydian, or the Blues. This requires changing both the scale and choosing the appropriate bass line. At the beginning try using familiar songs like "Twinkle, Twinkle, Little Star," "Hot Cross Buns" or "Mary had a Little Lamb" until students become comfortable in the new harmonic vocabulary.	• Students accurately perform melodies and songs in Dorian, Mixolydian, and the Blues. • Students correctly identify and perform the bass lines for each of the modes or scales. • Students correctly transpose songs from major or minor into another mode.

Standards Links:	

Resources and References:	

Category 2:	Musicianship Skills and Knowledge
Content Area:	2A—Tonal Aural Skills and Ear Training
Benchmark:	*Students demonstrate the following abilities: matching and manipulating pitch, playing with a sense of tonality, tonal--melodic and tonal--harmonic function (horizontal and vertical relationships/functions of tonality), ear-to-hand skills, aural and kinesthetic awareness of pitch accuracy and intonation, including and related to improvisation.*
Learning Task:	**4.2—Students improvise melodies and accompaniments in various modes and scales (e.g., Dorian, Mixolydian, Blues, etc.) and meters.**

Learning Sequences & Processes	Indicators of Success
General Information, Prior Knowledge and Precursors • In Learning Tasks 3.1–3.4 above, students performed and improvised rote patterns and melodies containing chromatic alterations or simple modulations, and primary harmonies (I, IV, and V chords). In Learning Task 4.1 above, students *performed* songs using Dorian, Mixolydian, and Blues scales/modes. In this exercise, students are asked to *improvise* melodies and accompaniments in various modes and scales. • Other activities related to improvisation may be found in Content Area 2C—Creative Musicianship. Sequence of Activities • Choose a song that uses Dorian, Mixolydian, or Blues. Using a pre-recorded harmonic background or constructing a riff with the musicians in the ensemble, establish the harmonic context for the piece. • Perform the basic scale notes (with variations, passing tones, etc.) over the repeated harmonic background. Allow various students to solo individually (or even in a group jam) over the background. • As a second option, have students practice the various chord tones (i.e., root, third, fifth, and seventh, as appropriate) over the chord changes (using arpeggios or simple alternating patterns) • As students gain experience, they will begin to identify which notes from the scale sound best over given chords. • Divide the class into groups. The first group plays the root of each chord during the riff. The second group plays the third of the chord and the fourth group plays the fifth of the chord, etc. At the beginning this progression will not necessarily sound as nice as later progressions, but it helps students understand the chord sequence. Next, have students move to the next closest chord tone during the chord changes. For example, the root of the tonic chord moves down to the third of the dominant chord, since those are neighboring tones. • As students grow comfortable with the background, have them practice improvising in the selected scale over the background, beginning first with just a few notes, and then slowly expanding the scale. The goal is for students to become comfortable in the new key area. • Ask the students to perform a familiar song in the selected mode, and then begin to make variations on the original tune. This helps jump-start the improvisation process. • The teacher directs students to create a new melody over the existing bass line. The melody may be a simple alteration of the known melody, or may be a completely new creation. • Students practice improvising new melodies over the bass line using the call-and-response approach between teacher and student, or between students.	• Students accurately improvise new melodies that relate to the given bass line. • Students are comfortable making mistakes and can recover from their mistakes during the performing. • Students are able to perform passing tones, neighboring tones, ornaments, or variations on the existing melody or tonal pattern. • Students change the melody at the appropriate time in the sequence of chord changes.

Standards Links:

Resources and References:

Content Area 2B—Rhythmic Aural Skills and Ear Training

Students perform simple and complex rhythm patterns/functions, with steady pulse/beat, correct sense of meter and metric organization and phrasing, in a variety of meters

General Discussion about Rhythmic Aural Skills and Ear Training

Before moving into the Learning Tasks related to Rhythmic Aural Skills, we believe it is essential to state the following:

- Rhythmic aural skills are as integrally tied to successful string playing as they are to successfully communicating in language (listening, speaking, reading, and writing). It is essential that string teachers place strong emphasis on the development of aural skills in the earliest stages of instruction.

- The foundation for strong rhythmic aural skills is closely tied to students' abilities to sing rhythm patterns and translate what is heard to the instrument (ear-to-hand skills). This includes the ability to play with a steady pulse, a clear sense of meter, and correct metrical direction; echo rhythm patterns and accompaniments; and improvise rhythm patterns and accompaniments.

- Accuracy in rhythm performance is not tied to a student's ability to correctly analyze or label rhythm values (or understand the definitions of rhythm notations), but rather to how students perceive rhythm. It is an internal sense of motion and time, rather than an arithmetic understanding of music theory related to rhythm. It is possible for students to correctly label complicated rhythm patterns (i.e., assign beat numbers or rhythm syllables), but still not perform those rhythm patterns with a steady pulse or clear sense of metrical direction.

- Students should develop a rich rhythm *vocabulary* that includes an understanding of and the ability to perform rhythm patterns in both duple and triple meters. In duple meters, the beat is divided into two equal portions. In triple meters, the beat is divided into three equal portions. This differs from the approach to categorize meter as *simple* or *compound* as is frequently done in music theory. The use of *simple* and *compound* is based on arithmetic values rather than on beat-function or how the rhythms actually feel and are perceived by the listener.

- The standard for rhythm in this curriculum states that students should…*perform simple and complex rhythm patterns/functions*…. For the purposes of this curriculum, simple patterns are those using only macrobeats and microbeats. Complex patterns are those that use elongations, (patterns containing note values that are longer than a macrobeat), subdivisions (patterns that contain note values that are shorter than a microbeat), syncopations, or other variations.

- The use of rhythm syllables provides a strong basis for understanding the relationship between meters and rhythm patterns and greatly enhances the ability to translate what is heard to what is performed.

- Students should develop a rich repertoire of songs at the beginning level, including songs in duple and triple meters. These songs will serve as the foundation for music literacy. Rhythm patterns derived from these songs may be used to teach basic ear-to-hand skills and beginning rhythm notation.

- Strong rhythmic aural skills lead to greater comprehension of written notation.

- Students should practice rhythm patterns and develop a strong foundation in rhythm skills from the first lessons. Common mistakes teachers make include:

  - Introducing notation too quickly (before students have a good aural and cognitive framework for what they are going to read)

  - Focusing on developing a theoretical understanding of rhythm before students can audiate and perform rhythm patterns by ear

  - Introducing too many new concepts at once (e.g., asking students to read notation, learn new rhythm patterns, play with the bow, etc.) before students have mastered any of those concepts individually.

  - Delaying rhythm skill teaching until students have developed the technical proficiency to play those patterns with the bow. Even while students are still acquiring basic executive skills (e.g., playing pizzicato on open strings in guitar position before they are able to use the bow), they are able to practice rhythm patterns vocally (chanting), using rhythmic movement activities, or playing pizzicato.

- Developing rhythmic aural skills at the outset of instruction is not a complex or difficult activity. Consider the following examples of aural skills activities:

<u>Sequence of Activities—Singing or chanting</u>

- Students echo simple rhythm (duple and triple) patterns on a neutral syllable
- Students sing simple folk songs in duple and triple meters tonalities. In addition, many beginning songs have a simple rhythmic structure that may be easily plucked on open strings while students sing the melody on solfège or using the words.
- Students change folk songs that are in duple meter into triple meter and vice versa
- Students improvise basic rhythm patterns on a single note

<u>Sequence of Activities—On the Instrument</u>

Note: Depending on the individual student or class progress on executive skills, these following activities may be performed in guitar position, playing position, pizzicato, or with the bow. For example, if students do not yet have the ability to hold the instrument in playing position for a long period of time, basic rhythm patterns may be performed in guitar position. Likewise, when a student has developed a good posture, playing position, and basic bow hold, new rhythm skills may be taught already in playing position.

- Students echo single-note patterns on an open string (pizzicato)
- Students echo single-note patterns on a fingered note (pizzicato). Patterns may be derived from the songs that will be taught, but should also include patterns not found in the songs, so that students develop the ability to *discriminate* aurally.
- Students perform simple folk songs in duple and triple meters.
- Students change folk songs that are in duple meter into triple meter and vice versa
- Students improvise basic rhythm patterns on a single note

What Syllable or Counting System Should I Use?

A wide range of rhythm syllable systems and counting systems are used across the country. It is important to note that the various systems in use have a variety of strengths (and in some cases, some substantial weaknesses). And, in any case, if the teacher does not accurately model the patterns in a rhythmic manner, it won't matter what system is used!

According to Hoffman, Pelto, and White (1996), there are six primary goals for any rhythm pedagogy:

1. It should lead to accuracy and musicality in performance, both studies and sight-read, including the ability to recognize and perform musical gesture.
2. It should require and reflect an understanding of rhythmic structure, recognition of metric and rhythmic interaction, and an awareness of precise contextual location of beats and at-tack points.
3. It should facilitate aural recognition and identification of rhythmic patterns and metric divisions.
4. It should provide a precise and consistent language for the discussion of temporal phenomena. There should be no need to create new terms or separate categories for performance, transcription, or analytical work.
5. It should address rhythmic issues presented by musics outside the realm of traditional tonal literature such as asymmetric meters, modulation of meter or tempo, complex syncopations, complex tuplet groupings, and passages that combine these in novel and challenging ways.
6. Like pitch solfège, it should be a system that is easily applied and adapts to broad applications, and it should be a tool for life-long use.[3]

Rhythm systems may be generally divided into the following categories:

- *Systems that emphasize beat or pattern function*, where the macrobeat receives the same syllable each time it occurs (e.g., the Gordon syllable system or the Takadimi system). In these systems, the macrobeat always receives the same syllable and students can easily transfer knowledge learned in one pattern to a new pattern. The syllables also reinforce and mirror the physical feeling associated with a specific rhythm pattern. Gordon uses a single syllable ("du") to represent the macrobeat, but then two different sets of syllables to indicate duple ("du-de") and triple ("du-da-di") meters, because those meters are perceived differently. This system is relatively easy for young children to use and has separate syllables for patterns in different beat functions and metrical feels.

  The Takadimi system developed by Hoffman, Pelto, and White also uses an elaborate system of syllables based on beat function, with unique syllables for each location within the beat ("ta-ka-di-mi" for duple and "ta-ki-da"

[3] Richard Hoffman, William Pelto, and John W. White, "Takadimi: A Beat-Oriented System of Rhythm Pedagogy." *Journal of Music Theory Pedagogy*, 10 (1996): 8.

for triple).[4] Both the Gordon and Takadimi systems have strengths and weaknesses, depending on complexity of the rhythm. Takadimi is a bit more complex than the Gordon system and may be more challenging for young children, though it should be usable by students at the middle- and high-school levels. It should also be noted that both systems are in use in musicianship classes in well known universities in the US.

- *Systems that emphasize arithmetic or note (time) values or counting systems*, where a numerical value is assigned to each rhythm. The counting system found in many instrumental music programs in the US and uses "1 e and a" is an example of this approach, as is the Cooley system ("1 and 2 and" for eighth notes and "1 a an a 2 a an a" for sixteenth notes). Both systems are useful for keeping track of the location of a specific rhythm or beat within a measure (e.g., "Please start on the 'and of 1'" to indicate beginning on the upbeat to the first beat of the measure), but do not emphasize beat function or the relationships between rhythmic patterns as the beat-function systems do.

- *Systems that combine time values and counting systems*, such as systems derived from the French (Galin-Paris-Chevé) system. In the French system, syllables are used to represent beat function (e.g., "Ta fa te fe"), but there is no distinction between syllables for duple and triple meters, and so the same problem exists as for systems that rely on counting, where a single syllable can have multiple meanings. This system was adapted by a variety of teachers for use outside of France, the most well known being teachers of the Kodály method. The French system is not encountered as frequently today, but is still used throughout the US.

  The Kodály system uses one syllable for the quarter-note ("ta") and two completely different syllables for the eighth-notes ("ti-ti"). In this system, there is no relationship between the function or feel of the quarter-note and the eighth-notes. It is a convenient system for quickly identifying rhythm values, but doesn't promote a sense of kinesthetic awareness of rhythm. Other examples of a French-type system include the McHose and Tibbs system, which uses "1 ta te ta,, 2 ta te ta."

- *Systems that use a linguistic or mnemonic device to learn rhythm patterns*. This practice has a history in eurthymics and associating a specific rhythm with a bodily motion (such as "run-ning"). This is commonly used in string programs where instruction begins at a very young age. Though this system provides for quick memorization of visual representations of rhythm patterns, the challenge is that there is not a convenient method for transferring knowledge from one rhythm pattern to another. For example, if one mnemonic phrase is used to describe a group of two sixteenth-notes followed by one eighth-note (such as "App-le Pie, App-le Pie"), when the student meets the opposite pattern (one eighth-note followed by two sixteenth notes), an entirely new set of words must be used, since using the old words in reverse (i.e., "Pie App-le, Pie App-le") makes no sense. In this system, any relationship between the two patterns is completely lost. Further confusion can result because the way a word is used in music (such as the word "strawberry" used to demonstrate triplets) may have a completely different rhythm in speech (where it may also sound like an eighth note and two sixteenth notes).

Summary

Because of the comprehensive nature of some of the counting systems, it is not possible here to give an adequate number of examples representing how the different counting systems may be used. We also do not want to minimize the work of those who have developed various rhythm systems by inadvertently omitting examples that may be distinguishing characteristics of a particular system. It would require several additional pages in this curriculum to fully represent the benefits (and negatives) of each system.

Ultimately, a rhythm syllable system must be implemented correctly if it is going to have any positive effect at all for the students. The system should be relatively easy to use and should help students develop their rhythm skills and knowledge. As shown above, there are many options for rhythm syllable systems and our desire is for the teacher to make an informed decision as to what system will best reinforce the rhythmic concepts to be taught at a specific grade level. Emphasis on beat function is a priority, especially for young children, but ease of communication is important during rehearsals. We have not specifically identified a counting system for this curriculum, but do place strong emphasis on the development of rhythmic audiation and perception, which seems to be best reinforced by beat function systems. We recognize that excellent teachers will use a wide range of systems, and it is our goal that this curriculum may be applied to a variety of teaching settings. The learning tasks listed below may be used with a variety of syllable systems, but are designed to be sequential in terms of process and content.

---

[4] Ibid., 14. Hoffman, et al, acknowledge the similarity between their syllables and the vocables used by North Indian tabla players, and credit other researchers and authors for introducing the possibility of using this system in teaching advanced rhythmic concepts.

Learning Tasks

1.1   Students maintain a steady pulse while *singing* or *chanting* rhythm patterns

1.2   Students demonstrate a sense of meter (determined by the division of macrobeats into microbeat groups of two or three) while singing or chanting rhythm patterns

1.3   Students maintain a steady pulse while playing (pizzicato or arco) rhythm patterns

1.4   Students demonstrate a sense of meter (determined by the division of macrobeats into microbeat groups of two or three) while playing (pizzicato or arco) rhythm patterns.

1.5   Students perform rhythm patterns containing rests

1.6   Students perform rhythm patterns containing ties

1.7   Students perform rhythm patterns containing upbeats

1.8   Students improvise rhythm patterns corresponding to Learning Tasks 1.1–1.7

2.1   Students perform rhythm patterns containing subdivisions

2.2   Students perform rhythm patterns containing elongations

2.3   Students perform rhythm patterns containing rests

2.4   Students improvise rhythm patterns corresponding to Learning Tasks 2.1–2.3

3.1   Students perform rhythm patterns in asymmetrical and unusual meters

3.2   Students perform rhythm patterns containing hemiolas

3.3   Students perform rhythm patterns containing enrhythmic notation

3.4   Students improvise rhythm patterns corresponding to Learning Tasks 3.1–3.3

4.1   Students perform rhythm patterns simultaneously from two

4.2   Students perform rhythm patterns in mixed meters

4.3   Students perform rhythm patterns containing syncopation within a single macrobeat

4.4   Students improvise rhythm patterns corresponding to Learning Tasks 4.1–4.3

Category 2:   Musicianship Skills and Knowledge

Content Area:	**2B—Rhythmic Aural Skills and Ear Training**
Benchmark:	*Students perform simple and complex rhythm patterns/functions, with steady pulse/beat, correct sense of meter and metric organization and phrasing, in a variety of meters*
Learning Task:	**1.1—Students maintain a steady pulse while singing or chanting rhythm patterns**

Learning Sequences & Processes	Indicators of Success
<u>General Information, Prior Knowledge and Precursors</u> • Rhythm skills are separate from tonal skills and fall within a different area of aptitude. Rhythm skills, therefore, need to be taught separately from the beginning. • Students in a single class may have a wide range of rhythm skills and aptitude. The teacher needs to be aware that students will progress at different levels and that instruction should be differentiated based on those skill levels. • Performing rhythm patterns with a steady beat is fundamental to all following rhythm tasks. Therefore, the development of a steady pulse must be a priority at the beginning level. • Pulse/beat and rhythm patterns must be experienced physically before learning notation or performing on instrument. • Demonstration of rhythm understanding must ultimately take place when there is no external reference (external pulse or beat, such as a metronome). • Demonstration of steady pulse and the ability to physically perform patterns subdivided into 2s or 3s should precede reading of rhythm patterns. • Initial patterns should include rhythms that are divided into 2s and 3s (duple and triple microbeats). Patterns should not include just quarter notes or eighth notes, but a combination of note values. This really helps students maintain an internal sense of rhythm (audiation) and understand the feel of the rhythm phrase and pattern. • Rhythm patterns may be selected from initial songs in the student's repertoire. This provides an excellent connection for developing the basic rhythm vocabulary needed to performing beginning songs. Because teachers use such a wide variety of beginning method books, we have not identified specific patterns to be used, but leave that at the teacher's discretion. A list of typical beginning method books may be found in the curriculum guide at the end of this document. <u>Sequence of Activities</u> • Students verbally and physically (e.g., knee taps, heel taps) maintain a steady pulse with an external reference, such as a recorded song with strong rhythmic feel. • Students physically respond (echo) subdivide music into two's (eighth-notes or duple microbeats) and three's (triplets or triple microbeats), keeping a steady pulse in heels while tapping knees in patterns divided into twos or threes. • Students verbally respond (echo) to patterns in twos or threes, using a syllable system that is based on beat function (such as ta, ta-ti, du, du-de, or takadimi) • Students verbally and physically improvise simple patterns in twos and threes (duple and triple microbeat).	• Students perform patterns vocally and physically (body percussion) with a steady pulse (pizzicato or arco). • Patterns are performed with sense of meter (triple or duple) • Patterns are performed with a sense of rhythmic phrasing. • Students perform with correct relative rhythm values (macrobeat, microbeats, etc., are performed with accuracy in relation to each other)

Standards Links:

Resources and References:

Category 2: Musicianship Skills and Knowledge

Content Area:	**2B—Rhythmic Aural Skills and Ear Training**
Benchmark:	*Students perform simple and complex rhythm patterns/functions, with steady pulse/beat, correct sense of meter and metric organization and phrasing, in a variety of meters*
Learning Task:	**1.2—Students demonstrate a sense of meter (determined by the division of macrobeats into microbeat groups of two or three) while singing or chanting rhythm patterns**

Learning Sequences & Processes	Indicators of Success
General Information, Prior Knowledge and Precursors • See notes from Learning Tasks 1.1 • A microbeat is the division of a macrobeat (the main pulse or "big beat") in music. • The terms "triple" and "duple" meter do not relate to a theoretical analysis of music, but on how students actually perceive music. • Duple meter: rhythm patterns that divide into groups of two microbeats • Triple meter: rhythm patterns that divide into groups of three microbeats • Students should early on perform patterns in both triple and duple meters. Students only fully understand what duple patterns are when they compare them to triple patterns. Activities should require students to discern what type of pattern is being performed. • The sequence for developing reading skills is based on language acquisition and the sound-before-sight concept. Students should be able to perform rhythms before reading them. However, reading should be introduced as soon as students perform basic patterns with mastery. Comprehension of rhythm notation does not begin with theoretical understanding (e.g., long explanations of note values and mathematical relationships), but from seeing how performed patterns look on the page. The use of flashcards is highly recommended. Sequence of Activities • Repeat activities from Learning Task 1.1. Add the following elements. • Students should understand that duple rhythm patterns have a specific set of rhythm syllables, which are different from the patterns in triple meter. (Du-de vs. Du-da-di, or similar). • When the teacher performs a duple rhythm pattern with body percussion, movement, or syllables, students answer "duple." When teacher performs a triple rhythm pattern, students answer "triple." Students also may perform patterns for each other. • The teacher uses flashcards to show the difference in notation between duple and triple patterns. • Students improvise patterns in duple and triple meter.	• Students perform patterns vocally and physically (body percussion) with a steady pulse (pizzicato or arco). • Patterns are performed with sense of meter (triple or duple) • Patterns are performed with a sense of rhythmic phrasing. • Students perform with correct relative rhythm values (macrobeats, microbeats, etc., are performed with accuracy in relation to each other)

Standards Links:

Resources and References:

Category 2:	Musicianship Skills and Knowledge
Content Area:	**2B—Rhythmic Aural Skills and Ear Training**
Benchmark:	*Students perform simple and complex rhythm patterns/functions, with steady pulse/beat, correct sense of meter and metric organization and phrasing, in a variety of meters*
Learning Task:	**1.3—Students maintain a steady pulse while playing (pizzicato or arco) rhythm patterns**

Learning Sequences & Processes	Indicators of Success
General Information, Prior Knowledge and Precursors • Once students can vocally demonstrate rhythm patterns with accuracy, they may move to the instrument. Pizzicato should be taught first, beginning with open strings or single, fingered notes. As students gain more fluency with their left-hand technique, the teacher may combine rhythm patterns with more complex fingering patterns, but only after students have mastered the basic performance of the rhythm patterns. Use patterns from beginning song repertoire. • Before students use the bow to demonstrate rhythm patterns, they should have a good basic bow hold that is flexible and relaxed. Performing rhythm patterns on the bow too early, i.e., when the bow arm is tense or the bow hold is incorrect, will only reinforce bad habits. • Once students can perform simple patterns verbally and physically (away from the instrument), students may perform the same patterns on the instrument using pizzicato and/or the bow (open strings before moving to fingered patterns). Note that incorrect bow hand position or tension in the bow arm may inhibit accurate performance of rhythms. The teacher should exercise care to determine if rhythm problems are due to a physical or audiation issue. Sequence of Activities • Repeat activities from Learning Tasks 1.1 and 1.2. • Using rhythm patterns that students already know, they should perform the same patterns now with the bow. • The teacher (or another student) should perform echo patterns first by ear before using flashcards, a rhythm sheet, or another form of notation, to show students the visual symbols for what they performed by ear. • Students should then read and perform the rhythm patterns at the same time. • Students may improvise their own duple and triple rhythm patterns. • Students should practice notating the patterns that they created	• Students perform patterns with a steady pulse (pizzicato or arco). • Patterns are performed with sense of meter (triple or duple) • Patterns are performed with a sense of rhythmic phrasing. • Students perform with correct relative rhythm values (macrobeat, microbeats, etc., are performed with accuracy in relation to each other)

Standards Links:

Resources and References:

Category 2:	Musicianship Skills and Knowledge
Content Area:	**2B—Rhythmic Aural Skills and Ear Training**
Benchmark:	*Students perform simple and complex rhythm patterns/functions, with steady pulse/beat, correct sense of meter and metric organization and phrasing, in a variety of meters*
Learning Task:	**1.4—Students demonstrate a sense of meter (determined by the division of macrobeats into microbeat groups of two or three) while playing (pizzicato or arco) rhythm patterns.**

Learning Sequences & Processes	Indicators of Success
General Information, Prior Knowledge and Precursors • As shown above, when students learn initial rhythm patterns, they may not immediately distinguish between patterns that move in duple or triple meters. Their basic comprehension is on simply echoing back what the teacher performed. • Once students can accurately identify and vocally demonstrate the difference between duple and triple patterns, they should repeat this activity on the instrument, pizzicato or arco. Sequence of Activities • Repeat activities from Learning Tasks 1.1–1.3. • Using rhythm patterns that students already know, they should perform the same patterns now with the bow. • The teacher (or another student) should perform echo patterns first, by ear, then use flashcards, a rhythm sheet, or another form of notation, to show students the visual symbols for what they performed by ear. • Students should then read and perform the rhythm patterns at the same time. • Students may improvise their own duple and triple rhythm patterns. • Students should practice notating the patterns that they created. • As students perform, the teacher should emphasize how duple and triple meters "feel" when they played. In other words, there should be a clear sense of metrical accent, rather than simple robotic imitation. • As students learn to play with the "feel" of the rhythm, this will also have a positive effect on their ability to be more musical and play with greater physical relaxation.	• Students perform patterns with a steady pulse (pizzicato or arco). • Patterns are performed with sense of meter (triple or duple) • Patterns are performed with a sense of rhythmic phrasing. • Students perform with correct relative rhythm values (macrobeat, microbeats, etc., are performed with accuracy in relation to each other)

Standards Links:

Resources and References:

Level:	**Baseline**

Category 2:	**Musicianship Skills and Knowledge**
Content Area:	**2B—Rhythmic Aural Skills and Ear Training**
Benchmark:	*Students perform simple and complex rhythm patterns/functions, with steady pulse/beat, correct sense of meter and metric organization and phrasing, in a variety of meters*
Learning Task:	**1.5—Students perform rhythm patterns containing rests**

Learning Sequences & Processes	**Indicators of Success**
General Information, Prior Knowledge and Precursors • As students develop a vocabulary of basic rhythm patterns in duple and triple meter, teachers should introduce the concepts of rests, upbeats, ties, syncopation, and dotted rhythms (elongations). • As with all previous rhythm activities, these concepts should first be introduced aurally. Students should then chant/sing, pizzicato, and, finally, use the bow to perform the selected rhythm patterns. Sequence of Activities • Using selected rhythm patterns already performed, replace sounding notes with rests. Students can do this vocally (leaving a beat empty), physically (using a new movement to indicate a rest), and then on the instrument (pizzicato, then arco). • Students should learn appropriate notation for rest values corresponding to selected note values. • Students should read and write rhythm patterns in duple and triple containing a combination of notes and rests.	• Students perform patterns with a steady pulse (pizzicato or arco). • Patterns are performed with sense of meter (triple or duple) • Patterns are performed with a sense of rhythmic phrasing. • Students perform with correct relative rhythm values (macrobeat, microbeats, etc., are performed with accuracy in relation to each other)

Standards Links:

Resources and References:

Category 2:	Musicianship Skills and Knowledge
Content Area:	**2B—Rhythmic Aural Skills and Ear Training**
Benchmark:	*Students perform simple and complex rhythm patterns/functions, with steady pulse/beat, correct sense of meter and metric organization and phrasing, in a variety of meters*
Learning Task:	**1.6—Students perform rhythm patterns containing ties**

Learning Sequences & Processes	Indicators of Success
General Information, Prior Knowledge and Precursors • As students develop a vocabulary of basic rhythm patterns in duple and triple meter, teachers should introduce the concepts of rests, upbeats, ties, syncopation, and dotted rhythms (elongations). • As with all previous rhythm activities, these concepts should first be introduced aurally. Students should then chant/sing, pizzicato, and finally, use the bow to perform the selected rhythm patterns. Sequence of Activities • Perform, first, rhythm patterns without ties (chanting or singing) and no notation. • Repeat the same pattern, but this time, include the tie, again without notation. • Because the students can read basic notation symbols by this point, have them notate both the first and second patterns. • Next, demonstrate how a longer note (such as a half note) is the same as two quarter-notes with a tie. (May link to a math problem, such as $1+1=2$.) • Perform echo patterns, moving a tie from one location in the pattern to another. • Finally, perform ties that hold over a bar line.	• Students perform patterns with a steady pulse (pizzicato or arco). • Patterns are performed with sense of meter (triple or duple) • Patterns are performed with a sense of rhythmic phrasing. • Students perform with correct relative rhythm values (macrobeat, microbeats, etc., are performed with accuracy in relation to each other)

Standards Links:

Resources and References:

Category 2:	Musicianship Skills and Knowledge
Content Area:	2B—Rhythmic Aural Skills and Ear Training
Benchmark:	*Students perform simple and complex rhythm patterns/functions, with steady pulse/beat, correct sense of meter and metric organization and phrasing, in a variety of meters*
Learning Task:	**1.7—Students perform rhythm patterns containing upbeats**

Learning Sequences & Processes	Indicators of Success
General Information, Prior Knowledge and Precursors • As students develop a vocabulary of basic rhythm patterns in duple and triple meter, teachers should introduce the concepts of rests, upbeats, ties, syncopation, and dotted rhythms (elongations). • As with all previous rhythm activities, these concepts should first be introduced aurally. Students should first chant/sing, then perform with pizzicato, and finally, use the bow to play the selected rhythm patterns. • An upbeat is also called an anacrusis. Sequence of Activities • First perform rhythm patterns, by ear, without upbeats (chanting or singing). • Repeat the same patterns, but this time add an upbeat, again without notation. • Next, demonstrate how the upbeat comes before the downbeat. Use movement activities to show the "feel" of the upbeat. • Because the students can read basic notation symbols by this point, have them notate both the first and second patterns, according to how they think the pattern should be written. • As students grow comfortable with the patterns, teach full songs that have upbeats (both single and double, or longer)	• Students perform patterns with a steady pulse (pizzicato or arco). • Patterns are performed with sense of meter (triple or duple) • Patterns are performed with a sense of rhythmic phrasing. • Students perform with correct relative rhythm values (macrobeat, microbeats, etc., are performed with accuracy in relation to each other)

Standards Links:

Resources and References:

Category 2:	Musicianship Skills and Knowledge
Content Area:	2B—Rhythmic Aural Skills and Ear Training
Benchmark:	*Students perform simple and complex rhythm patterns/functions, with steady pulse/beat, correct sense of meter and metric organization and phrasing, in a variety of meters*
Learning Task:	1.8—Students improvise rhythm patterns corresponding to Learning Tasks 1.1–1.7

Learning Sequences & Processes	Indicators of Success
General Information, Prior Knowledge and Precursors • The ability to improvise and create new rhythm patterns, within given guidelines, is the ultimate measure of a musician's mastery of rhythm understanding and comprehension. • The first levels of improvisation relate to primarily making basic alterations in known rhythm patterns, not necessarily relevant to a particular style or genre of music. • Rhythm improvisation is dealt with in much greater detail in the *Creative Musicianship* portion of this curriculum. Sequence of Activities • Perform echo patterns already known to the students as a warm-up activity. This is a basic "call-and-response" technique, which is an important part of improvisation performance in many genres. • Have individual students demonstrate rhythm patterns, to which the teacher provides a variation. Be sure to give specific guidelines at the beginning, such as, "move the eight notes from the beat that they are on to a different beat in the measure." • Other guidelines that may be used: if a rhythm pattern is in duple, your echo should also be duple. If the rhythm pattern is in triple, your echo should be in triple. If your rhythm pattern contains a rest, the echo should contain a rest, and so on. • Likewise, you may provide more complex echo requirements, such as, if the call was in duple, the response should be in triple. If the call contains a rest, your response should contain a tie. • As students gain mastery with this activity on single pitches, they may add additional pitches. • Students should also listen carefully for articulation of the pattern, as that relates to rhythm value and style. Practice the same rhythm patterns with short and long bowing styles, with straight and swung rhythms.	• Students perform patterns with a steady pulse (pizzicato or arco). • Patterns are performed with sense of meter (triple or duple) • Patterns are performed with a sense of rhythmic phrasing. • Students perform with correct relative rhythm values (macrobeat, microbeats, etc., are performed with accuracy in relation to each other)

Standards Links:

Resources and References:

Category 2:	Musicianship Skills and Knowledge
Content Area:	**2B—Rhythmic Aural Skills and Ear Training**
Benchmark:	*Students perform simple and complex rhythm patterns/functions, with steady pulse/beat, correct sense of meter and metric organization and phrasing, in a variety of meters*
Learning Task:	**2.1—Students perform rhythm patterns containing subdivisions**

Learning Sequences & Processes	Indicators of Success
General Information, Prior Knowledge and Precursors • As mentioned above, the macrobeat is the "big beat," the microbeat is the division of the macrobeat into groups of two or three, and subdivisions are the division of the microbeats into groups of two or three. For example, if a quarter-note is the macrobeat, then eighth-notes would be the microbeats and sixteenth-notes would be the subdivisions. Sequence of Activities • Do a movement sequence that includes macrobeats, microbeats, and subdivisions. • Chant rhythm patterns on a neutral syllable, then chant the same rhythm patterns using a rhythm syllable system. • Perform patterns on the instrument on a single note. • Perform patterns in a scale or in improvised echo patterns • Notate new subdivision patterns • Look at assigned music or repertoire for where subdivision patterns occur	• Students perform patterns with a steady pulse (pizzicato or arco). • Patterns are performed with sense of meter (triple or duple) • Patterns are performed with a sense of rhythmic phrasing. • Students perform with correct relative rhythm values (macrobeat, microbeats, etc., are performed with accuracy in relation to each other) • Subdivisions do not rush and maintain correct the metric accent

Standards Links:

Resources and References:

Category 2:	**Musicianship Skills and Knowledge**
Content Area:	**2B—Rhythmic Aural Skills and Ear Training**
Benchmark:	*Students perform simple and complex rhythm patterns/functions, with steady pulse/beat, correct sense of meter and metric organization and phrasing, in a variety of meters*
Learning Task:	**2.2—Students perform rhythm patterns containing elongations**

Learning Sequences & Processes	**Indicators of Success**
General Information, Prior Knowledge and Precursors • Elongations are the extension of rhythm values such as syncopation and dotted notes. These patterns may also occur with the use of the tied notes (see Learning Task 1.6 above). Sequence of Activities • Do a movement sequence that includes macrobeats, microbeats, and elongations. • Chant rhythm patterns on a neutral syllable, then chant the same rhythm patterns using a rhythm syllable system. • Perform patterns on the instrument on a single note. • Perform patterns in a scale or in improvised echo patterns • Notate new elongation patterns • Look at assigned music or repertoire for where elongation patterns occur	• Students perform patterns with a steady pulse (pizzicato or arco). • Patterns are performed with sense of meter (triple or duple) • Patterns are performed with a sense of rhythmic phrasing. • Students perform with correct relative rhythm values (macrobeat, microbeats, etc., are performed with accuracy in relation to each other) • Elongations do not rush and maintain correct the metric accent

Standards Links:

Resources and References:

Level:	Developing

Category 2:	Musicianship Skills and Knowledge
Content Area:	2B—Rhythmic Aural Skills and Ear Training
Benchmark:	*Students perform simple and complex rhythm patterns/functions, with steady pulse/beat, correct sense of meter and metric organization and phrasing, in a variety of meters*
Learning Task:	**2.3—Students perform rhythm patterns containing rests**

Learning Sequences & Processes	Indicators of Success
General Information, Prior Knowledge and Precursors • This is an extension of Learning Task 1.6, above. The change is in the difficulty of rhythm patterns associated with repertoire at this level. Rhythm patterns are going to be more complex, so it is essential that teachers continue to break new ideas down to their most basic levels. Sequence of Activities • Repeat Sequence of Activities, as applicable, from previous learning tasks.	• Students perform patterns with a steady pulse (pizzicato or arco). • Patterns are performed with sense of meter (triple or duple) • Patterns are performed with a sense of rhythmic phrasing. • Students perform with correct relative rhythm values (macrobeat, microbeats, etc., are performed with accuracy in relation to each other)

Standards Links:

Resources and References:

158

Category 2: Musicianship Skills and Knowledge

Content Area:	2B—Rhythmic Aural Skills and Ear Training
Benchmark:	*Students perform simple and complex rhythm patterns/functions, with steady pulse/beat, correct sense of meter and metric organization and phrasing, in a variety of meters*
Learning Task:	**2.4—Students improvise rhythm patterns corresponding to Learning Tasks 2.1– 2.3**

Learning Sequences & Processes	Indicators of Success
<u>General Information, Prior Knowledge and Precursors</u> • This is an extension of Learning Task 1.8, above. The change is in the difficulty of rhythm patterns associated with repertoire at this level. Rhythm patterns are going to be more complex, so it is essential that teachers continue to break new ideas down to their most basic levels. <u>Sequence of Activities</u> • Repeat Sequence of Activities, as applicable, from previous learning tasks. See also *Creative Musicianship* for more ideas.	• Students perform patterns with a steady pulse (pizzicato or arco). • Patterns are performed with sense of meter (triple or duple) • Patterns are performed with a sense of rhythmic phrasing. • Students perform with correct relative rhythm values (macrobeat, microbeats, etc., are performed with accuracy in relation to each other)

Standards Links:	

Resources and References:	

Category 2:	**Musicianship Skills and Knowledge**
Content Area:	**2B—Rhythmic Aural Skills and Ear Training**
Benchmark:	*Students perform simple and complex rhythm patterns/functions, with steady pulse/beat, correct sense of meter and metric organization and phrasing, in a variety of meters*
Learning Task:	**3.1—Students perform rhythm patterns in asymmetrical and unusual meters**

Learning Sequences & Processes	**Indicators of Success**
General Information, Prior Knowledge and Precursors • Asymmetrical patterns are those that are a combination of duple and triple patterns, such as 5/8, 7/8, 5/16, 7/16, and so on. • Unusual meters are those that are larger combinations of meters, such as 3/16+3/16+2/16, especially when there are frequent metrical changes. • In addition to encountering the meters and patterns listed above in contemporary classical music, many ethnic styles (especially dance music) have very complex rhythm patterns (especially music of Africa and the Balkan region of Europe). • Asymmetrical rhythm patterns create challenges not only in terms correctly perceiving and performing rhythms, but also in correctly distributing the bow for proper placement for tone production and also to produce the appropriate metrical accents. Sequence of Activities • Listen to music that contains asymmetrical patterns. Examples of pieces that are entry points into asymmetrical patterns include Take Five and Blue Rondo a la Turk by Dave Brubeck, "Mars" from The Planets, by Gustav Holst, *Allegro con grazia* (Movement II) from Symphony No. 6, by Tchaikovsky. • Students should first move to asymmetrical and unusual meters, so that they develop a physical and aural perception of what the meters feel like. • As with other rhythm patterns, students should chant/sing rhythm patterns before moving to the instrument. • Once students are comfortable with vocalizing the patterns, practice open string or single-note patterns, emphasizing correct bow distribution as students perform, so that they develop a correct feel for how the bow motion needs to be compensated during performance of these patterns. • Reading and notation of the patterns should come next. Students should create their own patterns and also their own meters; this is especially interesting when students recognize that they can create an infinite number of metrical combinations. • Practice moving from symmetrical patterns and meters to asymmetrical patterns and meters.	• Students perform patterns with a steady pulse (pizzicato or arco). • Patterns are performed with sense of meter (triple or duple) • Patterns are performed with a sense of rhythmic phrasing. • Students perform with correct relative rhythm values (macrobeat, microbeats, etc., are performed with accuracy in relation to each other)

Standards Links:

Resources and References:

Category 2:	Musicianship Skills and Knowledge
Content Area:	2B—Rhythmic Aural Skills and Ear Training
Benchmark:	*Students perform simple and complex rhythm patterns/functions, with steady pulse/beat, correct sense of meter and metric organization and phrasing, in a variety of meters*
Learning Task:	3.2—Students perform rhythm patterns containing hemiolas

Learning Sequences & Processes	Indicators of Success
General Information, Prior Knowledge and Precursors • A hemiola, in simple terms, in which the feel of the meter alternates between patterns of three and two, though the time signature doesn't change, to give a feeling of 1-2-3, 1-2-3, 1-2, 1-2, 1-2. This rhythmic device is encountered in music dating back to the Greeks and is found in both Western and non-Western musical forms. Sequence of Activities • Listen to musical examples containing hemiola, such as "America" from *West Side Story*, "O Fortuna" from *Carmina Burana*, waltzes by Brahms, dances by Dvorak and Smetana, in addition to numerous folk dances. • Repeat the sequence of activities listed in Learning Task 3.2.	• Students perform patterns with a steady pulse (pizzicato or arco). • Patterns are performed with sense of meter (triple or duple) • Patterns are performed with a sense of rhythmic phrasing. • Students perform with correct relative rhythm values (macrobeat, microbeats, etc., are performed with accuracy in relation to each other)

Standards Links:

Resources and References:

Category 2:	Musicianship Skills and Knowledge
Content Area:	**2B—Rhythmic Aural Skills and Ear Training**
Benchmark:	*Students perform simple and complex rhythm patterns/functions, with steady pulse/beat, correct sense of meter and metric organization and phrasing, in a variety of meters*
Learning Task:	**3.3—Students perform rhythm patterns containing enrhythmic notation**

Learning Sequences & Processes	Indicators of Success
<u>General Information, Prior Knowledge and Precursors</u> • Enrhythmic notation is when patterns that sound the same are written differently. This is parallel to the concept of an enharmonic note (such as G♭ and F♯). Examples include four quarter-notes in 4/4 time signature and four half-notes in 4/2 time signature; three quarter-notes in 3/4 and three half-notes in 3/2. • Students begin to encounter the concept of enrhythmic notation when they perform pieces in cut-time, especially when the half-note, instead of the quarter-note becomes the macrobeat. • In Baroque and Classical music, there is inconsistent usage of time signatures, so it is important for students to understand how to accurately read and interpret time signatures such as 3/16, 4/16, and so on. <u>Sequence of Activities</u> • This reading exercise is an excellent opportunity for students to understand that rhythm notation is sometimes ambiguous. The speed of the piece may dictate the feel of the meter, apart from the time signature. The teacher should play echo patterns and show students how to notate that same pattern in two or three different ways (such as 3/8, 3/4, and 3/2). • The teacher should allow students to create their own rhythm patterns and notate those same patterns with different time signatures. • Perform familiar pieces and songs using enrhythmic notation, rather than the standard notation (e.g., perform "Twinkle, Twinkle Little Star" with quarter-notes, eight-notes, and half-notes all receiving the main pulse).	• Students perform patterns with a steady pulse (pizzicato or arco). • Patterns are performed with sense of meter (triple or duple) • Patterns are performed with a sense of rhythmic phrasing. • Students perform with correct relative rhythm values (macrobeat, microbeats, etc., are performed with accuracy in relation to each other) • Students can transition between meters and enrhythmic patterns without hesitation.

Standards Links:

Resources and References:

162

Category 2:	**Musicianship Skills and Knowledge**
Content Area:	2B—Rhythmic Aural Skills and Ear Training
Benchmark:	*Students perform simple and complex rhythm patterns/functions, with steady pulse/beat, correct sense of meter and metric organization and phrasing, in a variety of meters*
Learning Task:	**3.4—Students improvise rhythm patterns corresponding to Learning Tasks 3.1– 3.3**

Learning Sequences & Processes	Indicators of Success
<u>General Information, Prior Knowledge and Precursors</u> • This level is an extension of early improvisation skills. Students should continue to create (write and improvise) rhythm patterns that include the elements listed in Learning Tasks 1.8 and 2.4. See the *Creative Musicianship* portion of this curriculum for specific activities tied to rhythm improvisation. <u>Sequence of Activities</u> • See the Sequence of Activities for Learning Tasks 1.8 and 2.4, but use material from level 3. • Listen to improvisations that contain elements from Level 3, and have students practice improvising using hemiola and asymmetrical and unusual meters.	• Students perform patterns with a steady pulse (pizzicato or arco). • Patterns are performed with sense of meter (triple or duple) • Patterns are performed with a sense of rhythmic phrasing. • Students perform with correct relative rhythm values (macrobeat, microbeats, etc., are performed with accuracy in relation to each other).

Standards Links:

Resources and References:

Category 2:	Musicianship Skills and Knowledge
Content Area:	**2B—Rhythmic Aural Skills and Ear Training**
Benchmark:	*Students perform simple and complex rhythm patterns/functions, with steady pulse/beat, correct sense of meter and metric organization and phrasing, in a variety of meters*
Learning Task:	**4.1—Students perform rhythm patterns in irregular meters and polymeters**

Learning Sequences & Processes	Indicators of Success
General Information, Prior Knowledge and Precursors • Students will encounter music that does not follow the standard metrical division into twos or threes in music from a variety of musical practices including classical music, folk music, rock, and jazz. • In early classical music (prior to the mid-seventeenth century), pieces did not always have bar-lines, or when they did, the bar line was not always placed right before the main beat of the music. Instead, the rhythm of the piece followed the poetic meter of the lyric. Editors of early music often placed bar-lines based on their individual preferences or interpretation. However, multiple editions of a single work may reveal different bar-line placement. The concerto grosso from the Baroque era is an excellent tool for teaching this concept. • Irregular meters are sometimes called *additive* or *asymmetrical*. These meters are not repeating groups of twos or threes, but are meters where the rhythm alternates between groups of twos or threes, such as 5/8, 7/8, 9/16, etc. Very complex rhythms may be found in the folk music of southeastern Europe, particularly Bulgaria, Macedonia, Greece, and other Balkan countries. • Polymetric music is a piece that contains two simultaneously occurring, but contrasting meters in different voices (e.g., 5/8 in the first part and 4/4 in the second part). Sequence of Activities • Listen to examples of Baroque music that contains lyrics and also to Baroque (or earlier) pieces that are only instrumental. Listen, in particular, to slow movements and ask students to determine the meter of the piece based on how it is performed by the singers and/or instrumentalists. • Give students musical examples (containing both pitch and rhythm), without any bar lines. Ask them to create possible bar-line placements based on how the piece sounds or feels. • Students should compare different interpretations of a single piece. Recordings by early music ensembles may provide the best resource for comparing different styles of performance of a single work. • A second option is to select a piece that is written in an asymmetrical meter, and teach that piece to the students by ear. Practice rhythm patterns vocally or using movement exercises first, so that students internalize the rhythm. Examples of music from the classical tradition that incorporates asymmetrical meters includes Symphony No. 5, by Tchaikovsky and "Mars" from The Planets, by Gustav Holst.	• Students perform with a correct sense of phrasing and metrical accent, based on the lyric of the piece or the overall melodic structure of the phrase. • Students demonstrate different metrical options for a single phrase. • Students discuss and demonstrate understanding of why different interpretations of a single phrase are viable, or why one is better than another. • Students perform asymmetrical meters with a clear sense of rhythmic flow and direction. • Students maintain rhythmic accuracy during performances of pieces with polymeters.

Standards Links:

Resources and References:

Category 2:	Musicianship Skills and Knowledge
Content Area:	**2B—Rhythmic Aural Skills and Ear Training**
Benchmark:	*Students perform simple and complex rhythm patterns/functions, with steady pulse/beat, correct sense of meter and metric organization and phrasing, in a variety of meters*
Learning Task:	**4.2—Students perform rhythm patterns in mixed meters**

Learning Sequences & Processes	Indicators of Success
General Information, Prior Knowledge and Precursors • Mixed meters occur when composers move from one time signature/meter to another, based on the length of the melody. This is particularly found in twentieth century and later techniques, when composers allowed the meter to serve the melody, rather than the other way around. This is also similar to the idea of the irregular or asymmetrical meters from Learning Task 4.1. Some consider additive meters (unusual meters) to be another form of mixed meter. • Examples of mixed meter occur in works like *The Rite of Spring*, by Stravinsky, *The Firebird*, by Prokofiev, and "Promenade" from Pictures at an Exhibition, by Mussorgsky. Other pieces that contain hemiola are sometimes also written as mixed meters. • The ability to read enrhythmic patterns is a crucial skill when performing pieces that are in mixed meters. Sequence of Activities • Listen to examples of pieces containing mixed meter. • As done in the precious learning task (4.1), give students musical examples (containing both pitch and rhythm), without any bar lines. Ask them to create possible bar-line placements based on how the piece sounds or feels. There will be multiple possible answers. • Students should perform rhythm excerpts from selected repertoire (such as those pieces listed above) on a single note before adding the actual pitches. • Students should strive to maintain a sense of flow and fluency as they perform. There is frequently a tendency to overemphasize the down-beat when performing mixed meters, and as a result, the intent of the composer is lost. • Avoid over-emphasizing the conducting beat; the ability to perform mixed meters correctly is not a visual issue, but an aural issue. Students should be able to perform the selected patterns without requiring a conductor to keep the pulse.	• Students perform the mixed meters without hesitation between time signature changes. • Students perform the selected rhythm patterns with a clear sense of rhythmic flow and direction. Though the pulse should remain steady, the overall sense of pulse may be diminished by the metrical changes of the piece. For example, the change between duple and triple meters should be fluid (emphasizing horizontal, linear motion), rather than simply emphasizing a strong pulse on every beat of the measure (vertical motion). • Students maintain correct rhythm values between time signature changes.

Standards Links:

Resources and References:

Category 2:	Musicianship Skills and Knowledge
Content Area:	**2B—Rhythmic Aural Skills and Ear Training**
Benchmark:	*Students perform simple and complex rhythm patterns/functions, with steady pulse/beat, correct sense of meter and metric organization and phrasing, in a variety of meters*
Learning Task:	**4.3—Students perform rhythm patterns containing syncopation within a single macrobeat**

Learning Sequences & Processes	Indicators of Success
<u>General Information, Prior Knowledge and Precursors</u> • Syncopation at the elementary and intermediate levels is frequently found when there is a tie over a bar-line, or when the 2nd and 3rd beats in four-beat measure are combined. In this way, the syncopation occurs by combining several macrobeats together. • At this level, the students should perform syncopations within a single macrobeat, such as a sixteenth-eighth-sixteenth pattern in a single beat (quarter-note is the macrobeat). • Syncopation within the beat is found both in classical/Western styles of music and also in complex rhythms from ethnic dance music (including Latin, African, and other styles), jazz, ragtime, and fiddle music. • The ability to accurately perform syncopations that occur this quickly requires that students have a well-developed bow arm, and are able to play with a relaxed and balanced bow stroke. Fatigue, especially when performing repeated patterns, can be an issue for younger players. <u>Sequence of Activities</u> • Listen to examples of pieces containing syncopation within a single beat. Ragtime dances by Scott Joplin are excellent examples, as are dances like the Cakewalk, and multiple Latin dance styles. • Students may create single, repeated syncopation patterns that can serve as a "riff" for improvisation in various styles, including rock, jazz, and other forms of ethnic music. • Students should create several riffs and alternate between two or three riffs, while improvising melodies or rhythmic variations over the riff. • In order to accurately perform fast syncopations, the teacher may need to start at a very slow tempo, gradually increasing the tempo while minimizing the bow stroke motion, so that students can perform the patterns while remaining relaxed. • Find examples from works to be performed and list them on a single rhythm excerpt sheet. Ask students to perform the patterns and then identify where the patterns occur in the music.	• Students perform the mixed meters without hesitation between time signature changes. • Students perform the selected rhythm patterns with a clear sense of rhythmic flow and direction. Though the pulse should remain steady, the overall sense of pulse may be diminished by the metrical changes of the piece. For example, the change between duple and triple meters should be fluid (emphasizing horizontal, linear motion), rather than simply emphasizing a strong pulse on every beat of the measure (vertical motion). • Students maintain correct rhythm values between time signature changes.

Standards Links:

Resources and References:

Category 2: Musicianship Skills and Knowledge

Content Area:	**2B—Rhythmic Aural Skills and Ear Training**
Benchmark:	*Students perform simple and complex rhythm patterns/functions, with steady pulse/beat, correct sense of meter and metric organization and phrasing, in a variety of meters*
Learning Task:	**4.4—Students improvise rhythm patterns corresponding to Learning Tasks 4.1– 4.3**

Learning Sequences & Processes	Indicators of Success
General Information, Prior Knowledge and Precursors • This level is an extension of early improvisation skills. Students should continue to create (write and improvise) rhythm patterns that include the elements listed in Learning Tasks 1.8, 2.4, and 3.3. See the *Creative Musicianship* portion of this curriculum for specific activities tied to rhythmic improvisation. Sequence of Activities • See the Sequence of Activities for Learning Tasks 1.8, 2.4, and 3.3 but use material from level 4. • Listen to improvisations that contain elements from Level 4, and have students practice improvising using hemiola and asymmetrical and unusual meters.	• Students perform patterns with a steady pulse (pizzicato or arco). • Patterns are performed with sense of meter (triple or duple) • Patterns are performed with a sense of rhythmic phrasing. • Students perform with correct relative rhythm values (macrobeat, microbeats, etc., are performed with accuracy in relation to each other).

Standards Links:

Resources and References:

Content Area 2C—Creative Musicianship

*Students demonstrate **creative musicianship** skills at all stages of development, including the ability to improvise variations of rhythmic, melodic, and harmonic patterns, within the traditions and standards of a variety of genres and practices; arrange and compose melodies and harmonies according to specific criteria and guidelines.*

General Discussion about Creative Musicianship

Music should be an artistic, expressive, and creative activity, a means of exploring the world around us and expressing thoughts, emotions, meaning, and ideas in ways that transcend the written word. Improvisation was historically an expected ability of musicians and composers even during the earliest eras in which string instruments are found. It is well documented that the great composers of the Baroque and Classical eras (such as Bach, Corelli, Mozart, Beethoven, and others) were outstanding improvisers themselves and expected that those who would perform their music would also display their virtuosity as masters not only of the written music, but also in the area of improvisation. Early musical forms, such as the toccata, theme and variations, sonatas, and the concerto grosso, contained sections where the musicians was expected to improvise or provide ornamentation and variation to the originally composed melody. During the nineteenth and twentieth centuries, this historic emphasis on the development of a musician's ability to improvise and add one's own ideas and thoughts to a composition (or even to compose original or arrange existing works) slowly decreased as teachers and musicians within the classical tradition became more focused on "re-creating" music, rather than creating music. Improvisation and creative musicianship remained a strong part of non-classical musical styles, such as jazz, rock, folk, and various forms of world music. At the beginning of the twenty-first century, our profession has seen a resurgence in creative musicianship through the increasing popularity of eclectic strings styles, in addition to an increased understanding of the importance of creativity for performers at all stages of development.

Creative Musicianship comprises a large number of potential musical skills and knowledge, including those needed for improvisation, composing, arranging, and musical expression. Because this curriculum focuses on the performance of string instruments within ensemble settings, we have narrowed this presentation of creative musicianship to skills and knowledge in four primary areas: rhythmic, tonal (melodic and harmonic), textural, and compositional.

In addition, we have added a fifth element called *creative leadership*, which is included here because each time students are encouraged to assume a position of leadership, they are compelled to think for themselves, hone their communication skills, and have an experience of empowerment. In the case of assuming the position of conductor, that students gain first-hand knowledge of the challenges and craft involved in that role; this can potentially change their perception of the string director. This unit blends improvisation and leadership, while highlighting the lessons students have already mastered in the earlier units on creativity.

Learning Tasks

1.1   Rhythmic: Students derive rhythm patterns from speech and environmental sounds and link them with the motion of the bow-hand

1.2   Tonal (Melodic & Harmonic): Students create one-note solos against a class-generated accompaniment

1.3   Textural: Students reproduce sound effects from their environment on their instruments (exploratory focus)

1.4   Compositional: Students invent scoring techniques based on common objectives

1.5   Creative Leadership: Students invent their own physical language for conducting

2.1   Rhythmic: Students teach each other short original rhythm phrases through call-and-response

2.2   Tonal (Melodic & Harmonic): Students use the root, third, and fifth of a chord to solo over student-generated accompaniment

2.3   Textural: Students translate a visual or experiential narrative into original sounds on their instruments (music as storytelling)

2.4   Compositional: Students add traditional notation into their original scores

2.5   Creative Leadership: Students rehearse conducting the group with individually created hand signals

3.1   Rhythmic: Students layer individual rhythm phrases to create an original group piece

3.2   Tonal (Melodic & Harmonic): Students create solos using the notes of the scale as stepping-stones between chord tones

3.3   Textural: Students translate a visual or experiential narrative into original sounds on their instruments and add rhythm components (rhythmic focus)

3.4   Compositional: Students add a second instrument to their original scores

3.5   Creative Leadership: Student conductors lead extemporaneous sound stories using nonverbal signals

4.1   Rhythmic: Students analyze rhythm phrases for tonal content and improvise over class-generated accompaniments

4.2   Tonal (Melodic & Harmonic): Students create solos using three scales over class-generated three-chord harmonic motion

4.3   Textural: Students improvise descriptive stories, including melody and harmony (harmonic focus)

4.4   Compositional: Students add third and fourth parts to their original scores

4.5   Creative Leadership: Students combine original scores with student-conducted improvised sections

Category 2:	Musicianship Skills and Knowledge
Content Area:	2C—Creative Musicianship
Benchmark:	*Students demonstrate **creative musicianship** skills at all stages of development, including the ability to improvise variations of rhythmic, melodic, and harmonic patterns, within the traditions and standards of a variety of genres and practices; arrange and compose melodies and harmonies according to specific criteria and guidelines*
Learning Task:	**1.1—Rhythmic: Students derive rhythm patterns from speech and environmental sounds and link them to the motion of the bow-hand**

Learning Sequences & Processes	Indicators of Success
General Information, Prior Knowledge and Precursors • See Content Area 2B—Rhythmic Aural Skills and Ear Training for units on basic rhythm skills • The part of the brain that processes rhythm is separate from the part of the brain that processes tonal (pitch) elements. For that reason, it is essential that students learn and practice rhythmic ideas separate from their melodic partners Sequence of Activities • Teacher invites class to call out examples of rhythmic sounds from their homes and from nature (e.g., a dripping faucet, the clothes washer, a woodpecker, etc.) • Teacher invites each student to emulate the example they've chosen vocally and/or via tapping, clapping, thumping, stamping. • Teacher chooses one of the examples and challenges the class to try to imitate it through pizzicato and then arco on their instruments. • Teacher invites a student to describe a dream, something the student did over the weekend, or something the student will do after school. Teacher picks out one sentence from the description that has a workable rhythmic shape and invites class to repeat the sentence a few times until it becomes a rhythmic chant. • Teacher invites class to substitute nonsense words into the rhythmic chant, and then to imitate the rhythmic phrase through clapping, tapping, pizzicato, and bowing. • Optional: Using call-and-response, teacher can apply accents and/or dynamics to the phrase to demonstrate the role these variables play in reshaping the feel of the phrase; students can take turns doing this as well.	• Student can emulate vocally (or via clapping or tapping) simple, short rhythmic phrases found in nature and speech patterns

Standards Links:

Resources and References:

Category 2:	Musicianship Skills and Knowledge
Content Area:	2C—Creative Musicianship
Benchmark:	*Students demonstrate **creative musicianship** skills at all stages of development, including the ability to improvise variations of rhythmic, melodic, and harmonic patterns, within the traditions and standards of a variety of genres and practices; arrange and compose melodies and harmonies according to specific criteria and guidelines*
Learning Task:	**1.2—Tonal (Melodic & Harmonic): Students create one-note solos against a class-generated accompaniments**

Learning Sequences & Processes	Indicators of Success
<u>General Information, Prior Knowledge and Precursors</u> • When musicians improvise, they create a melodic/rhythmic idea in their musical brain, and then externalize that idea onto their instrument. • In order to successfully accomplish this art of translation, the player must first learn how to identify pitch in relationship to the tonal range of their instrument. • Even though this learning sequence doesn't directly foster the creative process, it provides the tools through which the creative psyche can channel individually crafted musical ideas. • The six basic note values used in this task are: half-notes, quarter-notes, quarter-note triplets, eight-notes, eighth-note triplets, and sixteenth-notes. <u>Sequence of Activities</u> • Teacher chooses a key that's related to current repertoire. • Teacher explains that, like the skeleton and muscles that define the human body, chord tones are notes that help define the melody and are the building blocks for the accompaniment. • Teacher defines the chord tones of the chosen key (the root, third, and fifth) by first using call-and-response to establish the sound; half of the group can sing, pluck, or bow the tonic, while the other half sings, plucks, or plays each of the chord tones by ear against the tonic; repeat this exercise while naming the fingerings; repeat this exercise while naming the notes, and then switch the groups and repeat. Teacher can point out that each chord tone skips a note of the scale and that these intervals are called thirds if these topics are new to the class. • Teacher divides the group into three sub-groups and assigns one chord tone to each group to be sung or bowed as a group in order to sound out the full chord (this exercise can be applied to major, minor, and diminished depending on level). • Each student is given four beats to make up a rhythmic solo using one note of their choice from the chord tones.	• Students are able to create musical ideas in front of the group with confidence and ease • Students can combine rhythmic skills with chord-tone awareness • Students can maintain structural awareness while improvising by tracking four-beat phrases

Standards Links:

Resources and References:

Category 2:	Musicianship Skills and Knowledge

Content Area:	**2C—Creative Musicianship**
Benchmark:	*Students demonstrate **creative musicianship** skills at all stages of development, including the ability to improvise variations of rhythmic, melodic, and harmonic patterns, within the traditions and standards of a variety of genres and practices; arrange and compose melodies and harmonies according to specific criteria and guidelines*
Learning Task:	**1.3—<u>Textural</u>: Students reproduce sound effects from the home environment on their instruments (exploratory focus)**

Learning Sequences & Processes	Indicators of Success

<u>General Information, Prior Knowledge and Precursors</u>
 	
• Textural improvisation includes elements of music that relate directly to things like timbre, articulation, shape, complexity of the piece, and so on.
 	
<u>Sequence of Activities</u>
 	
• Teacher invites students to choose something from their home environment that makes a sound (inanimate or living) and imitate that sound on their instrument. Students can use their voices or anything that generates sound in their immediate environment if they so choose.
 	
• Teacher challenges the class to try to identify the household sound represented.
 	
• Note: Teacher can demonstrate an example first; this exercise can also be applied to environmental or imaginative items like:
 	
  • "What does the grass growing sound like?"
 	
  • "What does an aging flower sound like?"
 	
  • "What does a light bulb sound like when it is turned on and emits light?"
 	
  • "How about just after you turn off the electricity?"
	• Students learn to translate every-day surroundings into sounds on their instruments.
	
	• Students explore the instrument as a vehicle for original sounds.
	
	• Students have an opportunity to perform solo in front of the group in a fun, unselfconscious manner.
	
	• Students have an opportunity to explore their instruments without concern for "right" and "wrong" technique.
	
	• Students can successfully translate sights and sounds from their home environment onto their instrument
	
	• Students are able to create musical ideas in front of the group with confidence and ease

Standards Links:

Resources and References:

Category 2: Musicianship Skills and Knowledge

Content Area:	2C—Creative Musicianship
Benchmark:	*Students demonstrate **creative musicianship** skills at all stages of development, including the ability to improvise variations of rhythmic, melodic, and harmonic patterns, within the traditions and standards of a variety of genres and practices; arrange and compose melodies and harmonies according to specific criteria and guidelines*
Learning Task:	**1.4—Compositional: Students invent scoring techniques based on common objectives**

Learning Sequences & Processes	Indicators of Success
Sequence of Activities • Teacher initiates a class discussion regarding why music notation was invented. For instance, thousands of Irish fiddle tunes were taught by ear for centuries and were first notated only fairly recently in the history of Irish fiddling. Why did some cultures invent music notation (e.g., the Chinese tablature system) while others maintained an aural tradition? • Teacher invites the class to initiate a list on the board of the information a written system endeavors to communicate to the musician or ensemble (e.g., pitch, harmony, rhythm, dynamics, and tempo should be included in this list). • Teacher hands out large pieces of paper and crayons or colored pencils and invites students to create their own scores using color, pictures, and any other method of communication they choose to score a one-minute piece of music. Students are not allowed to use staff notation. • Students exchange their scores and take turns playing each other's pieces. • Note: interpretations of scores will be fairly textural and will vary depending upon the skills and interpretation of each player.	• Students apply an authentic understanding of the purpose of music notation to design their own, original method of written musical communication. • Students share their ideas and learn from each other • Students explore new visual and aural ideas

Standards Links:

Resources and References:

Category 2:	Musicianship Skills and Knowledge
Content Area:	2C—Creative Musicianship
Benchmark:	*Students demonstrate **creative musicianship** skills at all stages of development, including the ability to improvise variations of rhythmic, melodic, and harmonic patterns, within the traditions and standards of a variety of genres and practices; arrange and compose melodies and harmonies according to specific criteria and guidelines*
Learning Task:	**1.5—Creative Leadership: Students invent their own physical language for conducting**

Learning Sequences & Processes	Indicators of Success
Sequence of Activities • Teacher initiates a class discussion about the role of the conductor, and the tasks they need to fulfill. • Students create a list on the board that describes the conductor's role (e.g., establishment of tempo, using the gesture to indicate meter, maintaining the cohesiveness of ensemble, dynamics, and interpretation of each piece). • Students create hand signals for changes in pitch (low, medium, high), bow techniques (depending on level of the student, this could include tremolo, pizzicato, spiccato, legato, etc.) and any hand signals they think might help communicate sounds they've explored during the rhythmic and textural Creative Musicianship units.	• Students are comfortable assuming a role of leadership. • Students are able to create spontaneous musical performances with confidence and ease by guiding the whole group. • Students have a more experiential idea of the role of the conductor in the success of a group's performance.

Standards Links:

Resources and References:

Category 2:	Musicianship Skills and Knowledge
Content Area:	2C—Creative Musicianship
Benchmark:	*Students demonstrate **creative musicianship** skills at all stages of development, including the ability to improvise variations of rhythmic, melodic, and harmonic patterns, within the traditions and standards of a variety of genres and practices; arrange and compose melodies and harmonies according to specific criteria and guidelines*
Learning Task:	**2.1—Rhythmic: Students teach each other short, original rhythmic phrases through call-and-response**

Learning Sequences & Processes	Indicators of Success
General Information, Prior Knowledge and Precursors • See Content Area 2B—Rhythmic Aural Skills and Ear Training for units on basic rhythmic skills. • The part of the brain that processes rhythm is separate from the part of the brain that processes tonal (pitch) elements. • For that reason, it is essential that students learn and practice rhythmic ideas separate from their melodic partners. Sequence of Activities • Students sit or stand in a circle and create a walking quarter note by marching in place, placing a stronger emphasis on the first of each group of four steps (and/or teacher can sound out a drum beat or use a back-up track). • Each student individually initiates a rhythmic phrase vocally on an agreed-upon sound and any sustained pitch they choose ("la" or anything the group chooses) that lasts 4 beats; the group sings the phrase back, and the student repeats it a second time, as does the group. • This exercise can be repeated using pizzicato or arco on an open string. • This exercise can be broadened to include the root, third, and fifth of the key that relates to a piece of music the class is about to work on after the rhythmic part of the exercise has been successfully rendered. • The rhythmic part of the brain is in a separate location from the center for pitch; it is extremely useful to introduce activities that constantly separate and partner these two brain functions. • Generating a rhythmic phrase requires the ability to audiate and actualize a short series of rhythmic values; repeating the phrase a second time ensures engagement of auditory memory as well as the analytical skills necessary to evaluate the components of that phrase.	• Students are capable of generating a unique rhythmic phrase and are also able to repeat it a second time in a role of leadership. • Students are capable of hearing diverse rhythmic phrases and repeating them back while walking a quarter-note pulse. • Students learn from each other through imagination and repetition.

Standards Links:

Resources and References:

Category 2:	Musicianship Skills and Knowledge
Content Area:	2C—Creative Musicianship
Benchmark:	*Students demonstrate **creative musicianship** skills at all stages of development, including the ability to improvise variations of rhythmic, melodic, and harmonic patterns, within the traditions and standards of a variety of genres and practices; arrange and compose melodies and harmonies according to specific criteria and guidelines*
Learning Task:	**2.2—Tonal (Melodic & Harmonic): Students use the root, third, and fifth of a chord to solo over student-generated accompaniments**

Learning Sequences & Processes	Indicators of Success
Sequence of Activities • Teacher chooses a key that's related to current repertoire but different than the key used in Learning Task 1.2. • Teacher challenges students to find the third and fifth of the new key. • Teacher divides the group into three sub-groups and assigns one chord tone to each group to be sung, plucked repetitively, or bowed as a group in order to sound out the full chord (this exercise can be repeated and applied to major, minor, and/or diminished depending on level). Optional: the class can create a rhythmic phrase or layer three phrases together to use for the accompaniment. • Each student is given four beats to make up a melody extemporaneously using <u>all three</u> notes from the chord and employing any rhythmic ideas he or she chooses. This exercise can be implemented vocally, with pizzicato, and/or bowed. • This exercise can be applied over time to all twelve keys. • Note: Teacher can combine this learning task with Learning Task 4.2 by challenging students to couple their chord tone accompaniment with a rhythmic ostinato (students can create a multi-layering of ostinatos, or choose to play an ostinato in unison).	• Students are familiar with the definition of major chords and can track their chord tones while improvising. • Students can track four-beat phrases while improvising with pre-designated chord tones—a skill necessary to improvisation over most American folk, blues, jazz, and rock structures.

Standards Links:

Resources and References:

Category 2:	Musicianship Skills and Knowledge
Content Area:	**2C—Creative Musicianship**
Benchmark:	*Students demonstrate **creative musicianship** skills at all stages of development, including the ability to improvise variations of rhythmic, melodic, and harmonic patterns, within the traditions and standards of a variety of genres and practices; arrange and compose melodies and harmonies according to specific criteria and guidelines*
Learning Task:	**2.3—**<u>Textural</u>**: Students translate a visual or experiential narrative into original sounds on their instruments (music as storytelling)**

Learning Sequences & Processes	Indicators of Success
<u>Sequence of Activities</u> • Teacher divides class into smaller groups. • Teacher gives students ten minutes to create a short story and plan how they will describe this story through sound. • Teacher encourages students to create sounds with their instruments, voices or anything that generates sound in their immediate environment to illustrate the story. • Teacher encourages students to use their bows and instruments any way they want as long as they do not harm them. • Teacher sends each group to a corner of the room and advises them to whisper so that other groups can't hear them plan. They can decide on what each member of the group will do, but they are not allowed to rehearse. The rest of the class will try to identify their story after they perform it. • Teacher walks from group to group to monitor progress. If a group is stuck, teacher can appoint a group leader to help facilitate planning. • Note: It's useful to give examples. For instance, the story can be something totally original, based on a dream, based on an experience someone has had, or be the story of an eco-system (e.g., a farm, the inner workings of a cell, the solar system, a thunder shower, etc.). • Optional: Teacher can assign a story to the entire group the first time around for the purpose of demonstration.	• Students work together as a team to plan and perform an improvised performance. • Students learn to translate every-day sounds onto their instruments. • Students explore the instrument as a vehicle for original sounds. • Students have an opportunity to perform solo and as a group in front of the class in a fun, unselfconscious manner. • Students have an opportunity to explore their instruments without concern for "right" and "wrong" technique. • Students can successfully translate sights and sounds from their home environment onto their instrument • Students are able to create musical ideas in front of the group with confidence and ease

Standards Links:

Resources and References:

Category 2:	Musicianship Skills and Knowledge
Content Area:	2C—Creative Musicianship
Benchmark:	*Students demonstrate **creative musicianship** skills at all stages of development, including the ability to improvise variations of rhythmic, melodic, and harmonic patterns, within the traditions and standards of a variety of genres and practices; arrange and compose melodies and harmonies according to specific criteria and guidelines*
Learning Task:	2.4—Compositional: Students add traditional notation into their original scores

Learning Sequences & Processes	Indicators of Success
<u>Sequence of Activities</u> • Teacher provides class with staff paper and asks them to mark out four measures, leaving room for four parts. • Teacher invites students to pick a clef, a key and type of scale (major, minor, modal, etc.) they wish to write in, and to invent a melody. The melody should be four measures long. • Students can cut out the melody and add it into their score or they can place a symbol in their original score (created during Category 2C Learning Task 4.1—Composition) that refers player to the melody on this separate page. • Teacher encourages students to figure out a way to join the melody into the ideas they have already created. • Students exchange melodies and/or entire scores to perform one another's ideas.	• Students apply an authentic understanding of the purpose of music notation to design their own, original method of written musical communication. • Students share their ideas and learn from each other. • Students explore new visual and aural ideas.

Standards Links:

Resources and References:

Category 2:	Musicianship Skills and Knowledge
Content Area:	2C—Creative Musicianship
Benchmark:	*Students demonstrate **creative musicianship** skills at all stages of development, including the ability to improvise variations of rhythmic, melodic, and harmonic patterns, within the traditions and standards of a variety of genres and practices; arrange and compose melodies and harmonies according to specific criteria and guidelines*
Learning Task:	**2.5—Creative Leadership: Students rehearse conducting the group with individually created hand signals**

Learning Sequences & Processes	Indicators of Success
<u>General Information, Prior Knowledge and Precursors</u> • Content Area 2C—Creative Musicianship—Textural Learning Tasks <u>Sequence of Activities</u> • Teacher explains that students will practice skills they will need to perform improvised pieces of music that are created through the imagination of each volunteer conductor. • Students take turns conducting a pulse of their determination, changes in tempo, and changes in volume utilizing the hand signals they created in Learning Task 1.5. • Teacher highlights techniques that achieve the greatest success with the group. It often looks easy to conduct and many students will realize, once they assume the position of leadership, that it's far more challenging than they thought. Teacher can stand next to student volunteers and coach them, while respecting and reinforcing their original ideas.	• Students feel comfortable stepping into a position of leadership. • Students are able to communicate their ideas through physical gesture and achieve the results they seek. • Student conductors are able to conceptualize musical ideas and conduct those ideas successfully. • Students have a more experiential idea of the role of the conductor in the success of a group's performance.

Standards Links:

Resources and References:

Category 2:	**Musicianship Skills and Knowledge**
Content Area:	2C—Creative Musicianship
Benchmark:	*Students demonstrate **creative musicianship** skills at all stages of development, including the ability to improvise variations of rhythmic, melodic, and harmonic patterns, within the traditions and standards of a variety of genres and practices; arrange and compose melodies and harmonies according to specific criteria and guidelines*
Learning Task:	**3.1—Rhythmic: Students layer individual rhythm phrases to create an original group piece**

Learning Sequences & Processes	Indicators of Success
<u>General Information, Prior Knowledge and Precursors</u> • See Content Area 2B—Rhythmic Aural Skills and Ear Training for units on basic rhythmic skills. • See Creative Musicianship Learning Task 2.1. <u>Sequence of Activities</u> • Students sit or stand in a circle and create a walking quarter note by marching in place, placing a stronger emphasis on the first of each group of four steps (and/or teacher can sound out a drum beat or use a back-up track). • One-by-one, each student layers in a rhythmic phrase vocally that lasts four beats, using any sound or single pitch they choose, and repeats their phrase over and over again, until the entire group is layered in, and has turned into a human "rhythm machine." • This exercise can be repeated using pizzicato or arco on an open string. • This exercise can be repeated using one, two, three, and four pitches at a time (vocally and/or instrumentally). The class can agree upon these pitches or generate them randomly. The combinations of pitches can be discussed after each rhythm machine is created in relationship to repertoire (primary chord tones from a piece of music), chord theory (as a tool to introduce them to the sound of major or minor three- or four-part chord), or blues/jazz improvisation (chord tones from a specific piece you wish to lead into for improvisation). • Note: if the group has trouble keeping a steady beat, use an external device (drum beat or back-up track) to help hold them to a steady pulse.	• Students are able to generate unique rhythmic phrases that layer together as a group. • Students are able to sustain a steady beat without speeding up or slowing down while repeating individual ideas as a group.

Standards Links:

Resources and References:

Category 2: Musicianship Skills and Knowledge

Content Area:	2C—Creative Musicianship
Benchmark:	*Students demonstrate **creative musicianship** skills at all stages of development, including the ability to improvise variations of rhythmic, melodic, and harmonic patterns, within the traditions and standards of a variety of genres and practices; arrange and compose melodies and harmonies according to specific criteria and guidelines*
Learning Task:	**3.2—Tonal (Melodic & Harmonic): Students create solos using the chord tones and the notes of the scale as stepping-stones between chord tones**

Learning Sequences & Processes	Indicators of Success
General Information, Prior Knowledge and Precursors • See Content Area 2A, Learning Tasks 3.1 through 3.4 for chromatic exercises. Sequence of Activities • Teacher chooses a key or invites class to choose a key. • Students review the root, third, and fifth of the key. • Teacher challenges class to play the scale octave to octave and back again; students repeat this exercise starting on the second note of the scale and playing through to the ninth and back again; then from the third to the tenth, and so on, until they've initiated a seven-note scale from each of its seven scale tones. This helps students feel comfortable hearing and visualizing the notes across the fingerboard in varying contexts. • Teacher divides the group into four sections and assigns one chord tone per group; the fourth group will sing or play the scale against the three sustained chord tones, starting from each degree of the scale. • Exercise can be repeated by rotating each group's role in the exercise. • Class discusses dissonance versus agreement based on the sounds they've just created. • Teacher challenges the fourth group to sing, pluck, or play the notes of the scale by rearranging the order of the notes and experimenting with repetition and rhythmic ideas, with the agreement that scale tones (and chromatic passing tones if the class is ready) will be used like ascending and descending stepladders to carry the musical idea home to any of the three chord tones. The groups can keep rotating so that each group has an opportunity to solo while fulfilling this assignment.	• Students can track chord tones while using scale tones as stepping-stones. • Students are aware of notes that sound dissonant versus agreeable due to their placement within the scale when played against a chordal accompaniment.

Standards Links:

Resources and References:

Category 2:	Musicianship Skills and Knowledge
Content Area:	2C—Creative Musicianship
Benchmark:	*Students demonstrate creative musicianship skills at all stages of development, including the ability to improvise variations of rhythmic, melodic, and harmonic patterns, within the traditions and standards of a variety of genres and practices; arrange and compose melodies and harmonies according to specific criteria and guidelines*
Learning Task:	**3.3—Textural: Students translate a visual or experiential narrative into original sounds on their instruments and add rhythmic components to their piece (rhythmic focus)**

Learning Sequences & Processes	Indicators of Success
General Information, Prior Knowledge and Precursors • See Content Area 2C—Creative Musicianship Rhythmic Creativity Learning Tasks. • See Content Area 2B—Rhythmic Aural Skills and Ear Training for units on basic rhythmic skills. Sequence of Activities • Teacher follows protocol in Learning Task 2.3 (Textural Improvisation) and adds the following: • Students are instructed to embed an image or add an aspect to their sound story that requires a rhythmic pulse or rhythmic phrase. This rhythmic aspect must include at least half the group in any manner they choose, and has to be performed without rehearsal, and without a conductor. • Example: Students perform a forest with animal and plant sounds; a storm moves in and the rain drips off a tree branch and hits a tree stump in a rhythmic pattern that is first barely audible, gradually becomes louder and fuller, and then subsides as the storm moves away. Meanwhile, we hear the sounds of the storm and the response of the animals in the forest.	• Students experiment with textural sounds combined with a rhythmic pulse. • Students learn how to spontaneously create an agreed-upon rhythmic pulse or phrase and perform it in unison without a conductor. • Students work together in small ensembles. • Students create improvised pieces of music that describe events and stories. • Students translate a visual or experiential narrative into original sounds on their instruments.

Standards Links:	

Resources and References:	

Category 2: Musicianship Skills and Knowledge

Content Area:	2C—Creative Musicianship
Benchmark:	*Students demonstrate **creative musicianship** skills at all stages of development, including the ability to improvise variations of rhythmic, melodic, and harmonic patterns, within the traditions and standards of a variety of genres and practices; arrange and compose melodies and harmonies according to specific criteria and guidelines*
Learning Task:	**3.4—Compositional: Students add a second instrument to their original scores**

Learning Sequences & Processes	Indicators of Success
General Information, Prior Knowledge and Precursors • See Content Area 2C—Creative Musicianship Compositional Learning Tasks 1.4 and 2.4. • See Content Area 2D—Music Literacy. • See Content Area 2C—Rhythmic Creativity. Sequence of Activities • Teacher invites students to add a second four-measure part that compliments the melody they composed during Learning Task 2.4. • Depending on level, students can be challenged to add a parallel harmony part on through to more complex harmonic ideas, counterpoint, etc. • The second part can be for any instrument they choose (e.g., two violins, two violas, two cellos, two basses, or mixed ensemble) • Students partner with each other in groups of two to perform one another's ideas.	• Students create a second melodic/harmonic line that compliments their original melody. • Students share their ideas and learn from each other. • Students explore new visual and aural ideas.

Standards Links:

Resources and References:

Category 2:	Musicianship Skills and Knowledge
Content Area:	2C—Creative Musicianship
Benchmark:	*Students demonstrate **creative musicianship** skills at all stages of development, including the ability to improvise variations of rhythmic, melodic, and harmonic patterns, within the traditions and standards of a variety of genres and practices; arrange and compose melodies and harmonies according to specific criteria and guidelines*
Learning Task:	**3.5—Creative Leadership: Student conductors lead extemporaneous sound stories using nonverbal signals**

Learning Sequences & Processes	Indicators of Success
General Information, Prior Knowledge and Precursors • See Content Area 2C—Creative Musicianship Creative Leadership Learning Tasks 1.5 and 2.5. Sequence of Activities • Teacher presents a short story or (preferably) leads group in creating a story. This story can be built on a chosen theme or created extemporaneously: "Once upon a time…" and then call on students to fill in, event by event. Note: Successful stories from the Textural Creativity section can be utilized. • Student conductor facilitates non-verbally by leading group in a sung/plucked/bowed representation of the story, using self-invented hand signals and assigning roles in the story to individuals and sub-groups (or the total group), at will. This is all done once the piece has begun, not beforehand. • Teacher highlights techniques that achieved the greatest success with the group after each volunteer conducts their version of the story. • Teacher revisits moments in each student's performance that didn't work and rehearses more effective techniques by eliciting suggestions from the group.	• Students feel comfortable stepping into a position of leadership. • Students are able to communicate their ideas through physical gesture and achieve the results they seek. • Student conductors are able to conceptualize musical ideas and conduct those ideas successfully. • Students have a more experiential idea of the role of the conductor in the success of a group's performance.

Standards Links:	

Resources and References:	

Category 2: Musicianship Skills and Knowledge

Content Area:	**2C—Creative Musicianship**
Benchmark:	*Students demonstrate **creative musicianship** skills at all stages of development, including the ability to improvise variations of rhythmic, melodic, and harmonic patterns, within the traditions and standards of a variety of genres and practices; arrange and compose melodies and harmonies according to specific criteria and guidelines*
Learning Task:	**4.1—Rhythmic: Students analyze rhythmic phrases for tonal content and improvise over class-generated accompaniments**

Learning Sequences & Processes	Indicators of Success
General Information, Prior Knowledge and Precursors • See Content Area 2B—Rhythmic Aural Skills and Ear Training for units on basic rhythmic skills. • See Content Area 2C—Creative Musicianship Rhythmic Learning Tasks 1.1, 2.1, and 3.1. Sequence of Activities • Teacher explains that a catchy, short melodic/rhythmic phrase that repeats is called an ostinato in classical music, a riff in blues, jazz, and rock, and clave in Latin music; and that each style of music has its own preference for the type of scale, the key it's in, and the rhythmic content. • Teacher presents examples of spicy rhythmic and melodic phrases from classical, rock, blues, jazz, and Latin styles (derive phrases from class repertoire, bass lines, and a scan of literature on iTunes or CD; this can also take the shape of an assignment by asking each student to bring in a musical example of a piece that has a short, repeating musical phrase that contains catchy rhythmic and melodic ideas). • Teacher teaches a riff by ear using call-and-response, note-by-note, until the class is comfortable with the phrase; teacher repeats this process with several other riffs from class repertoire and from different styles. • Teacher leads a class discussion re: the types of rhythm patterns used in the patterns they've just learned, the note values, and how those patterns are intertwined with melodic lines to create a successful, catchy phrase. • Teacher invites students to create their own phrases by 1) choosing one of the examples they've just learned, leaving the rhythms intact, and creating their own pitch-to-pitch motion (new melodies); and 2) leaving the melodies intact and changing the rhythms. • Teacher chooses one of the patterns and invites students to figure out what kind of scale they would use if they were going to make up a melody or an overlapping phrase against it. Half the class can sing, pluck, or play the pattern while the other half experiments to find notes that sounds good against the pattern, and then the two groups can switch roles until everyone has found at least one pitch that compliments the pattern. Teacher can compile their findings and give a name to the scale they've "unearthed." • Teacher chooses a successful result from the student-created ostinatos and invites the whole class to play it repetitively after analyzing the scale tones that sound most successful against it; teacher then challenges students (one-by-one or in small groups) to make up melodies on the spot over the repeating phrase.	• Students generate rhythmic phrases coupled with one—on up to—four pitches. • Students are introduced to the concept of a riff (blues, jazz, rock terminology), ostinato (classical terminology), or clave (Latin terminology) as a basis for composition, accompaniment, or soloing. • Students gain confidence as soloists through a structured, supportive exercise.

Standards Links:

Resources and References:

Level: **Advanced**

Category 2:	Musicianship Skills and Knowledge
Content Area:	**2C—Creative Musicianship**
Benchmark:	*Students demonstrate **creative musicianship** skills at all stages of development, including the ability to improvise variations of rhythmic, melodic, and harmonic patterns, within the traditions and standards of a variety of genres and practices; arrange and compose melodies and harmonies according to specific criteria and guidelines*
Learning Task:	**4.2—Tonal (Melodic & Harmonic): Students create solos using three scales over class-generated three-chord harmonic motion**

Learning Sequences & Processes	Indicators of Success
General Information, Prior Knowledge and Precursors • See Content Area 2A—Tonal Aural Skills and Ear Training, Learning Task 3.3. • Practice exercises from Content Area 2C—Creative Musicianship Tonal Learning Tasks 1.2, 2.2, and 3.2 before doing this exercise. Sequence of Activities • Teacher or students choose a key. • Students march or clap in 4/4 time with an emphasis on the first beat while they name the root note of each of the following chords: I, IV, V, I (e.g., If you've chosen the key of G, then they will say "G" as they march out four beats, then "C" as they march out 4 beats, then "D" as they march out 4 beats, and then "G" again, as they march out 4 beats. • Repeat this exercise and challenge students to sing the pitches as they name them. • Repeat this exercise and challenge students to pluck or play the pitches as they name them. • Repeat this exercise, and ask students to name the root and third of each of the three keys as they march. Then sing and name them. Then pluck or play and name them. • Repeat this exercise and add in the fifth of the key. • Note: you can also use a computer-run accompaniment from Band-in-a-Box or Garage Band as they practice the above steps. • Review the scales for each of the three keys. • Divide the group in half and challenge half the group to play the root notes while marching as the other half improvises creating melodic/rhythmic ideas using the appropriate scale over each chord. • Switch the groups so that the accompanying group now has a chance to solo and visa versa. • Divide the group into three sub-groups and give each group a chord tone (e.g., Group 1 plays the root of each of the three chords, Group 2 plays the third, etc., so that the appropriate three chord tones (root, third, and fifth) are sounded out into the room over the appropriate chord (I, IV, V, I), allocating four beats per chord; point to individuals and invite them to solo for four bars across the form on their own. If they say "no," assign them a partner and perform the exercise in groups of two. Remind them to use the appropriate scale for each chord. • Note: you can invite the class to come up with an interesting rhythmic groove to use for the accompaniment rather than holding long tones.	• Students are capable of tracking three chords over a four-bar structure. • Students are capable of applying the appropriate chord tones and scale tones over each of those chords across the four-bar structure. • Students are able to improvise using diverse rhythmic/melodic ideas while maintaining clarity about the structural requirements of the exercise.

Standards Links:

Resources and References:

Category 2: Musicianship Skills and Knowledge

Content Area:	2C—Creative Musicianship
Benchmark:	*Students demonstrate **creative musicianship** skills at all stages of development, including the ability to improvise variations of rhythmic, melodic, and harmonic patterns, within the traditions and standards of a variety of genres and practices; arrange and compose melodies and harmonies according to specific criteria and guidelines*
Learning Task:	**4.3—Textural: Groups improvise descriptive stories; each group must include a melody and harmony line at some point within the story**

Learning Sequences & Processes	Indicators of Success

General Information, Prior Knowledge and Precursors
 	
• See Content Area 2C—Creative Musicianship Learning Task 3.3.
• See Content Area 2D—Music Literacy.
 	
Sequence of Activities
 	
• Teacher follows protocol in Learning Task 3.3 (Textural Improvisation) and adds the following:
 	
   • Students are instructed to embed a melody and at least one harmony part in the performance. This component can be planned, but has to be performed without rehearsal, and without a conductor.
 	
   • Note: Depending on the level of the group, teacher can keep it as simple and as specific as 1) somewhere within the story, one individual will make up a short melody that they repeat; 2) another member of the group will pick up the melody by ear, repeat it three times, and then harmonize a third above the melody in parallel motion. Or, the teacher can challenge each group to create more complex interactions melodically/harmonically based on earlier learning tasks and experience developing mastery of those lessons.
	• Students perform using textural sounds combined with melody and harmony.
	
	• Students work together in small ensembles.
	
	• Students create improvised pieces of music that describe events and stories.
	
	• Students translate a visual or experiential narrative into original sounds on their instruments.

Standards Links:

Resources and References:

Category 2:	Musicianship Skills and Knowledge
Content Area:	2C—Creative Musicianship
Benchmark:	*Students demonstrate **creative musicianship** skills at all stages of development, including the ability to improvise variations of rhythmic, melodic, and harmonic patterns, within the traditions and standards of a variety of genres and practices; arrange and compose melodies and harmonies according to specific criteria and guidelines*
Learning Task:	**4.4—Compositional: Students add a third and fourth part to their original scores**

Learning Sequences & Processes	Indicators of Success
General Information, Prior Knowledge and Precursors • See Content Area 2C—Creative Musicianship Compositional Learning Tasks 1.4, 2.4, and 3.4. • See Content Area 2C—Creative Musicianship Rhythmic Learning Tasks. • See Content Area 2D—Music Literacy. Sequence of Activities • Teacher invites students to add a third and fourth four-measure part that compliments the melody and harmony parts they composed during Learning Tasks 2.4 and 3.4. • Depending on level, students can be challenged to add a parallel harmony part on through to more complex harmonic ideas, counterpoint, etc. • The third and fourth parts can be for any instrument they choose (e.g., four violins, four violas, four cellos, four basses, or mixed ensemble). • Students partner with each other in groups of four to perform one another's ideas. • Students perform entire creative score, including notated parts. • Note: By combining this process with other Learning Tasks, teacher can broaden the scope of this process, include feedback, time allocated to improve the original scores, and so on.	• Students create a second melodic/harmonic line that compliments their original melody. • Students share their ideas and learn from each other. • Students explore new visual and aural ideas.

Standards Links:

Resources and References:

Category 2: Musicianship Skills and Knowledge

Content Area:	2C—Creative Musicianship
Benchmark:	*Students demonstrate **creative musicianship** skills at all stages of development, including the ability to improvise variations of rhythmic, melodic, and harmonic patterns, within the traditions and standards of a variety of genres and practices; arrange and compose melodies and harmonies according to specific criteria and guidelines*
Learning Task:	**4.5—Creative Leadership: Students combine original scores with student-conducted, improvised sections**

Learning Sequences & Processes	Indicators of Success
General Information, Prior Knowledge and Precursors • See Content Area 2C—Creative Musicianship Compositional Learning Tasks 1.1–1.4, 2.1–2.4, 3.1–3.4, and 4.1–4.4 Sequence of Activities • Teacher explains that the group will be co-creating a piece of music for their school concert. • Teacher invites suggestions from students for melodic themes, rhythmic themes, stories, and any other material created over the course of the Creative Musicianship Learning Tasks in Content Area 2C, or teacher works with students to generate 1) a melodic theme; 2) a rhythmic theme; 3) a story-line; and 4) conducting techniques that will work effective with these ideas. Harmony lines and/or sub-themes can be developed by the class to use with selected melodic ideas. • Teacher chooses a student conductor for this piece and the class designs/agrees upon hand signals for the material they've developed. • Class rehearses piece and teacher makes suggestions and modifications as needed. • Note: It is possible to elicit a story from the audience at a concert and use a student conductor to lead a musical illustration of that story with or without narration.	• Students create an original group piece that's ready for performance in their school concert. • Students feel comfortable stepping into a position of leadership. • Students are able to communicate their ideas through physical gesture and achieve the results they seek. • Student conductors are able to conceptualize musical ideas and conduct those ideas successfully. • Students have a more experiential idea of the role of the conductor in the success of a group's performance.

Standards Links:

Resources and References:

Content Area 2D—Music Literacy

Students demonstrate sequential music literacy skills (decoding and comprehension), defined as an association of sound-to-symbol, in a given musical context, which includes: predictive components (understanding of reading based on audiation of written material) and knowledge of symbols and notation related to pitch, rhythm, dynamics, tonality, clef, articulation, etc.), based on the principle that sound comes before sight.

Learning Tasks

1.1 Students correctly identify and perform basic music notation and symbols associated with the following skills and understandings to each corresponding curricular level:
   a. musical alphabet
   b. staff (line notes and space notes)
   c. clef signs
   d. lines and spaces in clefs specific to instruments
   e. chromatic symbols (♮, ♯, ♭)
   f. key signatures
   g. relative note values
   h. time signatures
   i. quarter notes, eighth notes, half notes, dotted half notes, whole notes and related rests
   j. dynamic markings (*piano, forte*)
   k. articulation (up-bow, down-bow, slurs, staccato, ties, etc.)
   l. tempo markings (allegro, andante, allegretto, largo, moderato, etc.)

1.2 Students correctly sight-read basic music notation and symbols

1.3 Students understand chord symbols (root only)

1.4 Students correctly identify the following key signatures: C, G, D, and F Major (with their relative minors)

1.5 Students correctly identify accidentals (♮, ♯, ♭)

1.6 Students correctly identify musical forms: AB and ABA

2.1 Students correctly identify tonality (including key signature) and perform repertoire through three sharps and three flats

2.2 Students correctly identify interval labels (numbers only)

2.3 Students correctly identify musical forms: theme and variations, rondo, minuet and trio

3.1 Students correctly identify and perform chords from chord symbols (tonic, dominant, and subdominant)

3.2 Violists correctly identify and perform the pitches found on the treble-clef staff, for the D- and A-strings, through 3rd position

3.3 Cellists correctly identify and perform the pitches found on the tenor-clef staff, for the D- and A-strings, through 4th position

3.4 Bassists correctly identify and perform the pitches found on the tenor-clef staff, for the D- and G-strings

3.5 Students correctly identify and perform notes with double-sharps and double-flats

3.6 Students correctly identify tonality (including key signature) and perform repertoire through four sharps and four flats

3.7 Students correctly identify musical form: Sonata-Allegro

4.1 Students correctly identify tonality (including key signature) for all major and minor tonalities

4.2 Students correctly identify modes and scales: *Dorian, Mixolydian*, and *Blues*

4.3 Students understand and are able to perform notation associated with non-classical styles (e.g., twentieth century/modern, world music, other special effects)

4.4 Cellists and bassists correctly identify and perform the pitches found on the treble-clef staff

Category 2: Musicianship Skills and Knowledge

Content Area:	2D—Music Literacy
Benchmark:	*Students demonstrate sequential music literacy skills (decoding and comprehension), defined as an association of sound-to-symbol, in a given musical context, which includes: predictive components (understanding of reading based on audiation of written material) and knowledge of symbols and notation related to pitch, rhythm, dynamics, tonality, clef, articulation, etc.), based on the principle that sound comes before sight.*
Learning Task:	**1.1—Students correctly identify and perform basic music notation and symbols associated with the following skills and understandings to each corresponding curricular level**

Learning Sequences & Processes	Indicators of Success

General Information, Prior Knowledge and Precursors
 	
• The teacher will prepare students for learning notes, rhythms, articulations and dynamics through rote drills and exercises. Once students demonstrate an understanding of concepts aurally, written symbols will be presented and practiced. This process is sequential and spiraling.
 	
• Basic literacy elements include:
  • musical alphabet
  • staff (line notes and space notes)
  • clef signs
  • lines and spaces in clefs specific to instruments
  • chromatic symbols (♮, ♯, ♭)
  • key signatures
  • relative note values
  • time signatures
  • quarter notes, eighth notes, half notes, dotted half notes, whole notes and related rests
  • dynamic markings (*piano, forte*)
  • articulation (up-bow, down-bow, slurs, staccato, ties, etc.)
  • tempo markings (allegro, andante, allegretto, largo, moderato, etc.)
 	
Sequence of Activities
 	
• Teacher demonstrates the new note, rhythm, articulation or dynamic through rote exercises or call-and-response.
 	
• Teacher introduces the symbol for the new note, rhythm, articulation or dynamic by writing the symbol on the board.
 	
• Teacher presents the new note, rhythm, articulation or dynamic in printed music appropriate for the students' performance level.
 	
• Students practice using symbols for the new note, rhythm, articulation or dynamic in performance, composition or improvisation.
 	
• Students are given a written example of prior learned symbols along with the addition of new symbols and label all parts of the example including the clef sign, note names, how to count the rhythms, what the dynamic level means and what kind of articulations are used.
	• Students accurately echo or answer teacher demonstration as a group and individually.
	
	• Students verbally identify notes (or note patterns), rhythm patterns, articulations and dynamics demonstrated by the teacher.
	
	• Students match aural examples with symbols on the board or flashcards.
	
	• Students aurally identify the new note, rhythm, articulation or dynamic as a group or individually in printed music.
	
	• Students use the new note, rhythm, articulation or dynamic correctly in performance, composition or improvisation.
	
	• Students can decode and label all parts of the musical example provided to them.

Standards Links:

Resources and References:

Category 2:	Musicianship Skills and Knowledge
Content Area:	**2D—Music Literacy**
Benchmark:	*Students demonstrate sequential music literacy skills (decoding and comprehension), defined as an association of sound-to-symbol, in a given musical context, which includes: predictive components (understanding of reading based on audiation of written material) and knowledge of symbols and notation related to pitch, rhythm, dynamics, tonality, clef, articulation, etc.), based on the principle that sound comes before sight.*
Learning Task:	**1.2—Students sight-read basic music notation and symbols**

Learning Sequences & Processes	Indicators of Success

General Information, Prior Knowledge and Precursors
 	
• Accurate sight-reading includes both an understanding of how to translate the information from what is written to the instrument *and* comprehension (accurate aural concept) of what is notated on the page, even before the student performs the material on the instrument.
 	
• The first stages of sightreading should include familiar material in a new context. In other words, students should already have the musical vocabulary (i.e., understanding of harmonic, rhythmic, and melodic patterns) to perform the piece with comprehension. Sight-reading (whether in music or language) is generally successful only to the extent that the reader *already* understands the words/notes, patterns/vocabulary/syntax contained in the work.
 	
• Sight-reading is a complex process that includes melodic, rhythm, technical, stylistic, and harmonic elements, among others.
 	
• The earliest stages of sight-reading should focus on reading these elements separately (i.e., just rhythm patterns, etc.).
 	
Sequence of Activities
 	
• Teacher gives the students a new musical excerpt using the new note, rhythm, articulation or dynamic to decode and perform.
 	
• Students study the piece, looking for familiar patterns. The following order is generally helpful:
  • meter/time signature/rhythm patterns (with associated technical requirements)
  • tonality/key signature/melodic patterns (with associated technical requirements)
  • harmonic elements (with associated technical requirements)
  • articulation and other stylistic elements (with associated technical requirements)
  • dynamics and phrasing (with associated technical requirements)
 	
• Practice sight-reading each element separately. When each element is mastered, then combine elements (e.g., rhythm and articulation).
 	
• Move from simple to complex.
	• Students accurately read and perform rhythm patterns
	
	• Students accurately read and perform melodic elements
	
	• Students accurately read and perform harmonic elements
	
	• Students accurately read and perform articulations
	
	• Students perform with correct phrasing and style

Standards Links:

Resources and References:

Category 2: Musicianship Skills and Knowledge

Content Area:	2D—Music Literacy
Benchmark:	*Students demonstrate sequential music literacy skills (decoding and comprehension), defined as an association of sound-to-symbol, in a given musical context, which includes: predictive components (understanding of reading based on audiation of written material) and knowledge of symbols and notation related to pitch, rhythm, dynamics, tonality, clef, articulation, etc.), based on the principle that sound comes before sight.*
Learning Task:	1.3—Students understand chord symbols (root only)

Learning Sequences & Processes	Indicators of Success
General Information, Prior Knowledge and Precursors • As mentioned earlier, under tonal skills, students should learn both melodies and the accompanying bass lines even from the first days of instruction. • As students learn to read notation for the melodies of the songs, they should also learn to read the basic chord symbols above the staff (e.g., D or G, indicating a D-major chord or a G-major chord). Sequence of Activities The following sequence may be done with or without instruments, singing, chanting, or playing: • Teacher puts a chord sequence on the board and students practice switching from the root of the chord to the next using four beats per chord root tone. • Students accompany the melody reading the root tone of the chords progressing from one chord to the next with rhythmic accuracy. The teacher cues when to switch to the next chord. • Students notate chord sequences for familiar songs, either on the board or on staff paper. • Using a piece of notated music, containing both the melody and the chord symbols, students read first the melody, then the bass line, then practice switching back-and-forth between the two. • Some written songs do not contain chord symbols. A useful exercise is to have the students enter the chord symbols above the staff, where the chord changes take place. • Students work in pairs with one student playing the melody and one student playing the root of the chords in an accompaniment using a rhythm specified by the instructor. Then they switch parts. • Students should determine where the given chords change for the corresponding melody.	• Students accurately switch between chord roots, in rhythm, and in coordination with the melody. • Students switch from root tone to the next every four beats. • Students switch from root tone to the next on the teacher's cue. • Students perform in pairs with one student accompanying using chord changes and only the root tone. • Students change to the correct chord when they hear the harmony change.

Standards Links:

Resources and References:

Category 2: Musicianship Skills and Knowledge

Content Area:	**2D—Music Literacy**
Benchmark:	*Students demonstrate sequential music literacy skills (decoding and comprehension), defined as an association of sound-to-symbol, in a given musical context, which includes: predictive components (understanding of reading based on audiation of written material) and knowledge of symbols and notation related to pitch, rhythm, dynamics, tonality, clef, articulation, etc.), based on the principle that sound comes before sight.*
Learning Task:	**1.4—Students correctly identify the following key signatures: C, G, D, and F Major (with their relative minors)**

Learning Sequences & Processes	Indicators of Success
General Information, Prior Knowledge and Precursors • Solfege provides an excellent background for students as they begin to learn about tonality and key signatures. Students should understand that *Do* is the resting tone in major and *la* is the resting tone in minor (using a moveable-*Do*, *la*-based minor system). • Students should also understand that half-steps occur between *mi–fa* and *ti–do* (or, scale degrees 3–4 and 7–8 in major). • Theoretical understanding of keys should come after the development of the basic aural skills mentioned above. Sequence of Activities The following sequence may be done with or without instruments, singing, chanting, or playing: • As each key signature is studied, students learn about the naturally occurring half- and whole-steps in the major and minor scales. • Students should be able to identify the tonic chord in the key signature. • Using either the solfege or numerical systems above, students should be able to determine the correct notes for the given key signature. • Once this is understood, they write the letter names and sharps or flats of the complete scale (e.g., F–G–A–B♭–C–D–E–F) marking where half- and whole-steps occur. • Using a blank finger chart, students write in where each tone of the scale is placed noting that half steps are close together. • Students identify the name of the key signature of pieces or excerpts and can name what accidentals are included in the key. • Students perform a piece or excerpt using the correct pitches found in the key signature.	• Students will correctly write scale using letter names and flats and sharps marking in half- and whole-steps. • Students correctly write the tones of the scale on a blank finger chart. • Students know what note names and accidentals are included in the key signature of a piece or excerpt. • Students play the correct pitches of a piece or excerpt.

Standards Links:

Resources and References:

Category 2: Musicianship Skills and Knowledge

Content Area:	2D—Music Literacy
Benchmark:	*Students demonstrate sequential music literacy skills (decoding and comprehension), defined as an association of sound-to-symbol, in a given musical context, which includes: predictive components (understanding of reading based on audiation of written material) and knowledge of symbols and notation related to pitch, rhythm, dynamics, tonality, clef, articulation, etc.), based on the principle that sound comes before sight.*
Learning Task:	**1.5—Students correctly identify accidentals (♮, ♭, ♯)**

Learning Sequences & Processes	Indicators of Success
General Information, Prior Knowledge and Precursors • Students should already have performed songs, by ear, that contain chromatic alterations/non-key notes (*or*, accidentals) • The theoretical discussion of how accidentals affect a pitch should only come after students have an aural basis for how it sounds. Sequence of Activities The following sequence may be done with or without instruments, singing, chanting, or playing: • Teacher performs echo patterns and/or familiar melodies containing chromatic alterations or non-key notes. • Teacher asks students to identify which notes were altered, and how they were altered. It is likely that students may give multiple correct answers for the same thing (such as F♯ or G♭). Upon that aural foundation, teacher demonstrates how the symbols for sharp, natural, and flat change the way a note is played. Students apply this knowledge to their instrument changing from natural note to a sharp or flat note. Try changing from a sharp or flat note to the natural version of the note. • Students sight-read new material using accidentals	• Students accurately echo teacher model. • Students change the pitch in the correct direction— up or down a half-step • Students use the correct pitches when playing a piece or excerpt with accidentals

Standards Links:

Resources and References:

Level:	**Baseline**

Category 2:	**Musicianship Skills and Knowledge**

Content Area:	**2D—Music Literacy**
Benchmark:	*Students demonstrate sequential music literacy skills (decoding and comprehension), defined as an association of sound-to-symbol, in a given musical context, which includes: predictive components (understanding of reading based on audiation of written material) and knowledge of symbols and notation related to pitch, rhythm, dynamics, tonality, clef, articulation, etc.), based on the principle that sound comes before sight.*
Learning Task:	**1.6—Students correctly identify musical forms: AB and ABA**

Learning Sequences & Processes	**Indicators of Success**
<u>General Information, Prior Knowledge and Precursors</u> • Most beginning string songs are based on either AB (or, ABAB) and ABA forms. • Students should have an aural basis for form before they analyze a piece visually for formal elements. In other words, what they *hear* is more important than what they *see* at the beginning. <u>Sequence of Activities</u> The following sequence may be done with or without instruments, singing, chanting, or playing: • Teacher plays a piece with AB form on an instrument or a recording. Starting with a familiar song is efficient and allows the teacher to move directly into a discussion about the formal elements of the piece. After reviewing what the A and B sections sound like, students stand up (or raise their hands) when they hear the A section and sit down when they hear the B section. • To check for independence, have the students close their eyes so they can't see other students and repeat the above. • Teachers selects an AB or ABA piece to play and splits the class into two groups once they are able to play both A and B sections. Students take turns playing the A sections and B sections. • Students analyze existing repertoire for formal elements, determining whether or not the pieces they already know follow into one of the forms mentioned above.	• Students will identify the A and B sections by standing or sitting at the correct time. • Students will independently identify the A and B sections by standing or sitting at the correct time. • Students play the correct phrase at the correct time in the piece. • Students correctly identify formal elements in other familiar songs.

Standards Links:

Resources and References:

Category 2: Musicianship Skills and Knowledge

Content Area:	**2D—Music Literacy**
Benchmark:	*Students demonstrate sequential music literacy skills (decoding and comprehension), defined as an association of sound-to-symbol, in a given musical context, which includes: predictive components (understanding of reading based on audiation of written material) and knowledge of symbols and notation related to pitch, rhythm, dynamics, tonality, clef, articulation, etc.), based on the principle that sound comes before sight.*
Learning Task:	**2.1—Students correctly identify tonality (including key signature) and perform repertoire through three sharps and three flats**

Learning Sequences & Processes	Indicators of Success
<u>General Information, Prior Knowledge and Precursors</u> • The teacher will prepare students for learning notes, rhythms, articulations and dynamics through rote drills and exercises. Once students demonstrate an understanding of concepts aurally, written symbols will be presented and practiced. This process is sequential and spiraling. • An understanding of tonality is more important than simply understanding the name of the key signature. Tonality addresses function, harmony, and the overall context of the piece. <u>Sequence of Activities</u> The following sequence may be done with or without instruments, singing, chanting, or playing: • As each key signature is studied, students write the letter names and accidentals (e.g., F–G–A–B♭–C–D–E–F) marking where half- and whole-steps occur. Students should also indicate where the tonic note is for the piece. • Using a blank finger chart, students write in where each tone of the scale is placed noting that half steps are close together. • Students identify the name of the key signature of pieces or excerpts and name what accidentals are included in the key. • Students perform a piece or excerpt using the correct pitches found in the key signature. • Teacher introduces intervals with the concept that an interval is the distance between two pitches named by the number of pitch letter names including both the lower and upper notes.	• Students correctly notate scales using letters and accidentals marking in half- and whole-steps, with a correct indication of tonic. • Students correctly write the tones of the scale on a blank finger chart. • Students know what note names and accidentals are included in the key signature of a piece or excerpt. • Students play the correct pitches of a piece or excerpt. • Students visually identify intervals on the staff and begin to aurally recognize the sound of intervals.

Standards Links:

Resources and References:

Category 2: Musicianship Skills and Knowledge

Content Area:	2D—Music Literacy
Benchmark:	*Students demonstrate sequential music literacy skills (decoding and comprehension), defined as an association of sound-to-symbol, in a given musical context, which includes: predictive components (understanding of reading based on audiation of written material) and knowledge of symbols and notation related to pitch, rhythm, dynamics, tonality, clef, articulation, etc.), based on the principle that sound comes before sight.*
Learning Task:	**2.2—Students correctly identify interval labels (numbers only)**

Learning Sequences & Processes	Indicators of Success
General Information, Prior Knowledge and Precursors • As with many other activities, understanding intervals is aided by the use of solfege from the first days of instruction. Students should be able to hear intervals based on their solfege relationships before labeling them with interval titles. • The use of hand symbols can also assist in this process. Sequence of Activities • Define an *interval* for the students as the distance between two notes. Students should already be familiar with this term from their practice in solfege. • Certain intervals are easy to recognize, based on their association with songs, such as the Perfect-4th (*Here Comes the Bride*), the minor-3rd (Brahms, *Lullaby*), etc. Using these associations can help students identify intervals, but should not be overly relied upon, as students may struggle to identify the same interval when it occurs in a new context or a different place within the scale. • In order to provide a visual aid to the idea of the Major/Minor 3rd, write a scale on the board and mark in the half- and whole-steps. Ask eight students to go to the front of the class, and stand in a row, as if they were a major scale. The students who are at the half-step locations should stand next to each other, while the students who the whole-step notes should stand with a space between them. Make the 3rd pitch of the scale a half step lower when building the scale and then play a major and minor scale and have them hear how that 3rd pitch is adjusted. This same exercises may be repeated for teaching chords, or identifying different intervals within the scales. • On a fingering chart, notice that half steps are close together (fingers touching) and whole steps have a finger space between them. After the explanation, have students break into groups of four and give them four tones to physically demonstrate. For example, using the tone set A–B♭–C–D, students would stand close together for A and B♭ and the other students would stand apart. Repeat with a different tone set. • Using the root, third and fifth of a chord, write the three tones on the staff on the board or on a worksheet and show how the three notes go from line to line or space to space. They look like snowmen when stacked up on three lines or spaces. Have the students write thirds of a chord stacked above given pitches on staff paper using both line and space notes. Teacher selects a piece of music with thirds in it and students circle them with a pencil. • Using the root and fifth of a chord, write the tones on the board or a worksheet noting that it is similar to the thirds exercise but that you skip the third of a chord leaving a line or space blank when writing a fifth. Have the students write the root and fifth of a chord on staff paper using both line and space notes starting on given tones. Teacher selects a piece of music with fifths in it and students circle them with a pencil. • The exercises above may be repeated for 4ths, 6ths, 2nds, 7ths, and octaves.	• Students can sing various intervals using solfege syllables. • Students visually identify intervals on the staff and begin to aurally recognize the sound of intervals. • Students form half- and whole-steps correctly using a four-note tone set given by the teacher. • Students perform melodic and tonal patterns using half- and whole-steps. • Students correctly place thirds above given pitches on staff paper. • Students correctly identify and notate other given intervals as indicated by the teacher.

Standards Links:

Resources and References:

Category 2:	**Musicianship Skills and Knowledge**
Content Area:	**2D—Music Literacy**
Benchmark:	*Students demonstrate sequential music literacy skills (decoding and comprehension), defined as an association of sound-to-symbol, in a given musical context, which includes: predictive components (understanding of reading based on audiation of written material) and knowledge of symbols and notation related to pitch, rhythm, dynamics, tonality, clef, articulation, etc.), based on the principle that sound comes before sight.*
Learning Task:	**2.3—Students correctly identify musical forms:** *theme and variations, rondo, minuet and trio*

Learning Sequences & Processes	Indicators of Success
General Information, Prior Knowledge and Precursors • This activity builds upon the prior knowledge about form introduced in learning task 1.6. • The specific forms mentioned in this task may be addressed as students progress through various types of literature. Other forms may be included, based on the specific repertoire chosen by the teacher. Sequence of Activities • Teacher performs or plays a theme and variations piece for the students and explains how the theme is altered by changing the melody, harmony, or rhythm. As the students listen, have them identify what alteration is made to the theme. • Select a piece of music for the students to play that demonstrates theme and variations. • Teacher creates a theme that the students alter by changing the melody, harmony or rhythm. Students select their favorite variations to create a new piece that can be performed at a concert. • Teacher performs or plays a piece that portrays the rondo form. Play the A part one more time so students can identify the melody. As you play through the piece, have them raise an arm or stand each time the A section is played. Have them decide how many different sections there are in the piece (e.g., A–B–A–C–A–D–A–E). • Students learn to play a rondo piece. Divide the class up into groups (ABCDE) and have each group play their own section letter. For example, cellists play the A sections, violists play the B sections and so forth. • With an unfamiliar piece of music, have the students label the sections of the rondo. • Teacher talks about the history of the minuet (a dance in ¾ time) and trio (contrasting minuet). Note that this went from music for dancing to the standard third movement of a four-movement symphony. Teacher plays an example of minuet and trio for the students and the students determine where the trio starts and the minuet repeats. • Students perform a minuet and trio and identify each section.	• Students correctly identify how the theme is altered. • Students play and correctly identify how the theme is altered. • The variations that the students perform relate to the theme created by the teacher. • Students correctly identify all of the sections of the rondo form. • Students play their section at the appropriate time. • Students label all of the sections of the rondo correctly. • Students correctly identify where the trio begins and the minuet repeats. • Students perform and correctly identify the parts of a minuet and trio.

Standards Links:	

Resources and References:	

Category 2:	Musicianship Skills and Knowledge

Content Area:	**2D—Music Literacy**
Benchmark:	*Students demonstrate sequential music literacy skills (decoding and comprehension), defined as an association of sound-to-symbol, in a given musical context, which includes: predictive components (understanding of reading based on audiation of written material) and knowledge of symbols and notation related to pitch, rhythm, dynamics, tonality, clef, articulation, etc.), based on the principle that sound comes before sight.*
Learning Task:	**3.1—Students correctly identify and perform chords from chord symbols (tonic, dominant, and subdominant)**

Learning Sequences & Processes	Indicators of Success
<u>General Information, Prior Knowledge and Precursors</u> The teacher will prepare students for learning key signatures and intervals through rote drills and exercises. Once students demonstrate an understanding of concepts aurally, written symbols will be presented and practiced. This process is sequential and spiraling. <u>Sequence of Activities</u> • Using various major scales, demonstrate that the 1st, 4th and 5th tones of the scale determine the tonic, subdominant and dominant chords, respectively. Label the chords as I, IV and V. • Students practice playing the chord sequence using the three tones of the chord starting each sequence on a different note. • Students perform a song by dividing students into two groups, one playing the melody and one playing the chord progression. Try it with stand partners or two at a time. • Write the pitches to the I, IV and V chords on the board and have the students improvise using the tones of the chord along with the teacher signaling when to change to the next chord using 1 finger, 4 fingers or 5 fingers. • Listen to and analyze music that utilizes I, IV, and V chord progressions and have the students identify them as they hear them change from one to the next. • Select music for the students to play using I, IV, and V chords in various keys and in various progressions, and have the students identify the chord changes. • Give the students a melody and have them write the accompaniment based on I, IV and V chords.	• Students accurately recognize, write and play chord progressions using the I, IV and V chords. • Students changes to new chord correctly, as required by the harmonic progression in the song.

Standards Links:

Resources and References:

	Level:	**Proficient**

Category 2:	**Musicianship Skills and Knowledge**
Content Area:	**2D—Music Literacy**
Benchmark:	*Students demonstrate sequential music literacy skills (decoding and comprehension), defined as an association of sound-to-symbol, in a given musical context, which includes: predictive components (understanding of reading based on audiation of written material) and knowledge of symbols and notation related to pitch, rhythm, dynamics, tonality, clef, articulation, etc.), based on the principle that sound comes before sight.*
Learning Task:	**3.2—Violists correctly identify and perform the pitches found on the treble-clef staff, for the D- and A-strings, through 3rd position**

Learning Sequences & Processes	**Indicators of Success**
General Information, Prior Knowledge and Precursors The primary clef for the viola is the alto clef, but as the viola range extends upward, the treble clef is introduced, in order to reduce the number of ledger lines required to notate high pitches (frequently as the upper notes exceed three ledger lines). This is typically not encountered until high-school level literature, but it is something that is easily introduced in middle school. Sequence of Activities • Find music that uses a small excerpt of treble clef moving mostly step-wise on one string. Moving into III position on the A-string excerpts are a great place to start and then gradually move to excerpts on other strings. • Find music that uses a small excerpt of treble clef moving mostly step-wise across two strings. Repeat using a different set of two strings. • Find music that uses a small excerpt of treble clef moving in skips on one string then across two strings. • Use familiar tunes that the students know in alto clef, but ask them to read (or transcribe) into treble clef.	• Viola students begin to feel comfortable playing small excerpts in treble clef on all strings using stepwise and skipping movement. • Students are able to quickly and accurately transpose (perform) songs from alto to treble clef.

Standards Links:

Resources and References:

Category 2:	**Musicianship Skills and Knowledge**
Content Area:	**2D—Music Literacy**
Benchmark:	*Students demonstrate sequential music literacy skills (decoding and comprehension), defined as an association of sound-to-symbol, in a given musical context, which includes: predictive components (understanding of reading based on audiation of written material) and knowledge of symbols and notation related to pitch, rhythm, dynamics, tonality, clef, articulation, etc.), based on the principle that sound comes before sight.*
Learning Task:	**3.3—Cellists correctly identify and perform the pitches found on the tenor-clef staff, for the D- and A-strings, through 4th position**

Learning Sequences & Processes	Indicators of Success
General Information, Prior Knowledge and Precursors • The primary clef for the cello is the bass clef, but as the cello range extends upward, the tenor and treble clefs are introduced, in order to reduce the number of ledger lines required to notate high pitches (frequently as upper notes exceed three ledger lines). This is typically not encountered until high-school level literature, but it is something that is easily introduced in middle school. • Tenor clef is a Perfect-5th higher than notes written in bass clef and is typically used until from approximately 4th position on the A-string to the A that is one-octave above the open A-string. At various times, tenor clef will also be used on the D-string, or slightly higher on the A-string, but this is typically done to avoid switching clefs too frequently within the music. As students learn tenor clef, it may be easy for them to simply think of transposing the written notes by one string, since the strings are also tuned in 5ths. Sequence of Activities • Find music that uses a small excerpt of tenor clef moving mostly step-wise on one string. Using III position excerpts on the A-string excerpts is a great place to start before gradually moving to excerpts on other strings. Find music that uses a small excerpt of treble or tenor clef moving mostly step-wise on one string. Introduce tenor or treble clef notes on the A string before using the other strings. • Find music that uses a small excerpt of tenor clef moving mostly step-wise across two strings. Repeat using a different set of two strings. • Find music that uses a small excerpt of tenor clef moving in skips on one string then across two strings. • Use familiar tunes that the students know in bass clef, but ask them to read (or transcribe) into tenor clef. • Challenge: Ask students to perform songs in treble clef, in thumb position, with music originally notated for the violin.	• Students are comfortable playing small excerpts in tenor and treble clef on all strings using stepwise and skipping movement. • Students are able to quickly and accurately transpose (perform) songs from bass to tenor clef.

Standards Links:	

Resources and References:	

Category 2:	Musicianship Skills and Knowledge
Content Area:	2D—Music Literacy
Benchmark:	*Students demonstrate sequential music literacy skills (decoding and comprehension), defined as an association of sound-to-symbol, in a given musical context, which includes: predictive components (understanding of reading based on audiation of written material) and knowledge of symbols and notation related to pitch, rhythm, dynamics, tonality, clef, articulation, etc.), based on the principle that sound comes before sight.*
Learning Task:	**3.4—Bassists correctly identify and perform the pitches found on the tenor-clef staff, for the D- and G-strings**

Learning Sequences & Processes	Indicators of Success
General Information, Prior Knowledge and Precursors • The primary clef for the bass is the bass clef, but as the bass range extends upward, the tenor and treble clefs are introduced in order to reduce the number of ledger lines required to notate high pitches (frequently as upper notes exceed three ledger lines). This is typically not encountered until high-school level literature, but it is something that is easily introduced in middle school. • Tenor clef is typically used when the range of music stays between that is one-octave above the open G-string and the D above that string (this is also generally around the initial thumb position on the bass). At various times, tenor clef will also be used on the D-string, or slightly higher on the G-string, but this is typically done to avoid switching clefs too frequently within the music. • Be aware that bass sounding pitches continue to be one-octave lower than written pitches. Sequence of Activities • Find music that uses a small excerpt of tenor clef moving mostly step-wise on one string. Using 5th–7th position excerpts on the G-string excerpts is a great place to start before gradually moving to excerpts on other strings. Find music that uses a small excerpt of treble or tenor clef moving mostly step-wise on one string. Introduce tenor or treble clef notes on the G-string before using the other strings. • Find music that uses a small excerpt of tenor clef moving mostly step-wise across two strings. Repeat using a different set of two strings. • Find music that uses a small excerpt of tenor clef moving in skips on one string then across two strings. • Use familiar tunes that the students know in bass clef, but ask them to read (or transcribe) into tenor clef	• Students are comfortable playing small excerpts in tenor clef on all strings using stepwise and skipping movement. • Students are able to quickly and accurately transpose (perform) songs from bass to tenor clef.

Standards Links:

Resources and References:

Category 2: Musicianship Skills and Knowledge

Content Area:	2D—Music Literacy
Benchmark:	*Students demonstrate sequential music literacy skills (decoding and comprehension), defined as an association of sound-to-symbol, in a given musical context, which includes: predictive components (understanding of reading based on audiation of written material) and knowledge of symbols and notation related to pitch, rhythm, dynamics, tonality, clef, articulation, etc.), based on the principle that sound comes before sight.*
Learning Task:	**3.5—Students correctly identify and perform double-flats (♭♭) and double-sharps (𝄪)**

Learning Sequences & Processes	Indicators of Success
General Information, Prior Knowledge and Precursors • The use of double-flats (♭♭) and double-sharps (𝄪) can be visually confusing. Students may struggle to understand the concept in terms of fingering, and as a result, not use their ears to guide their finger placement. • Double-sharps and double-flats are used primarily because of the conventions of notation, and the function of a given note within a scale of chord. • Students should already understand what *enharmonic* pitches are before double-sharps and double-flats are introduced. Sequence of Activities • Begin with aural echo-pattern warm-ups. Provide a worksheet that shows how the echo patterns can be notated using enharmonic pitches, including double-sharps and double-flats. • Write various notes on the staff using a double sharp or double flat and explain that each sharp or flat moves the pitch by a half step. At another time, write notes on the board and have the students tell you what the pitch is when double sharps and flats are used. • Connect the double-sharp (𝄪) or double-flat (♭♭) to its numerical place (or solfege syllable) in the scale, so students have an aural concept of the pitch's function.	• Students accurately identify and perform enharmonic pitches, and notes that are written as double-sharps and double-flats.

Standards Links:

Resources and References:

Category 2: Musicianship Skills and Knowledge

Content Area:	**2D—Music Literacy**
Benchmark:	*Students demonstrate sequential music literacy skills (decoding and comprehension), defined as an association of sound-to-symbol, in a given musical context, which includes: predictive components (understanding of reading based on audiation of written material) and knowledge of symbols and notation related to pitch, rhythm, dynamics, tonality, clef, articulation, etc.), based on the principle that sound comes before sight.*
Learning Task:	**3.6—Students correctly identify tonality (including key signature) and perform repertoire through four sharps and four flats**

Learning Sequences & Processes	Indicators of Success
General Information, Prior Knowledge and Precursors • Follow the same general procedures listed on learning task 2.1. • As scales grow more complex, students will need to learn new fingerings (and positions) in order to execute the new notes. Sequence of Activities • Begin with aural warm-ups. Perform familiar songs in keys that have four sharps and four flats. This will familiarize students with the general location of the notes on the fingerboard and also orient their listening to the new tonality. • As each key signature is studied, students write the letter names of the tones in a scale along with the sharps and flats used, marking where half and whole steps occur. • Using a blank finger chart, students write in where each tone of the scale is placed noting that half steps are close together. • Select a piece or excerpt and individually check the use of the correct pitches found in the key signature • To aid cello and viola intonation, practice echo patterns that use thirds on the lower strings that employ extensions (D–F# on the C-string or A–C# on the G-string)	• Students can write the pitches of a scale corresponding to key signatures using up to four sharps and four flats and mark the half and whole steps in the appropriate places. • Students can fill in a finger chart for the key signatures using up to four sharps and four flats. • Students identify the key signatures that use four sharps and four flats in the music they are studying and play the correct pitches of the sharps and flats used in those keys. • Students perform music using the correct pitches found in key signatures of up to four sharps and four flats.

Standards Links:

Resources and References:

Category 2:	**Musicianship Skills and Knowledge**
Content Area:	2D—Music Literacy
Benchmark:	*Students demonstrate sequential music literacy skills (decoding and comprehension), defined as an association of sound-to-symbol, in a given musical context, which includes: predictive components (understanding of reading based on audiation of written material) and knowledge of symbols and notation related to pitch, rhythm, dynamics, tonality, clef, articulation, etc.), based on the principle that sound comes before sight.*
Learning Task:	**3.7—Students correctly identify musical form: Sonata-Allegro**

Learning Sequences & Processes	Indicators of Success

General Information, Prior Knowledge and Precursors
 	
 • Follow the same general procedures listed on learning task 2.3.
 	
 • Students should listen regularly to pieces in this particular musical form, so that they have a sense of the general structure of the piece.
 	
 • Be sure to connect this new form to the previous forms, as it is an outgrowth of them.
 	
 Sequence of Activities
 	
 • Play a theme-and-variations in preparation for listening to a piece in sonata form.
 	
 • Show how the Exposition and Development are closely linked to the idea of theme and variations, but with much greater length in general.
 	
 • Discuss the characteristics of the development section of the sonata form:
 	
     • Usually starts in the same key in which the exposition ended but can move through several key signatures
 	
     • Usually includes one or more themes of the exposition slightly varied but can introduce new themes
 	
     • Variations of the exposition themes can include different keys, different harmonic structures, or rhythmic variations
 	
     • At the end, it returns to the dominant key in preparation for the recapitulation
 	
 • Analyze the development in a sonata allegro piece of music labeling the techniques used and how the section transitions to the recapitulation.
 	
 • Assign a composition project with a given theme and have the student compose their own development section.
 	
 • Ask students to identify formal elements in works they are currently performing.
	• Students accurately understand, analyze and apply the techniques of development using the material from the exposition transitioning it through the development towards the recapitulation.

Standards Links:

Resources and References:

Category 2: Musicianship Skills and Knowledge

Content Area:	2D—Music Literacy
Benchmark:	*Students demonstrate sequential music literacy skills (decoding and comprehension), defined as an association of sound-to-symbol, in a given musical context, which includes: predictive components (understanding of reading based on audiation of written material) and knowledge of symbols and notation related to pitch, rhythm, dynamics, tonality, clef, articulation, etc.), based on the principle that sound comes before sight.*
Learning Task:	**4.1—Students correctly identify tonality (including key signature) for all major and minor tonalities**

Learning Sequences & Processes	Indicators of Success
General Information, Prior Knowledge and Precursors • The teacher will prepare students for learning key signatures and intervals through rote drills and exercises. Once students demonstrate an understanding of concepts aurally, written symbols will be presented and practiced. This process is sequential and spiraling. • Refer to exercises in learning tasks 2.1 and 3.6 for additional ideas. Sequence of Activities • Begin with aural warm-ups. Perform familiar songs in keys that have five or more sharps or flats. This will familiarize students with the general location of the notes on the fingerboard and also orient their listening to the new tonality. • As each key signature is studied for the first time, students write the letter names of the tones in a scale along with the sharps and flats used, marking where half and whole steps occur. • Using a blank finger chart, students write in where each tone of the scale is placed noting that half steps are close together. • In pieces or excerpts of music review the sharps and flats found in the key signature playing those pitches prior to rehearsing. Play finger patterns using the raised (sharp) or lowered (flat) notes in the key signature to create an awareness of finger placement. • Select a piece or excerpt and individually check the use of the correct pitches found in the key signature.	• Students can write the pitches of a scale corresponding to new key signatures and mark the half and whole steps in the appropriate places. • Students can fill in a finger chart for the key signatures for new key signatures. • Students identify the new key signatures in the music they are studying and play the correct pitches of the sharps and flats used in those keys. • Students perform music using the correct pitches found in key signatures.

Standards Links:

Resources and References:

Category 2: Musicianship Skills and Knowledge

Content Area:	2D—Music Literacy
Benchmark:	*Students demonstrate sequential music literacy skills (decoding and comprehension), defined as an association of sound-to-symbol, in a given musical context, which includes: predictive components (understanding of reading based on audiation of written material) and knowledge of symbols and notation related to pitch, rhythm, dynamics, tonality, clef, articulation, etc.), based on the principle that sound comes before sight.*
Learning Task:	**4.2—Students correctly identify and perform modes and scales: *Dorian*, *Mixolydian*, and *Blues***

Learning Sequences & Processes	Indicators of Success
General Information, Prior Knowledge and Precursors • Students should learn pieces in various modes from the first-year of instruction. Many beginning- and intermediate-level folk songs are in modes (e.g., "Old Joe Clark"—Mixolydian or "Scarborough Fair"—Dorian). • Students need to recognize that modes are a change not only of the melodic scale but also the underlying harmonic structure. • As with other tonal activities, the development of aural skills as a predecessor to theoretical understanding is crucial. Sequence of Activities • Begin with aural warm-ups. Perform melodic patterns and harmonic sequences found in modal songs, such as those listed above. • Demonstrate that the tonic in modes is not the same as it is in major or minor. Therefore, the arrival back to tonic sounds different than it does in those two scales. • Though it is possible to teach modes from the idea of what the order of half- and whole-steps is in a scale, it's important that students recognize the new primary chords that occur in modal pieces. The teacher may show that the Dorian mode, for example, seems like it begins and ends on the 2nd degree of the major scale. Relatively speaking, this is true, but the harmonic progression in Dorian is not the same as it is in major, so students need to learn both elements together. • Teacher finds or writes excerpts of music in which the students identify which mode is used. • Assign a short composition using one of the three modes—Dorian, Mixolydian, or Blues. • Select literature to perform that contains one of the three modes. • Select recordings of music for the students to aurally identify the correct mode being used. Popular music from the 1960s and is frequently written using modes. Encourage students to bring in examples of popular songs that use modes.	• Students understand how the Dorian, Mixolydian, and Blues scales are constructed, both melodically and harmonically. • Students aurally identify the correct mode and perform various modes and modal harmonic progressions. • Students compose using modes.

Standards Links:

Resources and References:

Category 2:	**Musicianship Skills and Knowledge**
Content Area:	**2D—Music Literacy**
Benchmark:	*Students demonstrate sequential music literacy skills (decoding and comprehension), defined as an association of sound-to-symbol, in a given musical context, which includes: predictive components (understanding of reading based on audiation of written material) and knowledge of symbols and notation related to pitch, rhythm, dynamics, tonality, clef, articulation, etc.), based on the principle that sound comes before sight.*
Learning Task:	**4.3—Students understand and are able to perform notation associated with non-classical styles (e.g., twentieth century/modern, world music, other special effects)**

Learning Sequences & Processes	**Indicators of Success**
General Information, Prior Knowledge and Precursors • Notation used by composers during the twentieth century and later contains many new symbols and techniques. It is easiest to introduce these as they are encountered in specific literature. However, it is important that the teacher program pieces that contain these techniques so that students *understand and are able to perform* the required elements when they find them in other situations. Sequence of Activities • Teacher shows examples of the progression of notation from the beginning of time (Gregorian chants, Classical, modern, etc.) • Teacher shows examples of notation for certain instruments such as guitar, percussion, figured bass, basso continuo, jazz, shape note systems etc. • Teacher shows examples of notation from other countries such as India, Russia, China, Japan or Indonesia. • Teacher shows various examples of notation systems, which may include solfege, tablature, Klavar, graphic, Braille music, 12-tone, TUBS, and integer. • Assign a short composition in which the students create their own notation system and other students play the composition. • Extension: Explore special techniques and notation systems by composers such as Heinrich Biber (1644–1704), who was a virtuoso violinist and composer, and innovated several new playing techniques in his works.	• Students recognize and can accurately perform special effects and techniques notated in assigned repertoire. • Students can create various types of non-Classical notation systems on their own.

Standards Links:

Resources and References:

Category 2:	**Musicianship Skills and Knowledge**

Content Area:	**2D—Music Literacy**
Benchmark:	*Students demonstrate sequential music literacy skills (decoding and comprehension), defined as an association of sound-to-symbol, in a given musical context, which includes: predictive components (understanding of reading based on audiation of written material) and knowledge of symbols and notation related to pitch, rhythm, dynamics, tonality, clef, articulation, etc.), based on the principle that sound comes before sight.*
Learning Task:	**4.4—Cellists and bassists correctly identify and perform the pitches found on the treble-clef staff)**

Learning Sequences & Processes	**Indicators of Success**
General Information, Prior Knowledge and Precursors • Cellists and bassists both perform music that frequently includes treble clef, especially beginning at the advanced high school level. For both instruments, treble clef may be encountered even in 3rd–5th positions, but is most frequently used when the range of the instruments stays in 7th position or higher. Sequence of Activities • See sequence of activities from learning tasks 3.3 and 3.4 and apply to introducing the treble clef.	• See learning tasks 3.3 and 3.4.

Standards Links:

Resources and References:

Content Area 2E—Ensemble Skills

Students perform in an ensemble, demonstrating sensitivity and the ability to adjust and maintain a uniform sense of rhythm, tempo, articulation, tone, blend, balance, and dynamics; understand conducting gestures, follow conductor and section leader, and are able to synchronize bowings.

Learning Tasks

1.1   Students match pulse and rhythm to stay together in an ensemble

1.2   Students adjust pitch within the ensemble

1.3   Students demonstrate self-discipline by working cooperatively with peers to produce a quality musical performance.

1.4   Students display appropriate etiquette for style and venue of musical performance (e.g., the difference between a classical concert hall and a fiddle jam session)

1.5   Students demonstrate well-disciplined personal and professional demeanor during rehearsals and performance.

2.1   Students perform various tempos with a steady pulse

2.2   Students adjust pitch within the ensemble

2.3   Students demonstrate understanding of appropriate balance of the melody and accompaniment lines.

2.4   Students imitate rhythm patterns at slow, medium, and fast tempos, following a conductor's beat pattern and cues.

2.5   Students match bow usage to the section and ensemble.

3.1   Students follow section leaders.

3.2   Students perform with style, articulation, and pitch, including adjusting dynamic level, according to the musical function of their part (e.g., melody, harmony, counterpoint, etc.)

3.3   Students follow conductor's more complex beat patterns, cues, and expressive gestures.

4.1   Students adjust pulse, rhythm, pitch, and dynamics for a unified sound within the ensemble

4.2   Students demonstrate: pre-rehearsal preparation and awareness of balance, blend, style, interpretation, and musical sensitivity.

Category 2:	**Musicianship Skills and Knowledge**
Content Area:	2E—Ensemble Skills
Benchmark:	*Students perform in an ensemble, demonstrating sensitivity and the ability to adjust and maintain a uniform sense of rhythm, tempo, articulation, tone, blend, balance, and dynamics; understand conducting gestures, follow conductor and section leader, and are able to synchronize bowings.*
Learning Task:	**1.1—Students match pulse and rhythm to stay together as an ensemble**

Learning Sequences & Processes	Indicators of Success
<u>General Information, Prior Knowledge and Precursors</u> • Notation and understanding of whole, half, quarter and eighth notes and corresponding rests • Knowledge of time signatures 4/4, 3/4, 2/4 • Conducting patterns of 4/4, 3/4, 2/4 • One octave scale • Good basic bow and instrument positions <u>Sequence of Activities</u> • Standing without instruments, students gently pulse (using their knees) to the tempo established by the director. • Continuing to pulse, the students slowly sit down on the front half of their chairs keeping good posture. • Following the director's beat, cello and bass players tap quarter notes while the violin and viola players tap half notes. On cue the students reverse parts. • Tap quarter notes with right hand on the right knee then add eighth notes with their left hand on left knee (starting the concept of beat subdivision). • With bow: Following the conductor's beat, students (horizontally) bow quarter notes. • With instruments: Using open strings students follow the director's beat pattern playing half notes, quarter notes and eighth notes. • One section plays eighth notes while other sections play quarter notes listening to and matching the eighth notes. • Students perform a round, maintaining independent parts, first in unison, then in parts with various groupings. • With eyes closed, students perform a scale with half the group playing a quarter note on each step of scale while remaining members play two eighth notes on each step of the scale. • Ensemble rhythmically reads a line in their music maintaining a steady pulse. • One section at a time bows their part while others pizzicato enabling students to discover how their part fits rhythmically in the ensemble.	• Students determine which ensemble members have the same rhythmic parts • Ensemble members watch and listen across the group to match bow direction and basic beat • Students understand division of the beat • Ensemble performs music and discusses how their parts fit rhythmically with the other sections of the ensemble

Standards Links:

Resources and References:

Category 2:	**Musicianship Skills and Knowledge**
Content Area:	2E—Ensemble Skills
Benchmark:	*Students perform in an ensemble, demonstrating sensitivity and the ability to adjust and maintain a uniform sense of rhythm, tempo, articulation, tone, blend, balance, and dynamics; understand conducting gestures, follow conductor and section leader, and are able to synchronize bowings.*
Learning Task:	**1.2—Adjusts pitch within a section and ensemble**

Learning Sequences & Processes	Indicators of Success

General Information, Prior Knowledge and Precursors

- Many "baseline" students are participating in ensembles for the first time or are still in a relatively new performing situation.
- The beginning heterogeneous strings class may serve also as the first ensemble experience for students.
- The development of pitch within an ensemble is directly linked to the development of individual aural skills (see Musicianship Skill & Knowledge/Aural Skills – Tonal 1.1). The sequence of activities below is designed to take place in tandem with overall aural skill development, and focuses on specific routines that might be useful within a larger ensemble setting.
- The ability to adjust pitch is primarily an aural issue; manipulating pitch to match a given pitch also requires an understanding of the physical/kinesthetic issues related to adjusting intonation.
- Incorrect left hand position or poor tone production will affect the ability to perform with good intonation.
- The use of tapes can help students on a short-term basis understand the relative physical differences and relationships between notes and help establish the basic left-hand position. However, overuse of tapes or asking students to visually identify if they are out-of-tune by checking to see if their fingers are on the tapes is detrimental.

Sequence of Activities

- Review the key signature of the piece being studied. (Students should have an aural concept of the tonality even as they begin to perform with notation.)
- Use an echo-pattern warm-up to establish tonality. This might include melodic patterns in major over background harmony (from piano, keyboard, or teacher.
- Play scales in the pieces being studied, preferably incorporating rhythms used in the piece as a warm-up exercise. Scales may be performed in unison, or in rounds.
- Use echo exercises to hone in on particular pitches. (Examples: A–D on the A-string; A–C#, A–C natural). Use interval recognition such as "Here Comes the Bride." Sing the interval and then play it.
- Rapidly add players by section, one player at a time to match a particular pitch. Tell students to "hide" in the other students pitch.
- Ask students to slowly take sustained notes out of tune and then bring them back in tune (glissando exercise).
- Demonstrate, using either a teacher or other students as a model, what it sounds like when two pitches match and when they do not match.
- Identify and then write out difficult intonation measures for all sections of the orchestra. Practice in unison to improve pitch.

Indicators of Success:
- Students correctly identify sharps or flats found in the key signature and can locate and finger those notes on the instrument and the notes found in the music.
- Echo patterns and scale are performed with accurate intonation.
- Students correctly identify when the pitch they perform does not match the given pitch. Descriptive words such as same or different are helpful at the baseline level.
- Students correctly manipulate pitch to match given note. This is primarily an aural exercise. At the baseline level, students are simply trying to sound like one single instrument when performing with other students. Ultimately students should begin to predict where fingers should be placed in order to play with good intonation.
- Problem pitches improve and students can accurately match pitch in a given section. Overall speed of intonation adjustment is increased.

Standards Links:

Resources and References:

Category 2:	**Musicianship Skills and Knowledge**
Content Area:	2E—Ensemble Skills
Benchmark:	*Students perform in an ensemble, demonstrating sensitivity and the ability to adjust and maintain a uniform sense of rhythm, tempo, articulation, tone, blend, balance, and dynamics; understand conducting gestures, follow conductor and section leader, and are able to synchronize bowings.*
Learning Tasks:	**1.3—Students demonstrate self-discipline by working cooperatively with peers to produce a quality musical performance** **1.4—Students display appropriate etiquette for style and venue of musical performance (e.g., the difference between a classical concert hall and a fiddle jam session** **1.5—Students demonstrate well-disciplined personal and professional demeanor during rehearsals and performances**

Learning Sequences & Processes	Indicators of Success

General Information, Prior Knowledge and Precursors
 	
• Learning Tasks 1.3–1.5 are not specific classroom "activities" and so a specific sequence of activities is not included below for these items. However, successful experiences in playing stringed instruments in groups of any size are built not only on technical, musical, and artistic prowess, but also on the personal and professional attitudes, expectations, and disciplines of the performers themselves. For that reason, we have included these three items as core outcomes for students in string programs.
• Sample elements to be addressed and evaluated include:
  • Being prepared for rehearsals and lessons (this must be intentionally taught by the teacher, as students may not be aware of expectations and protocol)
  • Being respectful of the other musicians in the ensemble, emphasizing good listening skills and cooperative teamwork.
  • Being attentive to professional demeanor and presentation during rehearsals and performances.
  • Effectively communicating within an ensemble and to an audience.
  • Treating the instruments with care and respect.
 	
Sequence of Activities
1.3 *Students demonstrate self-discipline by working cooperatively with peers to produce a quality musical performance.*
  • Students will work cooperatively within their orchestra section or class.
  • Students will contribute in a positive manner to the group effort of making music.
  • Students will work to the best of their ability towards quality musical performances.
1.4 *Students display appropriate etiquette for style and venue of musical performance (e.g., the difference between a classical concert hall and a fiddle jam session*
  • Students will practice and demonstrate proper concert etiquette as an actively involved performer and listener.
1.5 *Students demonstrate well-disciplined personal demeanor during rehearsals and performance.*
  • Students will follow the classroom rules established by school, class and teacher.
  • Students will attend class regularly with music and instrument, complete class assignments and actively participate in class and all performances.
	• Students will be actively participating during the class.
	• Students actively participating in class will demonstrate positive attitudes and work ethic.
	• Student performers will arrive in time for tuning/warm-up, will be in appropriate dress, will not chew gum or send text messages (or similar) during rehearsals or performances, and will exhibit respectful behavior at all times.
	• As audience members, students will exhibit respectful behavior.

Standards Links:	

Resources and References:	

Category 2: Musicianship Skills and Knowledge

Content Area:	**2E—Ensemble Skills**
Benchmark:	*Students perform in an ensemble, demonstrating sensitivity and the ability to adjust and maintain a uniform sense of rhythm, tempo, articulation, tone, blend, balance, and dynamics; understand conducting gestures, follow conductor and section leader, and are able to synchronize bowings.*
Learning Task:	**2.1—Students perform various tempos with a steady pulse**

Learning Sequences & Processes	Indicators of Success
General Information, Prior Knowledge and Precursors • Knowledge of time signatures and basic conducting beat patterns of 2/4, 3/4 and 4/4 • Natural pulse of measures in 4/4, 3/4, 2/4 • Define and perform the following notes and corresponding rests: whole, dotted half, half, dotted quarter, quarter and eighth Sequence of Activities • Students count two measures in 4/4 out loud, then two measures silently, then out loud without cues or beat pattern from the conductor • Students count beats while the conductor keeps a steady pulse (the conductor varies the beat using patterns of 2, 3 and 4) • Students say "one" on each downbeat. • Pizzicato open strings keeping with the ictus of the beat. • Stress the natural pulse of each measure while counting • Using a line in their music literature, students pizzicato only the notes on beat one. • Using the same literature, the conductor changes tempos (Andante, Moderato, Allegro) • Conductor gives two preparatory beats and students enter on beat one matching the new tempo • When the ensemble keeps a steady pizzicato pulse, transfer knowledge to the bow. Have one section use the bow while the remaining sections continue to pizzicato. Each section takes turn using the bow while the others pizzicato. Students using pizzicato should stress the natural pulse of the measures. • Change the bow speed on different rhythmic values to help keep the ensemble with the beat. Encouraging students to use more bow on longer note values sometimes avoids rushing. • Subdivide the beat to help maintain a steady pulse.	• While playing open strings students watch the baton and stay with the beat. • Bow speed changes with note variance to help keep a steady pulse • Students listen across the ensemble maintaining a steady pulse • Performing an appropriate level music selection students keep a steady pulse without a conductor

Standards Links:

Resources and References:

Level: **Developing**

Category 2:	Musicianship Skills and Knowledge

Content Area:	2E—Ensemble Skills
Benchmark:	*Students perform in an ensemble, demonstrating sensitivity and the ability to adjust and maintain a uniform sense of rhythm, tempo, articulation, tone, blend, balance, and dynamics; understand conducting gestures, follow conductor and section leader, and are able to synchronize bowings.*
Learning Task:	**2.2—Students adjust pitch within a section and ensemble**

Learning Sequences & Processes	Indicators of Success
General Information, Prior Knowledge and Precursors • Students recognize and know finger patterns for key signatures up to three flats and sharps. • Students are capable of playing Grade II and III literature or medium-easy to intermediate level music. • Students have participated in the ensemble setting and can follow the conductor. • Students can accurately tune their own instrument. Sequence of Activities • Review the tonality of the piece being studied. (Students should have an aural concept of the tonality.) • Use an echo-pattern warm-up to establish tonality. This might include melodic patterns over background harmony (from piano, keyboard, or performed by other members of the ensemble). Include backward and forward extensions and shifts. • Students need to learn to listen and judge their own intonation. Play an excerpt with some pitch issues and have the students identify the problem pitches using a thumbs-up for a sharp pitch and a thumbs-down for a flat pitch. • Add call-and-response to the warm-up and allow student leaders to lead these sessions. Have students use the finger patterns being studied. • Play two-octave scales in the pieces being studied, preferably incorporating rhythms used in the piece as a warm-up exercise. • Isolate difficult intonation spots and break them down to practicing the intervals in question. Demonstrate the correct pitch. Have students listen and then sing those intervals back before playing them. • Lower strings can hold a drone pitch while upper strings practice an individual pitch or interval and vice versa. • Build the chord from the bottom up, isolating the problem pitch (e.g., A–C♯–E–A). • Match the pitch within the section before going on, then add the rest of the phrase. • All sections of the ensemble should practice these difficult spots in unison. • These students should now be able to understand "ringing tones" and listening for the clear resonant sound found when notes are played with accurate intonation. • Have students practice matching pitch using octaves. Start with an open string and the same note one octave higher.	• Students will demonstrate the half-steps and whole-steps within the scale. • Students will echo back using accurate intonation. • Students will answer the call with a response including the notes being studied using accurate intonation. • Students will be able to play two octave scales with accurate intonation. • Students will accurately adjust pitch to make a tonic chord. • Octaves will be in tune.

Standards Links:

Resources and References:

Category 2:	Musicianship Skills and Knowledge
Content Area:	2E—Ensemble Skills
Benchmark:	*Students perform in an ensemble, demonstrating sensitivity and the ability to adjust and maintain a uniform sense of rhythm, tempo, articulation, tone, blend, balance, and dynamics; understand conducting gestures, follow conductor and section leader, and are able to synchronize bowings.*
Learning Task:	**2.3—Students demonstrate understanding of appropriate balance of the melody and accompaniment lines.**

Learning Sequences & Processes	Indicators of Success
General Information, Prior Knowledge and Precursors • Students should be able to play songs containing simple melodies and bass lines in ensemble settings. • Students should have control of basic tone production elements (weight, angle, speed, and placement) and perform basic dynamics (*piano, mezzo piano, mezzo forte,* and *forte*). Sequence of Activities • Students sing or play (pizzicato or arco, depending on the level of the group) a familiar folk song, for which they know both the melody ad the bass line. The following sequence may be used: • The entire group sings or plays the melody. • The entire group sings or plays the bass line. • Divide the group in half. One half of the ensemble plays the melody, the other half plays the bass line. Switch parts and repeat. • Ask the students which part of the song (i.e., the melody or the bass line) should be stronger. • Experiment with playing the melody and bass lines at different levels. The teacher may use hand signs to indicate dynamic levels (1 finger=soft, 2 fingers=medium, 3 fingers=loud) and make changes while the group is playing. Practice switching dynamic levels in the middle of the song or phrase. Ask the students which balance level is the most appropriate for the piece. • As an extension activity, the teacher demonstrates how the conducting gesture can indicate a soft, medium, or loud dynamic level. Rehearse the piece with the students responding to the conducting gesture.	• Students can appropriately modify dynamic levels according to the indication or gesture by the conductor • Students correctly identify that the melodic material should be louder. • Students adjust bass line dynamic level to changes in the dynamic level of the melodic line.

Standards Links:

Resources and References:

Level:	**Developing**

Category 2:	**Musicianship Skills and Knowledge**
Content Area:	2E—Ensemble Skills
Benchmark:	*Students perform in an ensemble, demonstrating sensitivity and the ability to adjust and maintain a uniform sense of rhythm, tempo, articulation, tone, blend, balance, and dynamics; understand conducting gestures, follow conductor and section leader, and are able to synchronize bowings.*
Learning Task:	**2.4—Students imitate rhythm patterns at slow, medium, and fast tempos, following a conductor's beat pattern and cues.**

Learning Sequences & Processes	Indicators of Success
<u>General Information, Prior Knowledge and Precursors</u> • Conducting patterns of 4/4, 3/4, 2/4 • Notation: whole, dotted half, half, dotted quarter, quarter, eighth notes and corresponding rests • Basic tempos: Andante, Moderato, Allegro • Bowing styles: Simple détaché, staccato <u>Sequence of Activities</u> • Select a rhythm pattern from a piece that students are studying. • Demonstrate the pattern and have students echo the pattern with exact duplication (amount of bow, point of contact and style). • Notate pattern on board for visual reinforcement of aural work. • Count pattern in meter of music selection the students will be rehearsing. • Demonstrate the rhythm segment within conducting pattern. • Following conductor's beat, students perform pattern in a moderate tempo. • Vary the tempo and have students adjust the bow usage to fit. • Demonstrate the rhythmic pattern in a different time signature. • Vary the style of beat having students change articulations to match (legato and martelé) while playing the rhythmic pattern. • Give one measure of prep with ensemble entering in the new tempo and style reflected by conductor's beat.	• Ensemble imitates director's rhythmic example using the correct part of the bow, amount and style. • Ensemble transfers pattern to various tempos • Ensemble performs pattern using different bow articulations • Ensemble transfers knowledge to new music selection with the same rhythm pattern

Standards Links:

Resources and References:

Category 2:	Musicianship Skills and Knowledge
Content Area:	2E—Ensemble Skills
Benchmark:	*Students perform in an ensemble, demonstrating sensitivity and the ability to adjust and maintain a uniform sense of rhythm, tempo, articulation, tone, blend, balance, and dynamics; understand conducting gestures, follow conductor and section leader, and are able to synchronize bowings.*
Learning Task:	**2.5—Students match bow usage to the section and the ensemble**

Learning Sequences & Processes	Indicators of Success
General Information, Prior Knowledge and Precursors • The ability to perform effectively as an ensemble requires students to listen carefully to the other musicians in the group and to match elements like intonation, rhythm, articulation, and dynamics. • Students generally begin playing in ensembles in the 2nd or 3rd year of playing an instrument. Though the initial experiences of playing in an ensemble can be challenging as students adjust to having many different parts playing at one time, it is important to include elements of ensemble performance like following the conductor and following the section leader in their training. Sequence of Activities • The teacher demonstrates the elements that students should be observing while they play, including bowing direction and bowing placement. • Using a familiar piece, the students should play individually and compare how each student performs the selection. Be sure to point out the differences rather than indicate that someone is doing it wrong. This helps students gain confidence in their individual playing skills in addition to become willing to take risks. • Ask individual students to make a change in one element of their bowing (such as weight, angle, speed, or placement). Ask the other students in the section to play exactly as the first student played. • Ask students to identify what changes they made in their performance in order to match the modeled sound. • Make similar changes with bowing placement (such as playing near the tip versus the frog, or using longer versus shorter bows) while students play. • The teacher secretly chooses one or two members of the section to make changes, and then as all students play, asks the all students to monitor the section and determine who is doing something different. As students gain skill in discerning changes, they will make adjustments in their own playing in order to play with a uniform sound across the section.	• Ensemble imitates section leader's bowing changes, using the correct part of the bow, amount and style. • Ensemble stays together while watching the section leader and the conductor. • Ensemble is able to play correct notes, rhythms, and other musical elements while watching the section leader.

Standards Links:

Resources and References:

Level:	Proficient

Category 2: Musicianship Skills and Knowledge

Content Area:	2E—Ensemble Skills
Benchmark:	*Students perform in an ensemble, demonstrating sensitivity and the ability to adjust and maintain a uniform sense of rhythm, tempo, articulation, tone, blend, balance, and dynamics; understand conducting gestures, follow conductor and section leader, and are able to synchronize bowings.*
Learning Task:	3.1—Students follow section leader

Learning Sequences & Processes	Indicators of Success
General Information, Prior Knowledge and Precursors • The ability to perform effectively as an ensemble requires both an aural awareness of tone production, blend, and balance and the visual ability to follow the section leader's adjustment in bow placement and also bowing direction (i.e., up- or down-bow). • Students generally begin playing in ensembles in the 2nd or 3rd year of playing an instrument. Though the initial experiences of playing in an ensemble can be challenging as students adjust to having many different parts playing at one time, it is important to include elements of ensemble performance like following the conductor and following the section leader in their training. Sequence of Activities • The teacher (or a section leader with some prior experience) demonstrates the elements that students should be observing while they play, including bowing direction and bowing placement. • Using a familiar piece, the teacher (or section leader) should make adjustments to some element of bowing (such as switching an up-bow to a down-bow (or vice versa) while students are playing. See how quickly students can make the change! This also requires students to listen *and* watch at the same time. • Make similar changes with bowing placement (such as playing near the tip versus the frog, or using longer versus shorter bows) while students play. • As students gain confidence and skill in doing watching the section leader, combine this activity with other activities like following the conductor, adjusting balance, etc.	• Ensemble imitates section leader's bowing changes, using the correct part of the bow, amount and style. • Ensemble stays together while watching the section leader and the conductor. • Ensemble is able to play correct notes, rhythms, and other musical elements while watching the section leader.

Standards Links:

Resources and References:

Category 2:	**Musicianship Skills and Knowledge**
Content Area:	**2E—Ensemble Skills**
Benchmark:	*Students perform in an ensemble, demonstrating sensitivity and the ability to adjust and maintain a uniform sense of rhythm, tempo, articulation, tone, blend, balance, and dynamics; understand conducting gestures, follow conductor and section leader, and are able to synchronize bowings.*
Learning Task:	**3.2—Students perform with style, articulation and pitch adjusting dynamics according to musical function of their part (i.e. melody, harmony, counterpoint, etc.)**

Learning Sequences & Processes	Indicators of Success

General Information, Prior Knowledge and Precursors
 	
 • Students have rehearsed their individual part.
 • Students understand the notes, rhythm and bowing.
 • Basic knowledge of I, IV, V chords
 • Musical period and style of selection
 • Students have their own music part and music stand.
 	
 Sequence of Activities
 	
 • Teacher presents style to the students, through recordings, demonstrations, or other forms of modeling.
 • Briefly rehearse music in typical ensemble seating arrangement
 • Section players match the bow style, placement, and direction of the section leader.
 • To develop musical independence, change the seating of the ensemble to string quartets throughout the ensemble with the string bass section in a line facing their peers.
 • Director starts the ensemble, then stops conducting so students must listen to each other. Emphasize by eye contact and careful listening.
 • The conductor directs the students to attend to different instrument sections with each repetition of the portion of the music being rehearsed.
 • The conductor directs the ensemble to adjust the dynamics making:
    • the accompaniment parts softer than the melody
    • moving parts are stressed more than stationary parts
    • entrances of imitative parts brought out
 • As an exercise, place the basses in front of the ensemble, which enables every player to hear the bass line as they practice building chords.
 • At the next rehearsal, change the seats back to a typical ensemble seating arrangement. The ensemble continues to listen for all parts.
	• Students describe style and/or music period of the selection.
	
	 • Members of the ensemble know when to bring out their part.
	
	 • Students balance and blend their parts with little or no help from the director.
	
	 • Members understand all the parts of the ensemble.

Standards Links:

Resources and References:

Category 2:	Musicianship Skills and Knowledge
Content Area:	**2E—Ensemble Skills**
Benchmark:	*Students perform in an ensemble, demonstrating sensitivity and the ability to adjust and maintain a uniform sense of rhythm, tempo, articulation, tone, blend, balance, and dynamics; understand conducting gestures, follow conductor and section leader, and are able to synchronize bowings.*
Learning Task:	**3.3—Students follow conductor's more complex beat patterns, cues and expressive gestures**

Learning Sequences & Processes	Indicators of Success
General Information, Prior Knowledge and Precursors • Knowledge of meters: 4/4, 3/4, 2/4, 6/8, 3/8, 5/4, 7/4 • Conducting patterns of above meters • Varying expressive baton styles (dynamics, tempos, articulations) • Conductors have greatly varying styles, and what one conductor may use to indicate staccato, for example, may be intended for something different by another conductor. Students will need to know what the conductor's gestures mean, which requires the conductor to give an explanation and/or provide a model of the desired outcome. Sequence of Activities • Conductor changes meters in random order with students saying "one" on the downbeats. This helps them recognize where the first beat is, especially in pieces that have frequent meter changes. • Varying prep beat tempo, students enter in correct tempo. • Perform rhythm patterns with mixed meters (teachers may develop their own rhythm pattern worksheets, based on the specific repertoire to be performed) • While rehearsing, change phrases and dynamics on spur of moment to encourage students to always watch the conductor. Be sure that students change together as an ensemble, and that they are using both their visual *and* aural skills. • Practice beginning and releasing notes together watching conductor's cues • Change phrase and dynamics on spur of the moment to encourage students to always watch the conductor. • Within a phrase, change speed (rubato) • Match bow articulations to conducting style • Each time a selection is rehearsed, make it a creative endeavor constantly trying new phrasing and articulations to improve selection.	• Ensemble is able to be flexible in response to conducting gestures, while performing a selection • Ensemble is able to make transitions to new meters within a selection • Ability to follow beat changes within a measure and stay together as a section/ensemble.

Standards Links:

Resources and References:

Category 2: Musicianship Skills and Knowledge

Content Area:	**2E—Ensemble Skills**
Benchmark:	*Students perform in an ensemble, demonstrating sensitivity and the ability to adjust and maintain a uniform sense of rhythm, tempo, articulation, tone, blend, balance, and dynamics; understand conducting gestures, follow conductor and section leader, and are able to synchronize bowings.*
Learning Task:	**4.1—Students adjust pulse, rhythm, pitch, and dynamics for a unified sound within the ensemble**

Learning Sequences & Processes	Indicators of Success
General Information, Prior Knowledge and Precursors • Chord structure • Melody, countermelody, bass line, motif Sequence of Activities • The ensemble sight-reads a selection listening for rhythmic similarities between parts. • After sightreading, the ensemble analyzes each section's part in relation to the whole: i.e. melody, countermelody, bass line, motif, rhythm pattern, or moving part. • The ensemble rehearses the first section of music listening across the ensemble adjusting the dynamics to balance the chord structure and melody line. • Determine which part is creating the underlying pulse. Play through the section without the melody lines, listening to the rhythmic pulse. Add the melody line back in and continue to listen for the underlying pulse. • Play only the notes on beat one of each measure. Slow the tempo so students have time to adjust the pitch. When necessary hold the chord or build the chord from the bass up to tune and balance the chord. • To assist cleaning up a difficult technical passage students should memorize the challenging measures. Perform the part with their eyes closed. • Have the students sing their part. If the ensemble can sing their parts accurately, the ensemble will adjust the pitch, rhythm and dynamics when performing.	• Students adjust pitch when working in ensemble. • Without teacher assistance, students adjust their dynamics to balance the ensemble harmony and accompaniment parts. • Students listen for part that is the primary rhythmic motor within the piece, and adjust tempos to that standard.

Standards Links:

Resources and References:

Category 2: Musicianship Skills and Knowledge

Content Area:	2E—Ensemble Skills
Benchmark:	*Students perform in an ensemble, demonstrating sensitivity and the ability to adjust and maintain a uniform sense of rhythm, tempo, articulation, tone, blend, balance, and dynamics; understand conducting gestures, follow conductor and section leader, and are able to synchronize bowings.*
Learning Task:	**4.2—Students demonstrate preparation, balance, blend, style, interpretation, and musical sensitivity**

Learning Sequences & Processes	Indicators of Success
General Information, Prior Knowledge and Precursors	• Students are able perform one phrase with a variety of stylistically appropriate interpretations
• At this point, students should have a good working knowledge and vocabulary about appropriate performance practice for different musical eras and genres.	
• Students should understand how changing one element (e.g., articulation) can create an entirely different stylistic feeling or sensibility.	• Students understand all the elements of music cannot be printed on the musical score and are able to identify, discuss, and determine correct performance practice
• Students should be able perform and adjust elements such as bowing (weight, angle, speed, placement) and vibrato, in order to affect different musical sounds and effects.	
Sequence of Activities	
• Students are given an 8–16 measure excerpt from an unidentified work (no information is given about the composer, tempo, style or bowings)	• The performer learns there are usually several different possible interpretations
• Each section of the orchestra is assigned a specific performance practice (e.g., Baroque) for the 8–16 measure excerpt.	• The students understand the performer must be thoughtful and intentional in determining the specific interpretation for a given work.
• Within their individual section, students determine appropriate bowings, tempo, dynamics, and phrasing to fit the assigned style.	
• Each section performs their interpretation for the class.	
• The section discusses their rationale for their decisions about their specific interpretation or technique choices	
• After each section has shared their individual interpretation, the class reviews the performance example in regards to stylistic appropriateness	
• The class performs each example, also being sure to perform with correct blend and balance.	
• The class should explore playing the excerpt with as many different styles and interpretations as possible. In many styles, there may be several correct interpretations that are stylistically appropriate.	
• Finally, the teacher identifies the work and the class determines the correct practice interpretation on their understanding of historical practice while incorporating their own ideas.	

Standards Links:

Resources and References:

Content Area 3A—Expressive Elements

Students employ expressive elements of music to communicate abstract thoughts, ideas, and meaning; to share the depth of the human experience; and for self-expression and understanding.

Learning Tasks

1.1	Students shape phrases with simple dynamic variation
1.2	Students alter tone by modifying bowing technique elements (i.e., *weight, angle, speed, placement/contact point*)
1.3	Students perform with articulations corresponding to baseline-level right-hand technical skills
2.1	Students evaluate and demonstrate multiple ways of performing a single melody
2.2	Students apply knowledge of performance practice to selected repertoire
2.3	Students perform with articulations corresponding to developing-level right-hand technical skills
3.1	Students perform with an expanded range of dynamics, tempos, and timbre/tone color
3.2	Students perform with a characteristic tone at all dynamic levels
3.3	Students apply knowledge of performance practice to selected repertoire
3.4	Students perform with articulation corresponding to proficient-level right-hand technical skills
3.5	Students use vibrato, when appropriate, to enhance timbre and tone
4.1	Students perform with consistent timbre and tone quality at all dynamic levels
4.2	Students independently interpret and perform musical selections, applying appropriate dynamics, tempos, and timbre.
4.3	Students understand and perform with correct performance practice for selected repertoire
4.4	Students perform with articulations corresponding to advanced-level right-hand technical skills
4.5	Students employ various styles of vibrato for enhancing the artistic interpretation of the piece, according to accepted performance practice.
4.6	Students use ornamentation, as appropriate to the performance practice and conventions of the period and style.

Category 3:	Artistic Skills and Knowledge
Content Area:	3A—Expressive Elements
Benchmark:	*Students employ expressive elements of music to communicate abstract thoughts, ideas, and meaning; to share the depth of the human experience; and for self-expression and understanding.*
Learning Task:	**1.1—Students shape phrases with simple dynamic variation**

Learning Sequences & Processes	Indicators of Success
General Information, Prior Knowledge and Precursors • Students should understand the concept of a phrase, as a musical thought or sentence. • Students perform with simple dynamic variations (*p*, *mp*, *mf*, *f*, *crescendo* and *decrescendo*) Sequence of Activities • Students listen to two examples of a phrase. The first performance without dynamics, the second time with dynamics. • Discuss which version they preferred and ask students to explain their reasoning behind their preference • Discuss how the loudness and softness can be achieved (e.g., through change of dynamics or the addition or deletion of players) • Students play a simple round observing the ensemble's dynamic changes as parts are added and deleted • Students determine where the first phrase of their music selection begins and ends • Once the phrase is isolated, the class determines how they will interpret the phrase. • The easiest phrase starts from a point of rest, builds tension then returns to a point of relative rest. Have students practice using a crescendo to build tension and a decrescendo to relax the tension. • If the melody has sequential or repetitive figures, students may use dynamic changes on each motif to build their phrase. • Ask several students to interpret a phrase using dynamic variations. The class votes or achieves consensus on dynamic choices and perform the phrase accordingly.	• The students volunteer to interpret their music selections using simple dynamics to shape phrases. • Students demonstrate tension and release through selected repertoire • When sightreading music, students apply dynamics according to the rise and fall of the phrase.

Standards Links:

Resources and References:

Category 3:	Artistic Skills and Knowledge
Content Area:	**3A—Expressive Elements**
Benchmark:	*Students employ expressive elements of music to communicate abstract thoughts, ideas, and meaning; to share the depth of the human experience; and for self-expression and understanding.*
Learning Task:	**1.2—Students alter tone by modifying bowing technique elements (i.e., WASP—** *weight, angle, speed, placement/contact point*)

Learning Sequences & Processes	Indicators of Success
General Information, Prior Knowledge and Precursors • Students demonstrate a relaxed, correct bow hold • Students demonstrate a balanced body position free of tension • Students demonstrate drawing the bow parallel to the bridge Sequence of Activities • Practice moving the bow to different points of contact (Zones) on the string. Zone 1 (close to the fingerboard) to Zone 5 (close to the bridge) • Practice producing a warmer, more resonant tone (Zone 3, less arm weight, medium speed bow) • Practice producing an intense tone (Zone 5, natural arm weight, slow bow speed) • Using the natural arm weight, angle of bow, bow speed and point of contact practice producing *p*, *mp*, *mf*, *f* dynamic levels • Using the four *WASP* components, develop different tones to match various musical styles. • Practice scales using various dynamic levels • Incorporating the *WASP* variables, play a one-octave scale: crescendo during ascending portion; decrescendo during the descending portion • Transfer technique to selected music selection with simple dynamic levels (*p*, *mp*, *mf*, *f*, crescendo and decrescendo)	• Students perform music selections using printed dynamic markings • In rehearsals, students vary the contact point, the speed of the bow and the arm weight, achieving varied dynamic levels to match printed dynamics in repertoire.

Standards Links:	

Resources and References:	

Category 3:	Artistic Skills and Knowledge
Content Area:	**3A—Expressive Elements**
Benchmark:	*Students employ expressive elements of music to communicate abstract thoughts, ideas, and meaning; to share the depth of the human experience; and for self-expression and understanding.*
Learning Task:	**1.3—Students perform with articulations corresponding to baseline-level right-hand technical skills**

Learning Sequences & Processes	Indicators of Success
General Information, Prior Knowledge and Precursors • Students demonstrate a relaxed, correct bow hold • Students demonstrate correct bow hold free of tension • Students understand bowing symbols for basic articulations (down bow, up bow, simple two note slur, accent) • Students can perform two note slurs and accents. Sequence of Activities • Students scan entire music selection to be performed • Discuss all bowing symbols to reinforce understanding of how to produce each bowing found in selection • Discuss the notes needing more emphasis and which beats of the measure need stressed • Discuss style of the music selection • Students review first phrase of music to select the best bowing to build the phrase keeping with the desired style • Students perform first phrase using simple slurs, détaché and accents where appropriate. • Perform selection matching conductor's baton style	• Students perform simple music selections incorporating correct articulations to create desired style. • Students identify and perform articulations and bowings, using correct terminology and bowing techniques.

Standards Links:

Resources and References:

Category 3: Artistic Skills and Knowledge

Content Area:	**3A—Expressive Elements**
Benchmark:	*Students employ expressive elements of music to communicate abstract thoughts, ideas, and meaning; to share the depth of the human experience; and for self-expression and understanding.*
Learning Task:	**2.1—Students evaluate and demonstrate multiple ways of performing a single melody**

Learning Sequences & Processes	Indicators of Success

<u>General Information, Prior Knowledge and Precursors</u>
• Students understand vocabulary: melody, ascending, descending, sequence, repetitive
• Students have previous experience isolating melody lines and phrases.
 	
<u>Sequence of Activities</u>
• Students study the different characteristics of a melodic line:
  • Pitch variation (ascending/descending)
  • Sequential or repetitive figures
  • Rhythmic and metric considerations
  • Style of music
• Students isolate the melodic line from a music selection in their method book or music folder.
• The students sing the melodic line
• The ensemble explores possible ways to perform the melodic line using the following variables:
  • Pitch: crescendo on ascending lines, decrescendo on descending lines
  • Sequential or repetitive figures: change dynamics on each sequence or repetition to build tension and relaxation in the melodic line
  • Rhythmic considerations:
    • Order of importance of beats, e.g., in 4/4 beat one is the strongest; beat three is the second strongest
    • The last beat of the measure has a tendency to lead to the first beat of the following measure.
    • In general, the longer the duration of the note, the more important; the shorter duration notes should be played softer
    • Style of selection (Minuet, March) will determine the stress of beats.
• Students describe the above items in reference to their melodic line.
• Several students perform the melody using the above variables.
• The class reaches consensus on which student interpretation best fits the style, tempo and rhythm of the selected melody.
• The class performs the melody in unison with the agreed upon interpretation.
	• Students present various options for how a melody may be performed.
	• Students discuss what emotion they were trying to portray when they played the phrase a certain way.
	• Students discuss the overall "affect" presented during the performance and experiment with different ways of changing the melody to change the feeling of the selection.

Standards Links:

Resources and References:

Category 3:	Artistic Skills and Knowledge
Content Area:	3A—Expressive Elements
Benchmark:	*Students employ expressive elements of music to communicate abstract thoughts, ideas, and meaning; to share the depth of the human experience; and for self-expression and understanding.*
Learning Task:	**2.2—Students apply knowledge of performance practice to selected repertoire.**

Learning Sequences & Processes	Indicators of Success
General Information, Prior Knowledge and Precursors • Students are able to create phrases using simple dynamics • Students are able to follow a conductor's beat pattern • Students understand the principles of blend and balance in an ensemble Sequence of Activities • Students are able to create phrases using simple dynamics • Students study the different characteristics of a melodic line: A new music selection is given to students • Review composer/arranger of selection and style desired • Students scan and identify all symbols/terms found in their part • Students discuss bowing style for selection • Students vote and/or reach consensus on bowings to use on like parts within the ensemble. Members mark parts accordingly. • Students find phrases and like rhythmic sections • Students share their interpretation of the first phrase noting similar parts across the ensemble • Each section of the ensemble works to blend their sounds • The ensemble determines what section has: the melody, countermelody, harmony, and bass line. • The ensemble works to ensure the balance of the group. • Members make sure the moving part is heard. • Students listen across the ensemble to match pitch and pulse of other sections. • The ensemble responds to the nuances of the conducting gesture.	• Ensemble works together to determine style and bowing of selection. • Ensemble listens to their section and across the ensemble to match pitch, phrasing and rhythm patterns.

Standards Links:

Resources and References:

Level:	Developing

Category 3:	**Artistic Skills and Knowledge**

Content Area:	**3A—Expressive Elements**
Benchmark:	*Students employ expressive elements of music to communicate abstract thoughts, ideas, and meaning; to share the depth of the human experience; and for self-expression and understanding.*
Learning Task:	**2.3—Students perform with articulations corresponding to developing-level right-hand technical skills**

Learning Sequences & Processes	**Indicators of Success**
General Information, Prior Knowledge and Precursors • Students demonstrate correct bow hold free of tension • Students understand bowing symbols for basic articulations (accent, staccato, slurred staccato, martelé, accented détaché, brush stroke and double stops) Sequence of Activities • Select a music excerpt that contains staccato bow markings • Discuss the composer and style of the music • The class first plays the selection using staccato bowing; then repeats the selection using a brush stroke • With teacher assistance the ensemble reaches consensus on appropriate bowing to provide desired style and timbre. • The ensemble applies the bowing to the remainder of the music selection. • Students continue to develop *WASP* (arm weight, bow angle, bow speed and point of contact) techniques • Students apply the *WASP* principles to produce martelé, slurred staccato, accented détaché when marked in the music	• Students understand and apply correct bowing to match articulation symbols found in music selection. • Students demonstrate bowing styles expanding their range of expression

Standards Links:

Resources and References:

Category 3:	**Artistic Skills and Knowledge**
Content Area:	**3A—Expressive Elements**
Benchmark:	*Students employ expressive elements of music to communicate abstract thoughts, ideas, and meaning; to share the depth of the human experience; and for self-expression and understanding.*
Learning Task:	**3.1—Students expand the range of dynamics, tempi, timbre with increased sensitivity to phrasing**

Learning Sequences & Processes	**Indicators of Success**
General Information, Prior Knowledge and Precursors • Vocabulary expansion: *largo, adagio, larghetto, andante, andantino, allegretto, allegro, presto,* and *prestissimo.* • Understanding of *WASP* principles: (weight, angle, speed, point of contact). • Dynamic range: *ppp* to *fff* Sequence of Activities Select several phrases and explore the various methods that musicians may use to create musical drama: • Metronome markings hint at style. Additional adjectives help determine mood within a tempo and sensitivity to phrasing (e.g., *molto, assai, con brio, poco*) • Consider and explore how *accelerando, ritardando, allargando,* and *calando* will effect the phrase. • Tempo can also be influenced by certain technical demands of the piece (faster bowing requirements, etc.) • Add a slight breath/pause before the phrase • Increase dynamic range keeping steady tempo • Practice the echo effect *(f–p)* in repetitive figures. • Repeated notes or sustained tones in a melody may need a slight increase in dynamic to lead to height of phrase. • After reaching *forte,* drop the dynamic level back so the next phrase can be built. • Using the above ideas, record the selected phrases with varying tempi and dynamics.	• Students listen to the recorded phrase variations and determine which interpretation best fits the style of the music selection. • Students transfer phrase knowledge to the remaining phrases of selection

Standards Links:

Resources and References:

Category 3:	Artistic Skills and Knowledge
Content Area:	**3A—Expressive Elements**
Benchmark:	*Students employ expressive elements of music to communicate abstract thoughts, ideas, and meaning; to share the depth of the human experience; and for self-expression and understanding.*
Learning Task:	**3.2—Students perform with a characteristic tone at all dynamic levels**

Learning Sequences & Processes	Indicators of Success

General Information, Prior Knowledge and Precursors
• Overall instrument and bow quality will determine and impact the tone
• The following components of the set-up of the instrument are essential for students to be able to produce a good sound:
 • Bridge: set at the correct height, curve, placement
 • Soundpost placement
 • Condition and quality of strings
 • Bow:
  • Bow hair clean and in good condition
  • Rosin
• Students must have good body format, correct instrument position, and proper bow hand position, with relaxed arms, wrists, and fingers.
 	
Sequence of Activities
• In Andante tempo play a scale in whole notes using the entire bow on each step of the scale. Pure tones—no vibrato
• Maintain consistent tone from frog to tip
• Change bow direction smoothly without jerking or changing speeds.
• Start with *mf* dynamic; zone 3; medium arm weight and bow speed. As approaching tip move the bow slightly closer to the bridge, slightly slow the speed and add a little more natural arm weight.
• After accomplishing a quality *mf* tone throughout the bow stroke, work on *p* and *f* dynamic levels adjusting the arm weight, bow angle, speed and point of contact to maintain a characteristic tone from the frog to tip.
• Students should feel firm contact (tug or resistance) between the string and the bow hair.
• Practice double stops to develop a full tone
• Left hand fingers should be energetic dropping and lifting
• Portato bowing helps develop bow arm weight needed for a full tone. Apply weight using the leverage of the bow and the natural arm weight.
• Listen for sympathetic vibrations for intonation and resonance
• Vibrato is now added on all notes of the scale to enhance the tone.
	• Tone quality remains constant throughout stroke.
	• Tone retains quality when changing dynamic level
	• The tone is resonant and carries throughout the performance venue.
	• Bow speed, point of contact and arm weight change as bow is drawn from frog to tip to maintain the dynamic level.

Standards Links:

Resources and References:

Level:	Proficient

Category 3: Artistic Skills and Knowledge

Content Area:	3A—Expressive Elements
Benchmark:	*Students employ expressive elements of music to communicate abstract thoughts, ideas, and meaning; to share the depth of the human experience; and for self-expression and understanding.*
Learning Task:	**3.3—Students apply knowledge of performance practice to selected repertoire**

Learning Sequences & Processes	Indicators of Success

General Information, Prior Knowledge and Precursors
• Students are able to follow conductor's beat pattern.
• Students are able to blend and balance in the ensemble.
• Students understand how to create phrases varying the dynamics, tempo and bowing style.
 	
Sequence of Activities
• Students listen (no printed score) to an expressive excerpt and indicate their perceived dynamic and tempo contours by drawing on a chart.
• Students use colors to map the mood of excerpt.
• Students share and compare their interpretation charts.
• Students are provided the musical score of the expressive excerpt.
• The class now performs the selection making sure that:
  • Bowing usage is consistent (including WASP principles)
  • Phrasing is consistent between instruction sections
  • Tone is consistent and blended
  • Balance is accurate
  • Intonation, pitch, and rhythmic pulse are accurate and uniform across the ensemble
  • Performance relates to the conducting gesture
	• Ensemble works together to determine style and bowing of selection.
	• Students respond to the nuances of the conducting gesture.
	• Students listen to their section and across the ensemble to match pitch, phrasing and rhythm patterns.

Standards Links:

Resources and References:

Category 3:	Artistic Skills and Knowledge
Content Area:	**3A—Expressive Elements**
Benchmark:	*Students employ expressive elements of music to communicate abstract thoughts, ideas, and meaning; to share the depth of the human experience; and for self-expression and understanding.*
Learning Task:	**3.4—Students perform with articulation corresponding to proficient-level right-hand technical skills**

Learning Sequences & Processes	Indicators of Success
General Information, Prior Knowledge and Precursors • Students demonstrate correct bow hold that is free of tension. • Students demonstrate relaxed right bow arm and balanced posture. • Students understand symbols for articulations (accent, staccato, slurred staccato, martelé, accented détaché, brush stroke, louré, détaché lancé, tremolo, spiccato, double stops, chords, sul ponticello and sul tasto). Sequence of Activities • Select an excerpt from Classical era work to incorporate use of the following bowings: staccato, brush stroke and spiccato. • Review staccato, brush stroke and spiccato bowing on scales in the same key as the selected excerpt. • The ensemble plays the excerpt with each of the three different bowing styles. • With teacher assistance, the ensemble determines the better articulation for the excerpt. • Select an excerpt from a work that uses special effect bowings (e.g., sul ponticello, sul tasto, or tremolo). • Practice the special effect bowings using sustained notes (including chords within the orchestra) on scale patterns, or other echo patterns. • The ensemble plays the excerpt applying the special effects. • Students continue to refine bowing techniques (e.g., martelé, slurred staccato, accented détaché, détaché lance) using the WASP principles.	• Students understand and appropriately apply correct bowing to match articulation symbols found in music selection. • Students perform with a wider range of bowing styles and articulations.

Standards Links:

Resources and References:

235

Category 3:	Artistic Skills and Knowledge
Content Area:	**3A—Expressive Elements**
Benchmark:	*Students employ expressive elements of music to communicate abstract thoughts, ideas, and meaning; to share the depth of the human experience; and for self-expression and understanding.*
Learning Task:	**3.5—Students use vibrato, when appropriate, to enhance timbre and tone**

Learning Sequences & Processes	Indicators of Success
General Information, Prior Knowledge and Precursors • Vibrato is an artistic tool that should be used with consideration of the style of a given piece, performance practice, and an understanding of the musical context (e.g., solo versus ensemble performance). • As students develop skill in vibrato, their ability to control the consistency and style of vibrato is likely to be inconsistent from finger-to-finger (e.g., vibrato on the 4th finger on the violin or viola is much more difficult to master than on the 2nd or 3rd finger), and their ability to play with both wrist and arm vibrato is also likely to be somewhat limited. Nonetheless, students should be guided and encouraged to develop a consistent vibrato that can be used intentionally to enhance timbre and tone. • The ultimate goal for the use of vibrato is not that students simply play all the time with an indiscriminate vibrato motion, but that they are able to adjust vibrato speed, width (amplitude), and warmth (by adjusting the contact point of the finger to the string), depending on the demands of the piece. Too frequently, young and inexperienced musicians play with a non-stop vibrato that can actually interfere with the overall musicality and artistry of a piece. Sequence of Activities • Using a simple melody or a selection from the repertoire that the group is currently performing, the teacher (or another student) demonstrates how variations in vibrato speed can affect tone and timbre. The teacher should demonstrate incorrect vibrato (such as extremely wide or too fast) in addition to a variety of options that are appropriate. • Compare various recordings of the same work, listening specifically for differences in vibrato. • Practice an excerpt with different vibrato styles. The section should strive for uniform tone first without vibrato and then add a uniform vibrato. • Select pieces for which a variety of vibrato styles may be used (such as works with great dynamic variation). • Practice adjusting vibrato speed for higher ranges (generally faster, narrow vibrato) and lower ranges (generally slower and slightly wider).	• Students can adjust vibrato speed, width, and finger contact point to effect changes in timbre and tone. • Students can adjust vibrato to match others within the section. • Students can adjust vibrato in order to make changes in dynamics and interpretative elements. • Students adjust vibrato appropriately for the range of the instrument.

Standards Links:

Resources and References:

Category 3:	**Artistic Skills and Knowledge**
Content Area:	**3A—Expressive Elements**
Benchmark:	*Students employ expressive elements of music to communicate abstract thoughts, ideas, and meaning; to share the depth of the human experience; and for self-expression and understanding.*
Learning Task:	**4.1—Students perform with consistent timbre and tone quality at all dynamic levels.**

Learning Sequences & Processes	**Indicators of Success**
General Information, Prior Knowledge and Precursors • At this advanced level, students should be playing with consistently correct right- and left-hand technique. Students should have control of the four bowing variables (weight, angle, speed, and placement) and be able to adjust all of those elements to make adjustments in tone and timbre. Sequence of Activities • Select a scale, etude, excerpt, or other ensemble exercise. Even as students are learning the notes and rhythms, the teacher should emphasize equal attention on performing with consistent timbre and tone quality. • Practice the given selection with exaggerated dynamics (such as *ppp* or *fff*) even though the written dynamics may be different. • Work to sustain a centered, uniform, and characteristic tone quality throughout the performance. • Repeat the selection, this time making changes in another musical element, such as articulation style, bowing length, intensity of sound, vibrato speed, etc. • The conductor (or section leader) should indicate changes in phrase, dynamic level, or stylistic elements (such as accents or other articulation). Students should respond to these changes while focusing on keeping a balanced and uniform sound across the ensemble. • Apply these concepts to a selected work that the ensemble will perform.	• Students perform at all dynamic levels with consistent timbre and tone quality. • Students control bowing variables at all dynamic levels and when performing various articulation styles. • Students perform with uniform rhythm, intonation, balance, and tone production (blend).

Standards Links:

Resources and References:

Category 3: Artistic Skills and Knowledge

Content Area:	3A—Expressive Elements
Benchmark:	*Students employ expressive elements of music to communicate abstract thoughts, ideas, and meaning; to share the depth of the human experience; and for self-expression and understanding.*
Learning Task:	**4.2—Students perform with a characteristic tone at all dynamic levels**

Learning Sequences & Processes	Indicators of Success
General Information, Prior Knowledge and Precursors • Understanding of and ability to perform at dynamic levels (*ppp* to *fff*) • Understanding tempo markings (*Largo* to *Presto*) • Ability to perform a wide range of bowings • Knowledge of articulation markings Sequence of Activities • Hand out a music example without any articulations, dynamics, or tempo indications. • The ensemble plays the example, as written. • The ensemble sings the melody to determine phrasing. • Discuss how the shaping of the phrase fits into a larger section and the total music unit. • Ensemble determines bowings and fingerings to help create the desired phrasing and style. • Independently students write articulations, dynamics and tempo choices in their part. • Each student performs their interpretation and the ensemble discusses the effectiveness of the expressive choices. • Students consider how the timbre would change if written in a different musical era.	• Student-selected bowings match the phrasing requirements. • Student-selected fingerings permit ease of performance of selected materials. • Because the technical demands of the piece have been addressed, students are able to focus on the musical and interpretive elements of the performance.

Standards Links:

Resources and References:

Category 3: Artistic Skills and Knowledge

Content Area:	3A—Expressive Elements
Benchmark:	*Students employ expressive elements of music to communicate abstract thoughts, ideas, and meaning; to share the depth of the human experience; and for self-expression and understanding.*
Learning Task:	**4.3—Students understand and perform with correct performance practice for selected repertoire**

Learning Sequences & Processes	Indicators of Success
General Information, Prior Knowledge and Precursors • As students progress to higher levels of repertoire, they are likely to play fewer arrangements and more often play the original work by the composer (such as the actual concerto grosso as written by the composer rather than a simplified arrangement for younger orchestras). Because arrangements are frequently written to provide access to great musical works for younger students, the subtle details of performance practice are often omitted. For example, students may only play basic martelé or détaché strokes when they play a grade-2 arrangement of a work by Corelli, but when they play the original work, they may have to use various forms of détaché (such as louré) to correctly perform the work. • There is a drastic difference between the technical capabilities of period instruments and modern instruments. In addition, the conditions or venues where the original work was intended to be performed may vary greatly from the situation where the ensemble is going to play the work now (e.g., performing the concerto grosso with a large orchestra in a concert hall versus performing the work with 6–8 string players and a harpsichord in a small salon). As a result, conductors need to determine which aspects of authentic performance practice are appropriate for their specific ensembles. (Note: though this learning task focuses on historical performance practice, authentic performance practice also applies to non-classical music, such as jazz, folk, and other types of music.) Sequence of Activities • Compare multiple recordings of a selected piece, such as a performance on modern instruments versus a performance on period instruments. • Analyze differences in articulation styles, general dynamic range, tempos, intonation (the period performance is likely to be tuned much lower), tone (especially the use of vibrato), ornamentation and overall affect of the piece. • Discuss the historical and social context in which the piece was performed. Was it a large concert hall or a small chamber? Who was present? What was the size of the ensemble? What types of instruments were in the ensemble? What are the differences between period instruments and modern instruments? • Choose one of the elements, such as articulation style from the analysis conducted by the class to apply to the piece. Is it possible to replicate the articulation from a period performance on a modern instrument? What adjustments can and should be made? Is it possible to hold the bow differently, for example, to achieve a lighter martelé sound? • Repeat the selection, applying a different element each time (dynamics, speed, etc.). • Determine as an ensemble, under the guidance of the conductor, how much the final interpretation will reflect a period performance. • This is an excellent opportunity, as well, to coordinate with other departments in the school (such as art, literature, and history) in a discussion of the living, social, and political conditions that existed at the time the piece was performed.	• Students correctly identify and discuss differences in performance practice for the given work. • Students are able to adjust elements of their performance to fit the requirements of the piece. • Students understand the living, social, and political conditions at the time that the piece was written and can apply that knowledge to their performance of the work.

Standards Links:

Resources and References:

Category 3:	**Artistic Skills and Knowledge**
Content Area:	3A—Expressive Elements
Benchmark:	*Students employ expressive elements of music to communicate abstract thoughts, ideas, and meaning; to share the depth of the human experience; and for self-expression and understanding.*
Learning Task:	**4.4—Students perform with articulations corresponding to advanced-level right-hand technical skills**

Learning Sequences & Processes	Indicators of Success
General Information, Prior Knowledge and Precursors • Students demonstrate correct bow hold that is free of tension. • Students demonstrate relaxed right bow arm and balanced posture. • Students understand symbols for articulations (accent, staccato, slurred staccato, martelé, accented détaché, brush stroke, louré, détaché lancé, tremolo, spiccato, double stops, chords, sul ponticello, sul tasto, ricochet, sautillé and flying spiccato). Sequence of Activities • Select an excerpt with fast scale-like passages. • Review flying staccato and slurred-staccato bowing. • Apply flying staccato and slurred-staccato bowing to the excerpt. • Select an excerpt with short, light articulations and quick rhythms as in Rossini's William Tell Overture. • Practice ricochet bowing on open strings. • Apply ricochet bowing to excerpt. • Students apply bow articulations to works such as "Mars" from *The Planets*, by Gustav Holst. • Students continue to develop bowings (martelé, slurred staccato, accented détaché, détaché lancé, louré, chords, sul ponticello, and sul tasto) using the WASP principles.	• Students understand and apply correct bowing to match articulation symbols found in music selection. • Students demonstrate bowing styles expanding their range of expression.

Standards Links:

Resources and References:

Category 3: Artistic Skills and Knowledge

Content Area:	**3A—Expressive Elements**
Benchmark:	*Students employ expressive elements of music to communicate abstract thoughts, ideas, and meaning; to share the depth of the human experience; and for self-expression and understanding.*
Learning Task:	**4.5—Students demonstrate artistic applications of vibrato**

Learning Sequences & Processes	Indicators of Success

General Information, Prior Knowledge and Precursors
• Left hand is relaxed and free of tension
• Left hand fingers are flexible and elastic
• Left arm well balanced
 	
Sequence of Activities
• Students work for a consistent vibrato on each finger.
• Practice varying the width and speed of the vibrato.
• Students practice cycles (forward and backward movement) on each tone. Four, five, six, seven cycles per second.
• Practice carrying the vibrato over from one note to the next.
• Students practice varying the speed, width and intensity:
  • *Forte* passages may incorporate a more intense and wider vibrato
  • *Piano* passages may incorporate a narrow, subdued vibrato
  • Narrow vibrato: on soft passages and music which is simple and pure
  • Medium width vibrato: *mf* and *f* passages for expressive music of all types
  • Wide vibrato: very loud passages, passionate, romantic music
• Students practice varying the width and speed of the vibrato in the extreme ranges of their instrument. For higher pitches, a faster, narrower vibrato is usually implemented.
• Students practice varying their vibrato to fit the dynamic level. For violin and viola, the stronger the dynamics, the more that arm vibrato is used. Likewise, the softer the dynamics, the more that wrist vibrato is used.
	• Students adjust the speed, width and intensity of their vibrato to fit the musical demands of the selections
	• Students demonstrate a gradual transition from one vibrato to another with subtlety
	• The student's vibrato demonstrates even oscillations
	• Finger joints bend a little

Standards Links:

Resources and References:

Category 3:	**Artistic Skills and Knowledge**
Content Area:	**3A—Expressive Elements**
Benchmark:	*Students employ expressive elements of music to communicate abstract thoughts, ideas, and meaning; to share the depth of the human experience; and for self-expression and understanding.*
Learning Task:	**4.6—Students use ornamentation, as appropriate to the performance practice and conventions of the period and style**

Learning Sequences & Processes	**Indicators of Success**
General Information, Prior Knowledge and Precursors • Left and right hands are relaxed and free of tension; fingers are flexible and student performs with purposeful flexion in bow hand • Left arm well balanced • In this learning task, the goal for the left-hand is that students will be able to discern between core melody and options for the embellishment of that melody with the left hand; students learn to visualize team relationships between fingers. • The goal for the right hand is that students will be able to discern between core melody and options for the embellishment of that melody with the bow. Sequence of Activities—Left Hand • Teacher supplies class with a sentence (e.g., "I can't believe how hot it is outside."). • Teacher invites each (or chosen) student(s) to say this sentence as differently as possible by changing the order of the words, emphasizing certain words, replacing certain words, changes in vocal sounds/pitch, etc. • Teacher presents the several examples of ornamentation (through demonstration or recordings): grace note, turn, trill, slide, vibratrill, and vibraslide. • Students compare and contrast the sounds, imitating the teacher's demonstration and also creating their own variations. Sequence of Activities—Right Hand • Teacher supplies class with a sentence (e.g., "I can't believe how hot it is outside."). • Teacher invites each (or chosen) student(s) to say this sentence as differently as possible by changing the order of the words, emphasizing certain words, replacing certain words, changes in vocal sounds/pitch, etc. • Teacher presents the following several of ornamentation (through demonstration or recordings): tremolo, accentuation, martelé, spiccato, and chop technique. • Students compare and contrast the sounds, imitating the teacher's demonstration and also creating their own variations.	• Students apply style appropriate left-hand ornamentation to the core melody • Students can apply style-appropriate right-hand ornamentation to the core melody

Standards Links:

Resources and References:

Content Area 3B—Historical and Cultural Elements

Students listen to, respond to, and perform music from a wide range of genres in a culturally authentic manner, reflecting the diverse nature of people groups and cultures across the world and in the US; performances demonstrate an understanding of historical and cultural contexts and reflect stylistic traditions and practice.

Learning Tasks

1.1	Students listen to selected music from diverse cultures and musical eras
1.2	Students identify, describe and compare distinguishing characteristics of composers and styles from selected repertoire
1.3	Students perform music from diverse styles
2.1	Students listen to selected music from diverse cultures and musical eras
2.2	Students identify, describe and compare distinguishing characteristics of composers and styles from selected repertoire
2.3	Students perform music from an expanding repertoire of diverse styles
3.1	Students listen to selected music from diverse cultures and musical eras
3.2	Students analyze and classify music according to style, composer, and genre
3.3	Students perform music from a large repertoire of diverse styles
4.1	Students listen to selected music from diverse cultures and musical eras
4.2	Students analyze and classify music according to style, composer, and genre
4.3	Students perform a comprehensive repertoire of eclectic styles in a manner that reflects understanding of cultural and stylistic traditions.

Category 3:	Artistic Skills and Knowledge
Content Area:	**3B—Historical and Cultural Elements**
Benchmark:	*Students listen to, respond to, and perform music from a wide range of genres in a culturally authentic manner, reflecting the diverse nature of people groups and cultures across the world and in the US; performances demonstrate an understanding of historical and cultural contexts and reflect stylistic traditions and practice.*
Learning Task:	**1.1—Students listen to selected music from diverse cultures and musical eras** **1.2—Students identify, describe and compare distinguishing characteristics of composers and styles from selected repertoire** **1.3—Students perform music from diverse styles**

Learning Sequences & Processes	Indicators of Success
General Information, Prior Knowledge and Precursors • The teacher must set the stage in the classroom so that students learn more than just the musical and technical elements of any piece. This needs to be started at the baseline level and continued through high school. • Teachers will need to give students opportunities to compare/contrast styles needed for the pieces found in their first and second volume of their text as well as in the pieces being studied. Sequence of Activities—Learning Task 1.1 • Play recordings of the music the students are playing. This could be the exact piece or arrangement they are playing or an excerpt of a larger work from which they play a theme. • Play recordings of other contrasting pieces by composers whose music the students are playing. • Play recordings of other music from a variety of cultures other than the pieces the students are playing. • Feature a composer or country of the month in which students can begin to explore the great wealth of music available to string players. Sequence of Activities—Learning Task 1.2 • When introducing new pieces from the textbook, ask students what is new and have them contrast it with a piece learned earlier. Depending on the age of the students, questions could be very basic such as the feeling that major might evoke compared to minor tonality (students might use "happy" and "sad" though those two terms are not always accurate, especially for different cultures who view tonality through non-Western eyes), short vs. longer bow stroke, folk song or a classical theme. Begin to introduce relevant terminology as they progress through the text learning new skills and styles of music. • Using echo patterns, demonstrate the bowing style and have students echo back. • Ask the students to locate the given style in the music being studied. Sequence of Activities—Learning Task 1.3 • Literature performed at this level should be folk songs from various countries, short arrangements of famous melodies, original works that match the concepts presented in the beginning method book, and also styles such as boogie-woogie, jazz or rock. Curricular Extension • Provide opportunities and resources for students to independently gain more information about the music, culture and history of music being learned.	• Students can articulate that their excerpt or arrangement may be a portion of a larger work or an original composition by a contemporary composer. • Students understand that composers use a variety of musical concepts, compose for a variety of instruments and in varying styles. • Students describe basic stylistic similarities in music from a particular culture. • Students demonstrate awareness that there are many famous composers from many different countries composing many styles of music. • When music calls for specific bow strokes such as shuffle bowing or a Baroque staccato, students will be able to demonstrate this in a musical context and locate it in the printed music.

Standards Links:

Resources and References:

Category 3:	Artistic Skills and Knowledge
Content Area:	**3B—Historical and Cultural Elements**
Benchmark:	*Students listen to, respond to, and perform music from a wide range of genres in a culturally authentic manner, reflecting the diverse nature of people groups and cultures across the world and in the US; performances demonstrate an understanding of historical and cultural contexts and reflect stylistic traditions and practice.*
Learning Task:	**2.1—Students listen to selected music from diverse cultures and musical eras** **2.2—Students identify, describe and compare distinguishing characteristics of composers and styles from selected repertoire** **2.3—Students perform music from an expanding repertoire of diverse styles**

Learning Sequences & Processes	Indicators of Success
General Information, Prior Knowledge and Precursors • The teacher must set the stage in the classroom so that students learn more than just the musical and technical elements of any piece. This needs to be started at the baseline level and continued through high school. • Teachers will need to give students opportunities to compare/contrast styles needed for the pieces found in their first and second volume of their text as well as in the pieces being studied. Sequence of Activities—Learning Task 2.1 • Play recordings of music from various cultures and eras asking students to describe the instrumentation, rhythm, melody, form, timbre/tone color, and harmony. • Show pictures of the instruments used in music from a particular culture. • When listening to music of other cultures, students know the characteristics and traditions that correlate to this music. • Use simple listening maps when listening to works by famous composers. Have the students create their own listening map and share with others in the class. Sequence of Activities—Learning Task 2.2 • As each new piece is introduced, the teacher should discuss the style needed for the piece, how it is notated and should compare it to other pieces being studied. Each new style should be modeled for the students. • Define simple Baroque bowing, demonstrate it and have students imitate. Sequence of Activities—Learning Task 2.3 • Literature performed at this level should begin to teach musical styles based on the historical and cultural elements of the music. Music should include simple Baroque, Classical, fiddling, swing and jazz. Begin to integrate decorations, customs, descriptive readings, other authentic instruments or costumes into the concert to enhance and ingrain details about music that the students have learned. Curricular Extension • Provide opportunities and resources for students to gain more information about the music, culture and history of music being learned on their own.	• Students articulate characteristics of music when writing or talking about what they hear. Note that a word bank is helpful when learning to describe musical attributes. • Students understand that there is a wide variety of string instruments used in musical cultures around the world. • Students comprehend that other cultures also have music for various events, celebrations or traditions. • Students use and create listening maps. • Students can describe and demonstrate the style required by the music being studied. • Students will demonstrate simple Baroque bowing and will be able to locate where in the piece it is used. • Students perform music in the style that it was intended and experience music in other multi-sensory manners.

Standards Links:

Resources and References:

Category 3:	Artistic Skills and Knowledge
Content Area:	**3B—Historical and Cultural Elements**
Benchmark:	*Students listen to, respond to, and perform music from a wide range of genres in a culturally authentic manner, reflecting the diverse nature of people groups and cultures across the world and in the US; performances demonstrate an understanding of historical and cultural contexts and reflect stylistic traditions and practice.*
Learning Task:	**3.1—Students listen to selected music from diverse cultures and musical eras** **3.2—Students analyze and classify music according to style, composer, and genre** **3.3—Students perform music from a large repertoire of diverse styles**

Learning Sequences & Processes	Indicators of Success
<u>General Information, Prior Knowledge and Precursors</u> • Many teachers opt for concert-only preparation and there are many opportunities for learning to be critical thinkers as they analyze what they are playing. Before beginning new concert music, the teacher could assign students one piece and ask students to research it online in preparation for class discussion. <u>Sequence of Activities—Learning Task 3.1</u> • After listening to selected repertoire, discuss when and where the piece was composed (the musical era), and what was happening historically during this time. Post pictures of the composer, other composers of the era, famous people and inventions from the era. On a map, locate the country in which the composer lived. Identify how that country is similar or different to our country. Identify what was occurring in our country when the piece was composed. • Listen to other pieces written by the composer being studied. Look for commonalities of the composer's style (or characteristics of the genre). • Compare classical music styles with other styles within strings, such as blues, rock, bluegrass, Celtic, jazz, world music, etc. <u>Sequence of Activities—Learning Task 3.2</u> • Because students have listened to a variety of music in class, they should now be ready to discuss whether it is a classical piece, film music or an eclectic style. Terminology should be introduced as they listen to music so they can identify the characteristics found in any genre of music. • Students should be introduced to Baroque, Classical, Romantic, and Modern music and should be familiar with composers from those eras. They should become familiar with the types of music written: symphonies, opera, overtures, tone poems, concerti, quartets – all forms of music they should be capable of performing in either an arranged or original version. • The teacher should discuss the form of the music being studied, highlighting characteristic elements of the form and style. • Using fiddling as an example of an eclectic form, students should know the parts of a fiddle tune as well as various types of fiddle music. <u>Sequence of Activities—Learning Task 3.3</u> • Literature performed at this level should include styles such as concerti grossi, operatic overtures, jazz charts with improvised solos, small ensembles, full orchestra, pieces in mixed meters, have sound effects, and electronic music. <u>Curricular Extension</u> • Provide opportunities and resources for students to gain more information about the music, culture and history of music being learned on their own.	• Students know the basic eras of music and recognize photos of composers. They also understand the events that occurred simultaneously in our country and the country in which the music was composed. • Students recognize other famous melodies by specific composers studied. • Students become familiar with non-classical musical styles and learn the style in which the music is to be played. • Students can have an informed discussion about a piece of music by identifying what type of music it is and what characteristics it uses • When sight-reading music for upcoming concerts, students should be able to name what period it comes from and answer questions about the form of the piece. • Students begin to master specific artistic techniques used in a wide variety of styles of music.

Standards Links:

Resources and References:

Level:	Advanced

Category 3: Artistic Skills and Knowledge

Content Area:	3B—Historical and Cultural Elements
Benchmark:	*Students listen to, respond to, and perform music from a wide range of genres in a culturally authentic manner, reflecting the diverse nature of people groups and cultures across the world and in the US; performances demonstrate an understanding of historical and cultural contexts and reflect stylistic traditions and practice.*
Learning Task:	**4.1—Students listen to selected music from diverse cultures and musical eras** **4.2—Students analyze and classify music according to style, composer, and genre** **4.3—Students perform a comprehensive repertoire of eclectic styles in a manner that reflects understanding of cultural and stylistic traditions**

Learning Sequences & Processes	Indicators of Success
General Information, Prior Knowledge and Precursors • Artistic development and success at the advanced level is directly tied to the emphasis that the teacher places on artistry even during the beginning stages of performance on the instrument. The teacher must set the stage in the classroom so students learn more than just the notes for a particular piece. • By this point, students should be able to clearly articulate the differences between the major periods of Western classical music (e.g., Baroque, Classical, etc.) and also have a basic understanding of stringed instrument performance within traditional styles (folk music, etc.) Sequence of Activities—Learning Task 4.1, 4.2 • When listening to music, study the form (e.g., strophic, binary, medley, ternary, rondo, sonata etc.), texture (monophonic, homophonic and polyphonic), and harmonic structure of the piece. • Listen to a variety of musical examples from each specific composer studied. Compare the selected works, looking at both stylistic and compositional elements. • Identify a variety of musical styles when musical recordings are played and studied. • Listen to, analyze, and perform various examples of non-Western classical music. This should include the study of 12-tone, aleatoric, soul, electronic, experimental, fusion, neoclassical, new wave, salsa, samba, swing, world music and techno styles. Sequence of Activities—Learning Task 4.3 • Literature performed at this level should be a balance of literature that is original, culturally authentic, and reflects multiple styles and cultures, while honing in on artistic skills relevant to these specific styles of music	• Students recognize and identify several forms of music, texture or harmonic structure. • Students understand and can describe the compositional techniques of individual composers and for what instruments they composed. • Students begin to recognize the purpose a composer composed for such as a royal occasion, church, opera, the symphony or simply for personal enjoyment. • Students are able to describe and perform with an understanding of the depth, breadth and creativity in a wide range of musical styles. • Students master articulation, phrasing, accents, bowing techniques and other characteristics of a wide range of musical styles.

Standards Links:

Resources and References:

Content Area 3C—Evaluation of Music and Musical Performance

Students evaluate and analyze music for executive skill, musicianship, and artistic considerations; evaluate and analyze the individual and group performances based on appropriate criteria.

Learning Tasks

1.1 Students evaluate individual and group performance using established criteria.

1.2 Students describe personal preference in music listening and group performance.

2.1 Students evaluate individual and group performance using established criteria.

2.2 Students describe personal preference in music listening and group performance.

2.3 Students, with teacher assistance, establish criteria for evaluating individual and group performances based on the level of music performed

3.1 Students evaluate individual and group performance using established criteria.

3.2 Students describe personal preference in music listening and group performance

3.3 Students, with teacher assistance, establish criteria for evaluating individual and group performances based on the level of music performed

3.4 Students compare and contrast performances of various interpretations of the same piece, using appropriate terminology and informed value judgments

4.1 Students evaluate individual and group performance using established criteria.

4.2 Students describe personal preference in music listening and group performance

4.3 Students, with teacher assistance, establish criteria for evaluating individual and group performances based on the level of music performed

4.4 Students compare and contrast performances of various interpretations of the same piece, using appropriate terminology and informed value judgments

Category 3: Artistic Skills and Knowledge

Content Area:	**3C—Evaluation of Music and Musical Performance**
Benchmark:	*Students evaluate and analyze music for executive skill, musicianship, and artistic considerations; evaluate and analyze the individual and group performances based on appropriate criteria.*
Learning Task:	**1.1—Students evaluate individual and group performance using established criteria**

Learning Sequences & Processes	Indicators of Success
<u>General Information, Prior Knowledge and Precursors</u> • Students understand terms and symbols found in their music selection. • The evaluation form used needs to give specific feedback on the performance so the student(s) understand their score and how to improve future performances • The rubric/checklist needs to fit the age and experience level of student(s) • For less experienced players, select one area at a time to evaluate. • Select a list of criteria that exemplify musical works and styles. • Students should have been working on the music to be evaluated <u>Sequence of Activities</u> • Students watch and listen to their performance or a class rehearsal video. • Students share their constructive criticism of the performance. • The student observations of the ensemble's positive points and items needing improvement are placed on the classroom whiteboard • The techniques needed for "items needing improvement" are reviewed. • Specific passages are rehearsed applying strategies to improve. • Record students as they perform the selection trying to incorporate the class suggestions to enhance their playing. • The teacher explains the evaluation form with the criteria the student performers will be scoring as they listen the second time. • Students watch and listen to the second performance and score their performance. • After scoring, students share their observations with their peers. • The new recommendations for improvement are placed on a large post-it and placed in the room so students will be able to refer to the list during rehearsals. • The more specific the feedback, the better the students will be able to apply to improving their individual and group skills	• Students verbally assess a performance using the given criteria. • Students use correct terminology in evaluating a performance • Students give constructive criticism to enhance future performances • Student feedback is specific in praising accomplishments of peers • Students critique body format, intonation, rhythm, expression, balance, blend, tone, bowing • Students use evaluation tool accurately marking strong and weak parts of performance

Standards Links:

Resources and References:

Category 3:	Artistic Skills and Knowledge
Content Area:	3C—Evaluation of Music and Musical Performance
Benchmark:	*Students evaluate and analyze music for executive skill, musicianship, and artistic considerations; evaluate and analyze the individual and group performances based on appropriate criteria.*
Learning Task:	**1.2—Students describe personal preference in music listening and group performance**

Learning Sequences & Processes	Indicators of Success
General Information, Prior Knowledge and Precursors • Students understand terms and symbols found in their music selection • Teacher provides a *Listening Page* for the students that gives guidelines towards evaluating performances and includes items such as name of listening selection, composer, music period, date of composition, etc. • Suggestions of things to listen for at the bottom of page. • Teacher selects a wide range of literature for each grading period Sequence of Activities **First Idea:** *Music of the Week* • Once a week as students enter the classroom a recording is playing. (This music varies each week to cover many different musical genres.) • The name of the selection, composer, composer dates, music period, and style are on the board. • Students write five sentences on the music selection being played. • A listening form with suggested items to listen for is provided. • Students describe what instruments they hear, describe the sounds, rhythm patterns, harmony, etc. • Students state what they liked about the performance (and why they liked the performance). • Students keep a listening notebook containing all their *Music of the Week* writing logs. • At the end of each marking period, students reflect on the music examples they heard. • The students write a paragraph on which listening example was their favorite and why. **Second Idea:** *Group Music Performance Assessment/Festival* • After the orchestra has finished their event performance, the ensemble listens to three other performing groups. • Create a simple evaluation form for the students to fill out while listening. The form could request students list three positive things about the performing group and three areas needing improvement. Or, the form could be the same form used in the adjudication process. Questions could be: Would you like to perform one of the selections you heard today? Would you like to hear this group in the future?	• Students are forming their own ideas about the various music examples. • Through written logs, students express their preferences in music. • Students purchase a recording of a selection they heard or attend a local performance outside the school program. • Students describe preferences in performing groups at their own level of performance.

Standards Links:

Resources and References:

Level:	Developing
	Proficient
	Advanced

Category 3:	Artistic Skills and Knowledge
Content Area:	3C—Evaluation of Music and Musical Performance
Benchmark:	*Students evaluate and analyze music for executive skill, musicianship, and artistic considerations; evaluate and analyze the individual and group performances based on appropriate criteria.*
Learning Task:	**2.1, 3.1, 4.1—Students evaluate individual and group performance using established criteria**

Learning Sequences & Processes	Indicators of Success
General Information, Prior Knowledge and Precursors • Learning Tasks 2.1, 3.1, and 4.1 are all extensions of Learning Task 1.1. • In general, students should become more sophisticated in their use of musical terminology, in the depth and comprehensiveness of their critique, and their overall insight and understanding of the repertoire being performed and *how* it is being performed. • Additional activities to be included as students progress include: recording lessons and rehearsals and evaluating the recording compared to the perception the students had while they were playing; comparing recordings and/or performances of the same piece by different ensembles (including different levels of ensembles, such as a university orchestra as compared to a high school orchestra); use of technology and software to provide instant feedback about performance.	

Standards Links:

Resources and References:

Level:	Developing
	Proficient
	Advanced

Category 3:	Artistic Skills and Knowledge
Content Area:	3C—Evaluation of Music and Musical Performance
Benchmark:	*Students evaluate and analyze music for executive skill, musicianship, and artistic considerations; evaluate and analyze the individual and group performances based on appropriate criteria.*
Learning Task:	**2.2, 3.2, 4.2—Students describe personal preference in music listening and group performance**

Learning Sequences & Processes	Indicators of Success
General Information, Prior Knowledge and Precursors • Learning Tasks 2.2, 3.2, and 4.2 are all extensions of Learning Task 1.2. • In general, students should become more sophisticated in their use of musical terminology, in the depth and comprehensiveness of their description, and their overall insight and understanding of the repertoire being performed and *how* it is being performed. • Students should make deeper judgments about the affective aspects of musical performance, specifically, *why* a piece of music is important to them, and *what* aspects of the music influence their choice. • Students may not be able to fully articulate, with words, the power of music, but they should be able to communicate about the meaning of music to them, as individuals, as this is an important tool for developing self-understanding and the ability to communicate musical understanding to an audience.	

Standards Links:

Resources and References:

Developing

Proficient

Advanced

Category 3:	Artistic Skills and Knowledge
Content Area:	3C—Evaluation of Music and Musical Performance
Benchmark:	*Students evaluate and analyze music for executive skill, musicianship, and artistic considerations; evaluate and analyze the individual and group performances based on appropriate criteria.*
Learning Task:	**2.3, 3.3, 4.3—Students, with teacher assistance, establish criteria for evaluating individual and group performances based on the level of music performed**

Learning Sequences & Processes	Indicators of Success
General Information, Prior Knowledge and Precursors • As with other learning tasks in this content area, the levels of progress relate directly to the level of sophistication that individual students have. It is essential that the teacher provide regular opportunities, from the first lessons and rehearsals, for students to engage in critical thinking and evaluation about music and musical performances. • The teacher should provide students with examples of specific criteria, but also allow the students to determine criteria, so that they can learn to be creative and critical thinkers, when others aren't present to guide their performance and practice. • It is also helpful if students have had regular experience with evaluation processes, so that they are comfortable speaking about their performances and the performances of others; they should also have some knowledge of correct terminology to use in performance. Sequence of Activities • Students brainstorm items they observe when listening to a performance (including both visual and aural items) • All suggestions are accepted and placed on the board. • The teacher and students then group like ideas/areas. • The teacher selects one area for evaluation. • The class with teacher guidance composes an observation form focusing on one area to be evaluated, such as *bow hand*, *rhythm, balance* and *blend.* • The evaluation tool may be a rubric or checklist • The class brainstorms specific criteria for the area of evaluation, i.e., *bow hand* would define placement of each finger and the thumb. • Assign points for each criterion • The form(s) devised need to give specific feedback on each performance area so the student(s) understand their score and how to improve future performances.	• Students reinforce their knowledge as they determine criteria to be used in evaluations. • Students improve their areas of weakness due to understanding of criteria. • The class uses the criteria for future performances and evaluations

Standards Links:

Resources and References:

253

Category 3:	**Artistic Skills and Knowledge**
Content Area:	3C—Evaluation of Music and Musical Performance
Benchmark:	*Students evaluate and analyze music for executive skill, musicianship, and artistic considerations; evaluate and analyze the individual and group performances based on appropriate criteria.*
Learning Task:	**3.4, 4.4—Students compare and contrast performances of various interpretations of the same piece, using appropriate terminology and informed value judgments**

Learning Sequences & Processes	**Indicators of Success**
General Information, Prior Knowledge and Precursors • As with other learning tasks in this content area, the levels of progress relate directly to the level of sophistication that individual students have. It is essential that the teacher provide regular opportunities, from the first lessons and rehearsals, for students to engage in critical thinking and evaluation about music and musical performances. • Students have studied or played the music before listening to the performances. • Terms in the music have been defined and are understood by students. • General knowledge about the music selection is given: title, composer or arranger, era and/or style of music Sequence of Activities • Two performances of the same music selection are played, for example: 1. In an elementary string class, the teacher may perform the method book line demonstrating two different interpretations. 2. In middle and high schools, students may compare a MP3 recording from the publisher and a recording of their ensemble performing the same selection. 3. Two professional recordings of the same work may be used. • For each of the examples, students are provided with a diagram with areas of where performances are the same or different. First Performance · Same · Second Performance • The students list items that are the same or different as they listen. • Students share their assessment of the two performances, using appropriate terminology. • Items may include: timbre, tempo, phrasing, style of bowing, dynamics, quality of performance • The students support their preference of interpretation using past musical experiences.	• Working individually students describe their preference in music. • Students use appropriate terminology when writing and verbalizing their music choices. • Students support their choices in comparing music selections

Standards Links:

Resources and References:

Glossary

This glossary contains a basic overview of general terminology found in this curriculum. More specific descriptions and definitions of specialized terminology used in this book may be found in materials from the resource list or in general dictionaries of music.

Alternative Styles—Also known as Eclectic Styles, relates to a movement within the string education community to include non-classical styles in the curriculum. These styles include traditional music from around the world, in addition to non-classical Western styles. Examples include jazz, rock, blues, folk music, world music, fiddling styles, among others.

Artistic Skills & Knowledge—One of three categories of skills and knowledge in this curriculum. Artistic skills and knowledge refers to those elements that relate to the creative and expressive side of music-making, beyond mere performance, such as improvisation, performance with artistic understanding, etc.

Benchmark—Benchmarks are specific levels of objectives or outcomes related to the overall curriculum standard. Within this curriculum there are four benchmark levels: Beginning, Developing, Proficient, and Advanced. These benchmarks are not tied to a specific grade level, as the amount of resources and other program characteristics (including teaching time, instrument availability, scheduling, program support, administrative support, class size) vary greatly across the country. We also recognize that individual student progress within specific Standard areas will vary greatly. We recommend, however, that teachers and school districts that use this curriculum as a model do link the benchmarks to specific grade levels.

Bilateral movement—Bilateral movement is an extension of unilateral movement and leads to the development of the sequential bow stroke. In unilateral movement, the body moves in the same general direction as the bow. In bilateral movement, the body moves in the opposite direction of the bow.

Complex double stops—Complex double stops are created by playing fingered notes on two adjacent strings.

Enrhythmic Patterns—Rhythm patterns that sound the same to the listening ear, but are notated differently (e.g., a group of four eighth-notes and two quarter-notes in common time and a group of four quarter-notes and two half-notes in cut time).

Executive Skills and Knowledge—One of three categories of skills and knowledge in this curriculum. Executive skills and knowledge refers to those technical skills and understandings required to physically perform on the instrument, such as body format, bowings, etc.

Learning Task—A specific sequence of activities, prior knowledge, precursors, and indicators of success related individual elements found within the scope-and-sequence. In this curriculum, learning tasks provide a structural outline and possible teaching ideas for specific concepts.

Macrobeat—The macrobeat is the primary pulse or beat that is perceived in the rhythmic movement of a piece (sometimes called the "big beat"). The macrobeat is often perceived to be longer (because of the emphasis that is felt by the listener) than other beats in a measure, though this is not actually true in terms of measuring time.

Microbeat—The microbeat is the division of the macrobeat into two or three equal parts. In terms of notation, if the macrobeat is indicated as a quarter-note, then the microbeats will be two eighth-notes. If the macrobeat is a dotted quarter-note, then the microbeats would be three eighth-notes.

Musicianship Skills and Knowledge—One of three categories of skills and knowledge in this curriculum. Musicianship skills and knowledge refers to those elements, such as understanding of rhythms, aural skills, note-reading skills, etc., that relate to musical understandings.

Scope-and-Sequence—The specific list of skills and knowledge required in this curriculum, organized both sequentially (in terms of degree of difficulty) and by general content area.

Sequential Bow Stroke—The sequential bow stroke involves the coordinated movement of the body from lower body to the upper body, through the arms, into the hands and fingers, to the bow, in anticipation and response to the bow stroke. Though it is easier to show than describe, the sequential bow stroke generally has a naturally wavy shape, rather than angular, or simply having the body move in the opposite direction of the bow.

Shifting—The process of moving from one position to another on the fingerboard. Shifting is usually done for the purposes of convenience (such as avoiding difficult string crossings), to change timbre, or because it is required to access notes on the highest string that aren't playable in first position.

Simple double stops—Double stops are played by bowing or plucking two adjacent strings at the same time. Simple double stops consist of playing a fingered note on one string with the adjacent higher or lower open string.

Unilateral movement—Unilateral movement is the initial stage of bow arm movement in relation to the body. All elements move in the same direction (e.g., when the bow moves to the right, the body also moves to the right). Unilateral movement leads to bilateral movement and ultimately to the development of the sequential bow stroke.

Vertical technique—A term used to describe the general elements related to movement up-and-down the fingerboard (including facility in shifting, weight distribution, and the transference of weight between fingers in a single position or as the arm moves during the shifting process).

Vibrato—Vibrato is an oscillation of pitch that is an expressive or ornamental technique created by rolling the fingertip *below* the pitch and back, in a controlled and intentional motion. Vibrato is sometimes characterized as initiated by the finger, wrist, or arm. To perform any of these vibratos, the shoulder, elbow, wrist, thumb and finger joints must be free of excessive tension. It is used to intensify or add warmth and richness to the sound. Vibrato was not a standard part of performance practice on string instruments until the nineteenth century.

WASP—The basic bowing variables used to control tone production, including weight (the amount of weight placed by the player on the bow in order to control volume or intensity), *angle* (the angle of the bow to the string, which is generally 90 degrees, but may be changed as the player moves toward the fingerboard or toward the bridge, *speed* (directly related to the amount of the bow used, and influences the intensity, volume, and color of the tone), and *placement* (relates to the contact point on the bow itself—i.e., which part of the bow—and the contact point on the string—i.e., closer to the fingerboard or the bridge, or somewhere in-between).

Curriculum Resource List

Note: Inclusion in this list of resources does not denote an endorsement of any particular book, series, or other resource. Likewise, the absence of a specific resource does not indicate a lack of support for any particular book, series, or other method.

General Pedagogy, Program Design, and Related Resources

Allen, Michael, Louis Bergonzi, Jacquelyn Dillon-Krass, Robert Gillespie, James Kjelland and Dorothy Straub. Compiled and edited by David Littrell and Laura Reed Racin. *Teaching Music through Performance in Orchestra, Vol. 1.* Chicago: GIA Publications, 2001.

_____. *Teaching Music through Performance in Orchestra, Vol. 2.* Allen, Michael, Louis Bergonzi, Jacquelyn Dillon-Krass, Robert Gillespie, James Kjelland and Dorothy Straub. Compiled and edited by David Littrell. Chicago: GIA Publications, 2003.

_____. *Teaching Music through Performance in Orchestra, Vol. 3.* Chicago: GIA Publications, 2008.

Applebaum, Samuel. *The Art and Science of String Performance.* Sherman Oaks, CA: Alfred Publishing Co., Inc. 1986.

American String Teachers Association. *Basic String Maintenance: A Teacher's Guide.* Fairfax, VA: ASTA, 2005.

American String Teachers Association and MENC: The National Association for Music Education. *The Complete String Guide: Standards, Programs, Purchases and Maintenance.* Reston, VA: Music Educators National Conference, 1988. A joint publication of the American String Teachers Association with National School Orchestra Association and MENC: The National Association for Music Education.

Aten, Jane (ed.). *String Teaching in America: Strategies for a Diverse Society.* Fairfax, VA: ASTA, 2006.

Bergonzi, Louis. "Teaching Advanced-Beginning Students to Tune Their Instruments." Champaign-Urbana, IL: The University of Illinois. Accessed November 26, 2010. https://netfiles.uiuc.edu/**bergonzi**/core/TuningStrings.pdf.

Dick, William, and Laurie Scott. *Mastery for Strings: A Longitudinal Sequence of Instruction for School Orchestras, Studio Lessons, and College Methods Courses, Level One.* Van Nuys, CA: Alfred, 2007.

_____. *Mastery for Strings: Level Two: Navigating the Fingerboard.* Van Nuys, CA: Alfred, 2008.

Dillon, Jacquelyn, and Casey Kriechbaum. *How to Design and Teach a Successful School String and Orchestra Program.* San Diego, CA: Kjos West, 1978.

Dillon-Krass, Jacquelyn, and Dorothy A. Straub (comp.) *TIPS: Establishing a String and Orchestra Program.* Reston, VA: MENC: The National Association for Music Education, 1991. Developed by the Ad Hoc Committee on String and Orchestra Education.

Gardner, Robert D. "30 Songs for the Holiday Concert? No Problem! *American String Teacher,* 49 (1999): 23–25.

Gattiker, Irvin. *Complete Book of Rehearsal Techniques for the High School Orchestra.* West Nyack, NY: Parker Publishing. 1977.

Gillespie, Robert and Donald L. Hamann. *Strategies for Teaching Strings: Building a Successful String and Orchestra Program.* 2nd Ed. New York: Oxford University Press. 2009.

Gordon, Edwin E. *Learning Sequences in Music: Skill, Content, and Patterns.* Chicago: GIA Publications, 1997.
_____. *Taking a Reasonable and Honest Look at Tonal Solfege and Rhythm Solfege.* Chicago: GIA Publications, 2009.

Green, Elizabeth A.H. *Teaching Stringed Instruments in Classes.* Englewood Cliff, NJ: Prentice-Hall, 1966. Distributed by ASTA.

_____. *Orchestra Bowings and Routines.* Fairfax, VA: ASTA, 1990.

Hayes, Pamela Tellejohn (ed.). *The School Symphony Orchestra Experience.* Fairfax, VA: ASTA, 2003.

Kendall, John. D. *The Suzuki Violin Method in American Music Education: What the American Music Educator Should Know About Shinichi Suzuki.* Reston, VA: MENC: The National Association for Music Education, 1973.

Klotman, Robert. *Teaching Strings.* New York: Schirmer, 1996.

Kreitman, Edward. *Teaching From the Balance Point: A Guide for Suzuki Parents, Teachers, and Students.* Western Springs, IL: Western Springs School of Talent Education, 1998.

Lieberman, Julie Lyonn. *You Are Your Instrument.* Newtown, CT: Huiksi/Julie Lyonn Music, 1993. Distributed by Hal Leonard.

Littrell, David. *String Syllabus, Volume 1 (rev.).* Fairfax, VA: ASTA, 2009.

May, Joanne (ed.) *The String Teacher's Cookbook: Creative Recipes for a Successful Program.* Galesville, MD: Meredith Music Publications, 2007.

MENC: The National Association for Music Education. *Performance Standards for Music, Grades PreK–12: Strategies and Benchmarks for Assessing Progress Toward the National Standards.* Reston, VA: MENC: The National Association for Music Education, 1996.

_____. *The School Music Program: A New Vision—The K–12 National Standards, PreK Standards, and What They Mean to Music Educators.* Reston, VA: MENC: The National Association for Music Education, 1994.

_____. *Teaching String Instruments: A Course of Study.* Reston, VA: MENC: The National Association for Music Education, 1996. Developed by the MENC Task Force on String Education Course of Study.

O'Toole, Patricia. *Shaping Sound Musicians: An Innovative Approach to Teaching Comprehensive Musicianship through Performance.* Chicago. GIA Publications, 2003.

Rolland, Paul, Marla Mutschler, Marla. *The Teaching of Action in String Playing*, 2nd ed. Fairfax, VA: ASTA, 2000. Accompanying DVD series available from University of Illinois String Research Project, http://www.paulrolland.net/.

Straub, Dorothy, Louis Bergonzi and Anne Witt. *Strategies for Teaching: Strings and Orchestra.* Reston, VA: MENC: The National Association for Music Education, 1996.

Witt, Anne C. *A Rhythm A Week.* Belwin Publications, 1998

Young, Phyllis. *Playing the String Game: Strategies for Teaching Cello and Strings.* Austin: University of Texas Press. 1978.
_____. *The String Play: The Drama of Teaching and Playing Strings.* Austin: University of Texas Press. 1986.

Bowing

Berman, Joel, Barbara C. Jackson, and Kenneth Sarch. *Dictionary of Bowings and Pizzicato.* Bloomington: Tichenor Publishing, 1999. Distributed by ASTA.

Capet, Lucien. *Superior Bowing Technique.* Edited by Stephen B. Shipps and translated by Margaret Schmidt. Maple City, MI: Encore Music Publishers, 1993.

Cridge, Lisa. *Bow Games and Goals 1* Washington. D. C. Sound Post Publishers, 2004.

Erdlee, Emery. *The Mastery of the Bow.* Tamarac, Fl: Distinctive Publishing Corporation, 1988.

Gerle, Robert. *The Art of Bowing Practice.* London: Stainer and Bell, 1991.

Gigante, Charles. *Manual of Orchestral Bowing.* Bloomington, IN: Frangipani Press (ASTA), 1986.

Hodgson, Percival. *Motion Study and Violin Bowing.* Fairfax, VA: American String Teachers Association, 1958.

Kjelland, James. *Orchestral Bowing: Style and Function.* Van Nuys, CA: Alfred Publishing, 2003.

Lieberman, Julie Lyonn. *Rhythmizing the Bow.* DVD. Newtown, CT: Huiksi Music/Julie Lyonn Music, 2004. Distributed by Hal Leonard.

Rabin, Marvin, and Priscilla Smith. *Guide to Orchestral Bowing Through Musical Style.* Madison, WI: University of Wisconsin-Madison, 1984.

Violin Technique

Auer, Leopold. *Violin Playing As I Teach It.* New York: Frederick A. Stokes Co, 1921.

Costantakos, Chris A. *Demetrios Constantine Dounis: His Method in Teaching Violin*, rev. ed. New York: Peter Lang, 1997.

Dounis, D.C. *The Artist's Technique of Violin Playing.* Voorhess, NJ: Charles Dumont & Sons, 1921.

Fischer, Simon. *Basics: 300 Exercises and Practice Routines for the Violin.* London: Edition Peters, 1997.

Flesch, Carl. *The Art of Violin Playing. Book I, Technique in General, Applied Technique*, rev. ed. Chicago: Carl Fischer, 1939.

_____. *The Art of Violin Playing. Book II, Artistic Realization and Instruction.* Chicago: Carl Fischer, 1930.

Galamian, Ivan. *Principles of Violin Playing and Teaching.* London: Prentice Hall, 1985.

Galamian, Ivan, and Frederick Neumann. *Contemporary Violin Technique, Part 1: Scale and Arpeggio Exercises.* New York, NY: Galaxy Music, 1966.

_____. *Contemporary Violin Technique, Part 2: Double and Multiple Stops.* New York, NY: Galaxy Music, 1966.

Gerle, Robert. *The Art of Practising the Violin.* London: Stainer and Bell, 1983.

Havas, Kato. *A New Approach To Violin Playing.* London: Bosworth & Co., 1961.

Krayk, Stefan. *The Violin Guide.* Fairfax, VA: ASTA, 1995.

Lieberman, Julie Lyonn. *The Violin in Motion.* Newtown, CT: Huiksi Music/Julie Lyonn Music, 1994. Distributed by Hal Leonard.

_____. *Violin and Viola Ergonomics: Determining the Optimum Playing Position and Support for Your Body Type.* DVD. Newtown, CT: Julie Lyonn Music, 2010. Distributed by Hal Leonard.

_____. *Techniques for the Contemporary String Player.* DVD. Newtown, CT: Huiksi Music/Julie Lyonn Music, 1993. Distributed by Hal Leonard.

Menuhin, Yehudi, and William Primrose. *Violin and Viola.* New York: Schirmer Books, 1976.

Perkins, Marianne. M. *A Comparison of Violin Playing Techniques: Kato Havas, Paul Rolland, and Shinichi Suzuki.* Fairfax, VA: American String Teachers Association, 1995.

Rolland, Paul. *Basic Principles of Violin Playing.* Fairfax, VA: American String Teachers Association, 2000.

Rolland, Paul, Marla Mutschler. 2nd rev.ed. *The Teaching of Action in String Playing.* Urbana, Illinois: Illinois String Research Associates (available through ASTA), 2000.

Ross, Barry. *A Violinist's Guide for Exquisite Intonation (rev.)*. Fairfax, VA: ASTA, 2004.

Starr, William. *The Suzuki Violinst*, rev. ed. Van Nuys, CA: Alfred, 1999.

Viola Technique

Barnes, Gregory (ed.) *Playing and Teaching the Viola: Comprehensive Guide to the Central Clef Instrument and Its Music*. Fairfax, VA: American String Teachers Association, 2005.

Dalton, David. *Playing the Viola: Conversations with William Primrose*. New York: Oxford University Press, 1988.

Lieberman, Julie Lyonn. *Violin and Viola Ergonomics: Determining the Optimum Playing Position and Support for Your Body Type*. DVD. Newtown, CT: Julie Lyonn Music, 2010. Distributed by Hal Leonard.

Menuhin, Yehudi, and William Primrose. *Violin and Viola*. New York: Schirmer Books, 1976.

Cello Technique

Bunting, Christopher. *Essay on the Craft of 'Cello-Playing: Prelude, Bowing, Coordination*. Cambridge: Cambridge University Press, 1982. (Available from http://www.sjmusicpublications.co.uk/ or http://www.orpheusmusicshop.com/.)

Bunting, Christopher. *Essay on the Craft of Cello Playing: Left Hand* Cambridge: Cambridge University Press, 1983. (Available from http://www.sjmusicpublications.co.uk/ or http://www.orpheusmusicshop.com/.)

Carey, Tanya L. *Cello Playing is Easy, Part 1: Warm-ups*. Ann Arbor, MI: Shar Products, 2007.

Epperson, Gordon. *The Art of Cello Teaching*. Fairfax, VA: American String Teachers Association, 1986.

Potter, Louis. *The Art of Cello Playing*. Van Nuys, CA: Alfred, 1980.

Sazer, Victor. *New Directions in Cello Playing: How To Make Cello Playing Easier and Play Without Pain*, 3rd ed. Ofnote, 2007.

Smith, G. Jean. *Cellist's Guide to the Core Technique*, 2nd ed. Fairfax, VA: American String Teachers Association, 1974.

Stanfield, Millie Bernardine. *The Intermediate Cellist*. London: Oxford University Press, 1973.

Watkins, Cornelia. *Rosindust: Teaching, Learning and Life from a Cellist's Perspective*. Houston: Rosindust Publishing, 2007.

Young, Phyllis. *Playing the String Game: Strategies for Teaching Cello and Strings*. Austin: University of Texas Press, 1978.

Bass Technique

Benfield, Warren A., and James S. Dean. *The Art of Double Bass Playing*. Evanston, IL: Summy-Birchard, 1973.

Bradetich, Jeff. *Double Bass: The Ultimate Challenge*. Denton, TX: Music for All to Hear, 2009.

Brun, Paul. *A New History of the Double Bass*. Villeneuve d'Ascq, France: Paul Brun Productions, 2000.

Green, Barry. *The Fundamentals of Double Bass Playing*. Cincinnati, OH: Piper Co, 1971.

Rabbath, François. *Art of the Bow*. DVD, 2005. (Available from http://www.artofthebow.com/.)

Rabbath, François. *Art of the Left Hand*. DVD, 2009. (Available from http://www.artofthebow.com/.)

Reid, Rufus. *Evolving Bassist*. Van Nuys, CA: Alfred Publishing Company, 2000.

Vance, George and Costanzi, Annette. *Progressive Repertoire for the Double Bass, Vol. 1–3*. New York: Carl Fischer, 2000.

Zimmerman, Frederick. *A Contemporary Concept of Bowing Technique for the Double Bass*. Van Nuys, CA: Alfred Publishing Company, 1985.

Online Resources

Michael Hopkins: String Pedagogy Notebook (http://stringtechnique.com)

Mimi Zweig: StringPedagogy (http://www.stringpedagogy.com)

Violin Masterclass: The Sassmannshaus Tradition for Violin Playing (http://www.violinmasterclass.com/)

Method Book Series

Alfred Music Publishing

String Explorer, by Andrew H. Dabczynski, Richard Meyer, and Bob Phillips.

> Includes both level 1 and level 2 books for violin, viola, cello, and string bass; teacher's manual, teacher's resource kit, piano accompaniment, CD accompaniment recordings

Orchestra Expressions, by Kathleen DeBerry Brungard, Michael L. Alexander, Gerald E. Anderson, and Sandra Dackow

> Includes both level 1 and level 2 books for violin, viola, cello, and string bass; teacher's edition, curriculum package, piano accompaniment, CD accompaniment recordings

Sound Innovations, by Bob Phillips, Peter Boonshaft, and Robert Sheldon

> Includes levels 1 and 2; series is also designed to be customizable by the teacher

Strictly Strings, by Jacquelyn Dillon, James Kjelland, and John O'Reilly

> Includes level 1, 2, and 3 book for violin, viola, cello, and string bass; conductor's book, piano accompaniment, CD accompaniment recordings

FJH Music Company

New Directions for Strings, by Joanne Erwin, Kathleen Horvath, Robert D. McCashin, and Robert Mitchell

> Includes both level 1 and level 2 books for violin, viola, cello, and string bass; teacher's manual, piano accompaniment, CD accompaniment recordings

GIA Music

Do It! Play Strings, by James Froseth and Bret Smith

> Includes both level 1 and level 2 books for violin, viola, cello, and string bass; teacher's resource edition, CD accompaniment recordings

Jump Right In: The Instrumental Series, by Richard Grunow, Edwin Gordon, and Christopher Azzara

Includes both level 1 and level 2 books for violin, viola, cello, and string bass; teacher's resource edition, CD accompaniment recordings

Neil A. Kjos Music Company

All for Strings, by Robert Frost and Gerald Anderson

Includes levels 1, 2, and 3 books for violin, viola, cello, and string bass; conductor's score/teacher's manual, piano accompaniment, CD accompaniment recordings, and supplemental theory books

Artistry for Strings, by Gerald Fischbach and Robert Frost

Includes both level 1 and level 2 books for violin, viola, cello, and string bass (low- and middle-positions); full score, piano accompaniment, CD accompaniment recordings, and parent's guide

Müller-Rusch String Series, by Harold Rusch and J. Frederick Müller

Includes levels 1–5 books for violin, viola, cello, and string bass; conductor's score/teacher's manual/piano accompaniment book

Spotlight on Strings, by Albert Stoutamire and Doris Gazda

Includes both level 1 and level 2 books for violin, viola, cello, and string bass; teacher's score (w/piano accompaniment), CD accompaniment recordings

Hal Leonard

Essential Elements 2000, by Michael Allen, Pamela Tellejohn Hayes, and Robert Gillespie

Includes methods books 1 and 2, book 3/*Essential Technique*, *Advanced Technique*, and *Essential Musicianship* books for violin, viola, cello, and string bass; teacher's manual (with DVD), piano accompaniments, CDs

Northeastern Music Publications

Simply Strings, by Denese Odegaard

Includes both level 1 and level 2 books for violin, viola, cello, and string bass; teacher's manual.

Alternative Styles, Improvisation, & Creativity
<hr>

American String Teachers Association. *Alternative Styles in the Classroom*. DVD. Fairfax, VA: ASTA, 2007.

_____. *Ultimate Strings, Volume 1: Alternative Styles*. CD. Fairfax, VA: ASTA, 2005.

Anger, Darol. *All Star Bluegrass Jam-Along for Fiddle*. Milwaukee, MI: Hal Leonard, 2009.

_____. *Chops and Grooves: Strategies for String Rhythms*. DVD. Portland, OR: Homespun Tapes, 2005.

_____. *Fiddle Tunes*. Milwaukee, WI: Hal Leonard, 1996.

Azzara, Christopher, and Richard Grunow. *Developing Musicianship Through Improvisation*. Chicago, IL: GIA Publications, 2006.

Blake, John and Jody Harmon. *Jazz Improvisation Made Easy*. Westford, MA: JIME, 2002. Distributed by ASTA. Available for violin, viola, cello, and bass.

Dabczynski, Andrew, and Bob Phillips. *Fiddlers Philharmonic*. Van Nuys, CA: Alfred, 2009. Part of the "Philharmonic" series by Alfred, includes teacher's manual, individual instrument books (violin, viola, cello/bass), piano accompaniment, and cd.

_____. *Fiddlers Philharmonic, Encore*. Van Nuys, CA: Alfred, 2009. Part of the "Philharmonic" series by Alfred, includes teacher's manual, individual instrument books (violin, viola, cello/bass), piano accompaniment, and cd.

_____. *Basic Fiddlers Philharmonic: Celtic Fiddle Tunes*. Van Nuys, CA: Alfred, 2009. Part of the "Philharmonic" series by Alfred, includes teacher's manual, individual instrument books (violin, viola, cello/bass), piano accompaniment, and cd.

_____. *Basic Fiddlers Philharmonic: Old-Time Fiddle Tunes*. Van Nuys, CA: Alfred, 2007. Part of the "Philharmonic" series by Alfred, includes teacher's manual, individual instrument books (violin, viola, cello/bass), piano accompaniment, and cd.

Darling, David and Julie Weber. *The Darling Conversations.* , 3-CD set, Manifest Spirit Records, MSR-075, 2007.

Glaser, Matt. *Teach Yourself Bluegrass Fiddle*. Music Sales America, 1999.

Glaser, Matt and Mimi Rabson. *Berklee Practice Method*. Boston: Berklee Press, 2004.

Glaser, Matt and Stephane Grappelli. *Jazz Violin*. Music Sales America, 1992.

Gradante, William. *Foundations of Mariachi Education: Materials, Methods, and Resources*. Reston, VA: MENC: The National Association for Music Education, 2008.

Harmon, Jody. *Improvise! for Violin*. Westford, MA: JIME, 2002. Distributed by ASTA. Also available for viola, cello, and bass.

Lyonn Lieberman, Julie. *Alternative Strings: The New Curriculum*. Pompton Plains, NJ: Amadeus Press, 2004.

_____. *The Contemporary Violinist*. Newtown, CT: Huiksi Music/Julie Lyonn Music, 1999. Distributed by Hal Leonard.

_____. *The Creative Band and Orchestra*. Newtown, CT: Huiksi Music/Julie Lyonn Music, 2002. Distributed by Hal Leonard.

_____. *Improvising Violin*. Milwaukee, WI: Hal Leonard, 1997.

_____. *Planet Musician: The World Music Sourcebook for Musicians*. Milwaukee, WI: Hal Leonard, 1998.

_____. *Rockin' Out With the Blues Fiddle*. Newtown, CT: Huiksi Music/Julie Lyonn Music, 2000. Distributed by Hal Leonard.

_____. *Rhythmizing the Bow* (DVD). Milwaukee, WI: Hal Leonard, 2004.

Mathieu, W. A. *The Listening Book: Discovering Your Own Music*. Boston: Shambhala, 1991.

Nachmanovitch, Stephen. *Free Play: Improvisation in Life and Arts*. New York: Tarcher/Penguin, 1991.

Neel, Marcia, and Francisco Grijalva. *¡Simplemente Mariachi!* Glenmoore, Northeastern Music Publications. Includes teacher's manual, individual instrument books (trumpet, violin, guitar/vihuela, and guitarron), cd.

Nevin, Jeffrey. *Mariachi Mastery*. San Diego, CA: Neil A. Kjos, 2006. Includes teachers' manual, individual instrument books (trumpet, violin, viola, cello/bass, guitar, guitarron, vihuela, and harp)

Nieto, John and Bob Phillips. *Mariachi Philharmonic*. Van Nuys, CA: Alfred, 2006. Part of the "Philharmonic" series by Alfred, includes teacher's manual, individual instrument books (violin, viola, cello/bass, trumpet), piano accompaniment, and cd. Books also available in Spanish.

Norgaard, Martin. *Getting Into Gypsy Jazz Violin*. Pacific, MO: Mel Bay, 2008.

_____. *Jazz Wizard Series*. Pacific, MO: Mel Bay. Includes a number of books for developing jazz fiddling skills for all levels and string instruments: *Jazz Fiddle Wizard, Jazz Fiddle Wizard Junior, Book 1,* and *Jazz Fiddle Wizard Junior, Book 2*.

Oshinsky, Jim. *Return to Child: Music for People's Guide for Improvising Music and Authentic Group Leadership.* Goshen, CT: Music for People, 2008.

Sabien, Randy and Bob Phillips. *Jazz Philharmonic, Book 1.* Van Nuys, CA: Alfred, 2000. Part of the "Philharmonic" series by Alfred, includes teacher's manual, individual instrument books (violin, viola, cello/bass), piano accompaniment, and cd.

_____. *Jazz Philharmonic, Book 2.* Van Nuys, CA: Alfred, 2009. Part of the "Philharmonic" series by Alfred, includes teacher's manual, individual instrument books (violin, viola, cello/bass), piano accompaniment, and cd.

Wood, Mark. *Electrify Your Strings.* Cherry Lane, 2008.

College Texts

Gillespie, Robert, and Donald Hamann. *Strategies for Teaching Strings: Building a Successful String and Orchestra Program,* 2nd ed. New York: Oxford University Press, 2009.

Klotman, Robert. *Teaching Strings.* New York: Schirmer Books, 1988.

Lamb, Norman, and Susan Lamb Cook *A Guide to Teaching Strings*, 7th ed. New York: McGraw-Hill, 2001.

Curriculum and Assessment

Benham, Stephen. "Musical Assessment as an Impetus for Strategic, Intentional, and Sustainable Growth in the Instrumental Classroom." In *The Practice of Assessment in Music Education: Frameworks, Models, and Designs*, ed. Timothy Brophy, Chicago: GIA Publications, 2010.

Brophy, Timothy. *Assessing the Developing Child Musician.* Chicago: GIA Publications, 2000.

_____. *Assessment in Music Education: Integrating Curriculum, Theory, and Practice.* Chicago: GIA Publications, 2007.

_____. *The Practice of Assessment in Music Education: Frameworks, Models, and Designs.* Chicago: GIA Publications, 2010.

Culver, Robert. "Goals of a String Program." *American String Teacher* 56 (1981): 46–48.

_____. *The Master Teacher Profile: Elements of Delivery at Work in the Classroom.* Madison, WI: The University of Wisconsin–Madison, Division of University Outreach, Department of Continuing Education in the Arts, 2006.

Doerksen, David. *Evaluating Teachers of Music Performance Groups.* Lanham, MD: Rowman & Littlefield, Reston, VA: MENC, 2006.

Kimpton, Paul and Delwyn Harnisch. *Scale Your Way to Music Assessment.* Chicago: GIA Publications, 2009.

Lieberman, Julie Lyonn. *Alternative Strings: The New Curriculum.* Pompton Plains, NJ: Amadeus Press, 2004.

Odegaard, Denese. *Music Curriculum Writing 101: Assistance with Standards-based Music Curriculum and Assessment Writing.* Chicago: GIA Publications, 2009.

Adopted 2007

I. As a Musician

1. demonstrates high level of musicianship in performance
2. performs at an intermediate to advanced level on at least one string instrument
3. demonstrates at least basic to intermediate performance concepts on one string instrument and understands advanced and artistic concepts on other string instruments
4. demonstrates ability to play by ear and improvise
5. demonstrates a basic knowledge of performing and teaching the woodwind, brass, and percussion instruments at least at a basic level, with an understanding of intermediate to advanced concepts.
6. demonstrates orchestral conducting skills
7. demonstrates keyboard skills of at least a basic to intermediate level and accompanies melodies using at least I-IV-V chords
8. demonstrates aural discrimination skills
9. demonstrates the understanding of prevention of performance injuries
10. demonstrates the knowledge of a wide range of music repertoire for teaching diverse styles, genres, cultures, and historical periods.

II. As an Educator

1. understands and applies pedagogy for violin, viola, cello, and bass
2. demonstrates effective rehearsal techniques for string and full orchestra
3. demonstrates the knowledge of a variety of string and orchestral instruction materials at all levels
4. demonstrates the knowledge of repertoire for student performance, including solo literature, orchestra music and chamber music
5. demonstrates skill in arranging music for school orchestras
6. demonstrates strategies for integrating music with other disciplines
7. understands different student learning styles, levels of maturation, and special needs, and adapts instruction accordingly
8. demonstrates knowledge of comprehensive, sequential K–12 music curricula, including string and orchestra, with appropriate goals and expectations for all levels of proficiencies
9. demonstrates understanding of the principles of a variety of homogeneous and heterogeneous pedagogical approaches for teaching string classes (Suzuki, Rolland, Bornoff, e.g.)
10. exhibits effective classroom management skills and strategies
11. demonstrates understanding of how to teach students of diverse ages, socio-economic, ethnic, and geographic backgrounds
12. demonstrates effective methods of assessing and evaluating student achievement
13. knows about instrument rental and purchasing
14. knows current technology for instruction, research, and musical applications
15. knows of current music and general education policies, including current scheduling practices for successful string and orchestra programs
16. demonstrates ability to gather pertinent orchestra program data
17. understands the importance of maintaining a balance between personal and career interests
18. demonstrates ability to develop budgets for equipment and supplies
19. demonstrates understanding of effective advocacy strategies for comprehensive music programs which include string/orchestra programs
20. demonstrates clear communication in written and oral form
21. demonstrates understanding of the K–12 National Music Education Standards and other state and local standards for music

II. As a Professional

A. Musician

1. continues to perform
2. demonstrates concepts and understandings necessary for student achievement of Grade 12 National Music Education Standards
3. exhibits effective, on-going professional self-assessment
4. continues to pursue opportunities for learning as a musician

B. Professional Affiliations and Related Activities

1. maintains active involvement in professional associations, such as MENC, ASTA/NSOA, SSA, CMA
2. continues to interact with other music educators, observes other programs
3. demonstrates professional ethics, appearance, behavior, and relationships within the profession, the school, and the greater community
4. participates in ongoing professional development to improve teaching effectiveness
5. serves in leadership roles with state and local MEAs, ASTA/NSOA chapters

C. School and Community Relations

1. develops a healthy rapport with school administrators for nurturing a successful string and orchestra program
2. understands the value of positive interaction with other members of the music and arts community
3. establishes and maintains positive relations with school administrators, staff, and fellow teachers through communication and dialogue
4. articulates the positive aspects of the string/orchestra component of a school music program through writing and speaking
5. communicates effectively with parent support/booster groups, including clear and grammatically correct communication
6. advocates effectively for a strong school orchestra program